LEMURS OF MADAGASCAR
and the Comoros

The IUCN Red Data Book

IUCN - THE WORLD CONSERVATION UNION

Founded in 1948, IUCN - The World Conservation Union - is a membership organisation comprising governments, non-governmental organisations (NGOs), research institutions, and conservation agencies in 120 countries. The Union's objective is to promote and encourage the protection and sustainable utilisation of living resources.

Several thousand scientists and experts from all continents form part of a network supporting the work of its six Commissions: threatened species, protected areas, ecology, sustainable development, environmental law and environmental education and training. Its thematic programmes include tropical forests, wetlands, marine ecosystems, plants, the Sahel, Antarctica, population and natural resources, and women in conservation. These activities enable IUCN and its members to develop sound policies and programmes for the conservation of biological diversity and sustainable development of natural resources.

WCMC - THE WORLD CONSERVATION MONITORING CENTRE

The World Conservation Monitoring Centre (WCMC) is a joint venture between the three partners in the World Conservation Strategy, the World Conservation Union (IUCN), the World Wide Fund for Nature (WWF), and the United Nations Environment Programme (UNEP). Its mission is to support conservation and sustainable development by collecting and analysing global conservation data so that decisions affecting biological resources are based on the best available information.

WCMC has developed a global overview database of the world's biological diversity that includes threatened plant and animal species, habitats of conservation concern, critical sites, protected areas of the world, and the utilisation and trade in wildlife species and products. Drawing on this database, WCMC provides an information service to the conservation and development communities, governments and United Nations agencies, scientific institutions, the business and commercial sector, and the media. WCMC produces a wide variety of specialist outputs and reports based on analyses of its data.

UNEP

WWF

LEMURS OF MADAGASCAR
and the Comoros

The IUCN Red Data Book

Compiled by the
World Conservation Monitoring Centre
Cambridge, U.K.

by

Caroline Harcourt
with assistance from
Jane Thornback
(Project coordinator and editor)

Financial support from
Bristol Zoo
Conservation International
World Wildlife Fund (U.S.) Primate Program
Madagascar Fauna Captive Propagation Group
Jersey Wildlife Preservation Trust
and the
Parc Zoologique et Botanique de la Ville de Mulhouse

IUCN - THE WORLD CONSERVATION UNION
Gland, Switzerland and Cambridge, U.K.
1990

Published by IUCN, Gland, Switzerland and Cambridge, U.K.
with financial support from Bristol Zoo, Conservation International, the World Wildlife
Fund (U.S.) Primate Program, Madagascar Fauna Captive Propagation Group, Jersey
Wildlife Preservation Trust and the Parc Zoologique et Botanique de la Ville de Mulhouse.

A contribution to GEMS - The Global Environment Monitoring System.

Citation: Harcourt, C., and Thornback, J. (1990) *Lemurs of Madagascar and the
              Comoros. The IUCN Red Data Book*. IUCN, Gland, Switzerland and
              Cambridge, U.K.

ISBN: 2-88032-957-4
Printed by: Unwin Brothers Limited, The Gresham Press, Old Woking,
                  Surrey, U.K.
Cover illustration: Indri by: Brian Groombridge
Typesetting by: Richard Maling, IUCN Publications Services Unit

Available from: IUCN Publications Services,
                  219c Huntingdon Road, Cambridge CB3 0DL, U.K.

The designations of geographical entities in this book, and the presentation of the material,
do not imply the expression of any opinion whatsoever on the part of IUCN, or other
participating organisations concerning the legal status of any country, territory, or area, or of
its authorities, or concerning the delimitation of its frontiers or boundaries.

The views of the authors expressed in this publication do not necessarily reflect those of
IUCN or other participating organisations.

Dedicated to

Sir Peter Scott
(1909-1989)

who initiated Red Data Books and who gave boundless
enthusiasm and committment to the cause of conservation.

CONTENTS

PREFACE (1)

The *Lemur Red Data Book* carries on the tradition of careful compilation and sorting of information established in earlier *Red Data Books*. Its publication now is extremely timely. With a fauna and flora substantially and long different from continental Africa, the biota of Madagascar is recognized as one of the top priorities for conservation of biodiversity globally. Over the next decade many resources will be channeled into conservation efforts in Madagascar. The information contained in the *Lemur Red Data Book* should serve as an invaluable source for those who must make decisions about where specific resources are most needed and can best be used.

But perhaps even more important than the information contained in the *Red Data Book* is the information that it does not contain. There are tremendous gaps in knowledge of the taxonomy, ecology and behavior of most of the lemurs. Our ability to act quickly and wisely to conserve these animals is undeniably limited by this lack of knowledge. Identifying those areas where information is sorely lacking, and moving to upgrade data from these areas, has always been a basic goal of IUCN's conservation effort. I strongly urge that the need to expand the data base be foremost in our minds as we help develop conservation programs in Madagascar and that we make every effort to fill as many of the knowledge gaps as possible in the course of supporting conservation projects and programs.

This book could not have been compiled without support from Bristol Zoo, Conservation International, World Wildlife Fund (U.S.) Primate Program, the Madagascar Fauna Captive Propagation Group of AAZPA, Jersey Wildlife Preservation Trust and the Parc Zoologique et Botanique de la Ville de Mulhouse. They deserve a special thank you for making this volume possible.

George Rabb
Chairman
IUCN Species Survival Commission.

Notes on Authors

Caroline Harcourt is a primatologist affiliated with the Zoology Department, University of Cambridge, U.K. She specialises in the study of nocturnal prosimians, but now earns her living as a researcher and writer on conservation issues.

Jane Thornback has been compiler, and more recently editor, of the IUCN Mammal Red Data Book for fourteen years.

PREFACE (2)

The Primate Specialist Group of IUCN has long recognised Madagascar as its top priority and is now in the process of preparing an Action Plan for Primate Conservation in Madagascar to guide its activities there over the critical last decade of this century. As should be obvious from the species accounts here, one of the most glaring gaps in our knowledge of lemurs is often the most basic information on geographic distribution and conservation status. In spite of several centuries of observation and collection and more than three decades of research, we still are not clear as to the limits of the distribution of most species and have only the most subjective impressions of conservation status. The striking cases of two new species (*Hapalemur aureus* and *Propithecus tattersalli*) being discovered in the last three years and another, the aye-aye (*Daubentonia madagascariensis*), previously believed to be highly restricted and nearly extinct and now being found in many different parts of the island, are good indicators of how ignorant we still are. Clearly, much more thorough survey work is needed for all species, with special emphasis on the most endangered, among them *Hapalemur aureus, Hapalemur simus, Hapalemur griseus alaotrensis, Propithecus diadema candidus, Propithecus diadema perrieri, Propithecus tattersalli, Indri indri, Allocebus trichotis* and *Daubentonia madagascariensis*. Projects for all of these and many other species will be included in the Action Plan.

Another key feature of the Action Plan will be a wide variety of projects using these beautiful and unique species as "flagships" for public awareness and education campaigns, both to stimulate general interest for conservation within Madagascar and to focus ever more international attention on the importance of this country in global efforts to conserve biological diversity. Since lemurs are the most attractive, conspicuous and best known of Madagascar's wildlife, they are ideally suited to this purpose.

As with any other undertaking of this kind, putting together an effective Action Plan requires a view of all existing information on ecology, behaviour, distribution and conservation status. By doing this so effectively, this outstanding book comes at a very timely moment in the history of conservation in Madagascar and makes a major contribution to the survival of one of the most intriguing and unusual faunas ever to exist on our planet.

> Dr. Russell A. Mittermeier,
> Chairman,
> IUCN/SCC Primate Specialist Group.

ACKNOWLEDGEMENTS

IUCN and the compilers wish to thank the many individuals who have provided information about lemurs and their conservation status. Without their time, energy and forbearance in answering the numerous enquires generated during the project it would have been impossible to produce this book.

Many people commented on the draft data sheets, allowed access to unpublished information, provided photographs or generally assisted in the completion of this book. For this we thank the following: J. Andrews, S. Andriatsarafara, S. Barlow, R. Birkel, D. Brockman, R. Byrne, P. Chapman, P. Coffey, C. Deulofeu (BIOS), L. Durrell, S. Edmondson, N. Ellerton, N. Flesness, J. Ganzhorn, B. Grieser, A. Harcourt, D. Haring, J. Hartley, A. Hawkins, T. Iwano, K. Izard, A. Jolly, A. Katz, L. Kolter, J.-M. Lernould, J. Mallinson, N. Maskel, B. Meier, D. Meyers, J. Mikolai, S. Nash, M. Nicoll, S. O'Connor, E. Outlaw, F. Pang, J.-J. Petter, G. Rakotoarisoa, J. Ratsirarson, C. Raxworthy, G. Refeno, A. Richard, J. Sayer, H. Simons Morland, E. Stirling, R. Sussman, P. Thompson, S. Thompson, I. Thorpe, A. Walsh (Oxford Scientific Films), D. Wharton, J. Wilson, K. Winkelsträter, P. Wright and E. Zimmerman. Those requiring particular thanks for comments and discussion are Martin Jenkins, Olivier Langrand, Mark Pidgeon, Jonathon Pollock, Elwyn Simons and Ian Tattersall. Both the IUCN/SSC Primate Specialist Group and the IUCN/SSC Captive Breeding Specialist Group have contributed to this publication, particularly through the efforts of their Chairmen, Russell Mittermeier and Ulysses Seal respectively, who kindly commented on the manuscript as a whole. In addition, Russell Mittermeier, assisted by Rod Mast, provided many of the photographs.

Special thanks must go to the institutions who generously donated funds. These are Bristol Zoo (U.K.), Conservation International, Jersey Wildlife Preservation Trust, the Madagascar Fauna Captive Propagation Group, Parc Zoologique et Botanique de la Ville de Mulhouse and the World Wildlife Fund (U.S.) Primate Program.

IUCN THREATENED SPECIES CATEGORIES

The species identified as threatened by IUCN are assigned a category indicating the degree of threat as follows:

EXTINCT (Ex)
Species not definitely located in the wild during the past 50 years (criterion as used by the Convention on International Trade in Endangered Species of Wild Fauna and Flora)

ENDANGERED (E)
Taxa in danger of extinction and whose survival is unlikely if the causal factors continue to operate.

Included are taxa whose numbers have been reduced to a critical level or whose habitats have been so drastically reduced that they are deemed to be in immediate danger of extinction. Also included are taxa that may be extinct but have definitely been seen in the wild in the past 50 years.

VULNERABLE (V)
Taxa believed likely to move into the "Endangered" category in the near future if the causal factors continue to operate.

Included are taxa of which most or all the populations are decreasing because of over-exploitation, extensive destruction of habitat or other environmental disturbance; taxa with populations that been seriously depleted and whose ultimate security has not yet been assured; and taxa with populations that are still abundant but are under threat from severe adverse factors throughout their range.

In practice, "Endangered" and "Vulnerable" categories may include, temporarily, taxa whose populations are beginning to recover as a result of remedial action, but whose recovery is insufficient to justify their transfer to another category.

RARE (R)
Taxa with small world populations that are not at present "Endangered" or "Vulnerable", but are at risk.

These taxa are usually localised within restricted geographical areas or habitats or are thinly scattered over a more extensive range.

INDETERMINATE (I)
Taxa known to be "Endangered", "Vulnerable" or "Rare" but where there is not enough information to say which of the three categories is appropriate.

INSUFFICIENTLY KNOWN (K)
Taxa that are suspected, but, because of lack of information, are not definitely known, to belong to one of the above categories.

Habitat destruction in Madagascar is progressing so fast that many would argue that all primates on the island are threatened. However, a few species are still abundant - and we have debated extensively with specialists on Madagascar as to whether these species should be classified as NOT THREATENED. Finally, we have decided to designate these species as ABUNDANT.

INTRODUCTION

> *May I announce to you that Madagascar is the naturalists' promised land? Nature seems to have retreated there into a private sanctuary, where she could work on different models from any she has used elsewhere. There, you meet bizarre and marvellous forms at every step......What an admirable country, this Madagascar.*

> *(J.-P. Commerson, 1771)*

Lemurs evolved in Madagascar and are found nowhere else in the world, except on the Comoros, where there are two species that were probably introduced to the islands by man sometime within the past several hundred years. Man has lived on Madagascar for less than two thousand years and yet, in that comparatively short time, six genera and at least fourteen species of lemur have disappeared from the country and, therefore, from the world. Madagascar does, indeed, demonstrate very clearly that primate extinctions are a very real phenomenon.

While collecting information for this book, we have received pessimistic reports that all the forest within the country will be gone within 30 years, 25 years, or as little as ten years. To counter this is the great and increasing interest in the conservation of Madagascar's wildlife from individuals and institutions from both outside and inside the country. Without this interest it is likely that most of Madagascar's primates, perhaps all except the tiny mouse lemurs and the ubiquitous brown lemur, will disappear within the relatively near future. However, changes are occurring, international organisations are providing money and people to aid conservation, education and development in the country and the Malagasy Government is very keen to stop the destruction of its unique heritage and to secure the essential natural resources for the benefit of its people.

Madagascar, approximately 1600 km long and 580 km wide at its broadest point, with a surface area of around 587,000 sq. km, is the world's fourth largest island, surpassed only by Greenland, New Guinea and Borneo. It lies in the Indian Ocean, separated from the east coast of Africa by at least 300 km of the Mozambique Channel. The island falls almost entirely within the tropical zone, extending from latitude 11° 57'S to 25° 35'S, and it is between 43° 14'E and 50° 27'E longitude. It has a diverse geology, climate and vegetation and, because of this and its large size, it is often regarded as a microcontinent. Certainly, most of its flora and fauna is unique to the area and, botanically, it is one of the richest areas in the world. The origins of Madagascar are still disputed. It may have broken away from Africa as long as 200 million years ago, but mammals could have drifted across the channel up until 40 million years ago. After that time, the increased width of the Mozambique Channel apparently made this impossible. Not until man arrived, perhaps 2000 years ago, were more mammalian species introduced to the island.

The vegetation of Madagascar is both extremely rich and unique. Estimates of the numbers of species of plant vary between about 7000 to 12,000, approximately 80% of these are endemic. The country has been divided into two major floral zones (Humbert, 1959; Perrier de la Bathie, 1936; White, 1983), a moister Eastern Region and a dry Western area, and within these are a wide range of habitats (Figure 1). The Eastern Region covers just under half the island, extending westwards from the east coast to cover the central highlands and includes a small enclave, the Sambirano Domain, on the north-west coast. This unit was

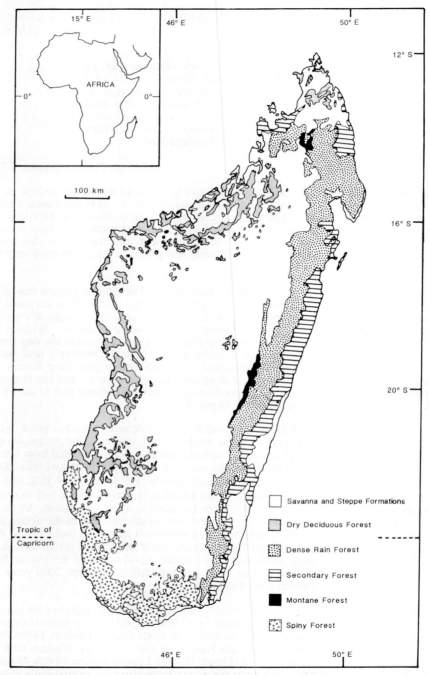

Figure 1: Approximate Distribution of Vegetation Types in Madagascar (adapted from Humbert and Cours Darne, 1965). There are, as yet, no more recent maps of remaining forest cover in the country.

probably originally all forested, but much of the forest has now been replaced by a mosaic of cultivation and secondary formations. The Western Region extends from the flat plains on the west coast eastwards up to about 800m. Within this area are the dry decidous forests, less dense with a lower, more open canopy than in most of the moister eastern forests. Lusher forests grow in riparian habitat along rivers. Included within the Western Region biogeographical zone is the semi-arid Southern Domain. This is characterised by thickets or forests of endemic, bushy, xerophytic vegetation, with Euphorbiaceae and Didiereaceae predominating.

Apart from the lemurs, Madagascar's mammalian fauna is relatively impoverished. Indeed, it has fewer mammal species (109) than any other comparably sized African country. The native living land mammals belong to only five orders: Primates, Carnivora, Rodentia, Insectivora and Chiroptera. There are eight species of native carnivore, all unique to the island and all belonging to the Viverridae; ten species of rodent, again all found only in Madagascar; 32 species in the order Insectivora, which are mostly endemic tenrecs; and there are 28 bat species, though only nine of these are unique to the island. There used to be a pygmy hippopotamus in the country but this became extinct sometime after man's arrival on the island. Similarly, the number of bird species found on Madagascar is low. There are a total of 250 species of which about half are endemic. The huge, flightless elephant bird, *Aepyornis maximus*, used to occur on the island but this too has vanished in the last few hundred years. In contrast to the birds and mammals, the reptile and amphibian fauna is rich compared to that in other African countries. There are around 260 reptile species which include one crocodile, 13 tortoises, 60 snakes and about 180 lizards. Madagascar contains two thirds of the world's chameleon species from the tiniest, the size of a thumb nail, to the largest at 60 cms. Though there are around 150 amphibian species on the island (all but two of which are endemic), they are all frogs; no toads or newts are found there. Madagascar is, without doubt, the world's highest major primate conservation priority, with astounding levels of primate diversity and endemism and more endangered and vulnerable primates than any other country. Madagascar is fourth on the world list of primate species (in spite of being only one seventh the size of Brazil, the world leader, and roughly one quarter the size of Indonesia or Zaire, second and third on the world list) and its level of endemism, 28 of 30 species, or 93.3%, is by far the highest in the world (Mittermeier, in litt and see Mittermeier and Oates, 1985). At the generic and familial levels, Madagascar's diversity is even more striking, with five primate families, four of which are endemic and 13 genera of which 12 are found nowhere else. Compare this to Brazil, which has only two families, neither of them endemic, while only two of 16 primate genera within the country are endemic. Of the 30 lemur species currently recognised for Madagascar, 10 are considered endangered in this book and another 15 are believed to be in some trouble, again a figure unmatched by any other country. The fourteen species of lemur that have vanished from Madagascar since the arrival of humans were all bigger than the present day species. Indeed, the largest (*Megaladapis edwardsi*) may have weighed two hundred kilogrammes, similar in size to a male orang-utan (Jolly *et al*, 1984). These species vanished before they could be studied at all, but even now very few of the existing primate species have been studied in any detail, their ability to tolerate the man-made disturbances of their habitat is generally unknown, even accurate distributions are not known. Almost invariably, there are also no estimates of population numbers. On this basis, an assessment of the conservation status of each species is very difficult. It is, however, sure that all the primates in Madagascar, except *Homo sapiens*, are declining each year.

The human population of Madagascar is estimated to be presently increasing at a rate of 2.9%; it has more than doubled in thirty years, from 5.4 million in 1960 to 11.2 million in 1989, and it is calculated that there will be 28.1 million people in the country by 2025 (World Resources Institute, 1988). The population is still mostly rural and the people depend on agriculture for their livelihood. To obtain more land the forests are destroyed by slash and burn (or tavy) cultivation. Areas are clear cut, the vegetation is dried and then fired some months later. Dry land rice is most commonly planted, but maize, manioc and

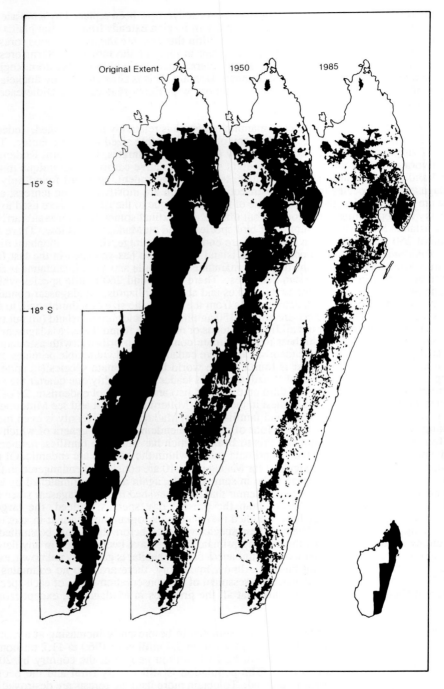

Figure 2: Maps of distribution of rain forest in eastern Madagascar through time. From Green and Sussman (in press).

other crops are also cultivated. These are grown for a year or two, then the land is left fallow and the process repeated elsewhere. Degraded vegetation types grow on the abandoned land and these are then cleared after an interval of ten years or so. Progressive deterioration of the soil structure and nutrient content finally leads to the area becoming grassland or being eroded to bare soil. This clearing of land for cultivation is the major threat to the rain forest in the east of Madagascar.

In the west, the principal agent of forest destruction is fire, much of it deliberately started to encourage new grass growth for the large herds of livestock raised in the area. The fires are usually set in the dry season when the forests are at their most vulnerable. Overgrazing frequently prevents any forest regeneration, instead bush or grasses colonise the cleared areas. Fires are also a hazard in the dry forests of the south, but the collection of wood for conversion to charcoal is generally considered to be the major threat in this area (Sussman *et al*, 1985). Clearing forests for agricultural land also occurs in the west and south, as does cutting down trees for fuel and building materials in all areas.

Some timber is removed by logging companies, but this is not a major threat in Madagascar, especially as now much of the remaining forest is in steep, isolated areas inaccessible to heavy machinery. It is not clear how much of Madagascar was originally covered in forest. Even now there are no accurate figures for the extent of surviving tree cover, though it is usually said that approximately 20% of the island is covered with forest. This is the figure estimated by Guichon in 1960, based chiefly on aerial surveys made in the late 1940s. Estimates in the 1980s record 10.3 million hectares of closed forest and 2.9 million hectares of open forest remaining (World Resources Institute, 1988), but these figures do not appear to be based on any new data. It is estimated that 1.2% of the closed forest is cut down every year (World Resources Institute, 1988), but, again, there are apparently no recent data to base this on. There are no up to date vegetation maps available for the whole country, but Green and Sussman (in press) have just produced a map of the eastern rain forest based on satellite images (Figure 2). They estimate that the rate of deforestation between 1950 and 1985 was 111,000 ha per annum and that, in 1985, only 3.8 million hectares of eastern rain forest remained. They consider that, if cutting continues at the same pace, only forests on the steepest slopes will survive the next 35 years.

Destruction of their habitat is almost certainly the main threat to the lemurs. Hunting does occur in some areas, mostly using traditional means such as nest raiding, snaring and stone throwing, though guns are now also used and may become a real threat. In several regions it is taboo to kill lemurs but, as human populations become more mobile, the lemurs in these areas are likely to be killed by people without the traditions of protecting the animals. The largest of the lemurs have already gone, quite possibly driven to extinction by hunting as well as habitat destruction, and now it is the largest of the surviving lemurs that could become menaced by hunting. The Black and White Ruffed Lemur (*Varecia variegata*) is probably the most at risk in this way. The one species which may be immediately threatened by hunting is the Aye-Aye (*Daubentonia madagascariensis*) as, to some local people, this animal brings bad luck and it is likely to be killed whenever it is seen. It does not, however, appear to be actively sought out and slaughtered. The smaller, nocturnal species are the least likely to be directly hunted but even they can be caught in snares.

Trade in lemurs is not considered to be a threat to any of the species (Kavanagh *et al*, 1987). All are listed on Appendix 1 of CITES and in Class A of the African Convention, which precludes trade in them or their products except for scientific purposes. In addition, both Madagascar and the Comoros have strict regulations controlling the export of lemurs.

Legal protection of nature in Madagascar began as long ago as 1881 when, under the ancient Hova Kingdom, those cutting down forests were condemned to be chained in irons! Madagascar has one of the oldest protected area networks in the African region, with ten Reserves Naturelles Integrales dating back to 1927. There are now 11 Nature Reserves, two National Parks and 23 Special Reserves in the country (Figure 3 and see section on protected areas). This system of protected areas is quite comprehensive and covers a good cross-section of key ecosystems. Unfortunately, however, much of this network exists only on paper. The Reserves are essential for conservation of the country's rich biological diversity, and this was recognised by the Malagasy Government during its 1985 Conference on the Conservation of Madagascar's Natural Resources for Development (Rakotovao *et al*, 1988). In 1986, a project to survey the protected areas was set up through WWF's programme in Madagascar in collaboration with a number of Government Ministries. The aims of this project are to evaluate the existing protected areas, to develop and implement management plans for priority protected areas, to recommend the establishment of new protected areas in key regions and to train Malagasy counterparts in protected area management and conservation biology. Recommendations for conservation and management have already been made for many of the protected areas (Nicoll and Langrand, 1989).

A number of proposals for the conservation of biological diversity in Madagascar have been put forward by R. Mittermeier (1986) in a preliminary Action Plan for the country. In addition to the survey of existing and potential protected areas, the following are suggested: the establishment of a conservation data centre and a biological inventory programme for Madagascar, possibly to be set up in Parc Tsimbazaza in Madagascar's capital, Antananarivo, and to be run with the University of Madagascar; a programme to increase public awareness and conservation education within the country; the training of Malagasy conservation professionals; the development of international wildlife tourism for Madagascar; the strengthening of the zoological park and botanical garden at Parc Tsimbazaza; surveys of the most endangered lemur species and the development of captive breeding programmes for key endangered species.

As has been stated many times, the survival of Madagascar's unique biota, including its primates, and ultimately the well-being of its people, depends on the continued presence of forests in the country. Given the political will in Madagascar, the expertise both within and outside the country and financial aid from richer countries and institutions, there is no reason why this should not be assured. It will, however, require great effort particularly in ensuring that the country's conservation needs are fully integrated with its overall development objectives.

References

Green, G.M. and Sussman, R.W. (in press). Deforestation history of the eastern rainforests of Madagascar with satellite images. *Science.*

Guichon, A. (1960). La superficie des formations forestières à Madagascar. *Revue forestières française* 6: 408-411.

Humbert, H. (1959). Origines présumées et affinities de la flore de Madagascar. *Mémoires de l'Institut Scientifique de Madagascar, Séries b (Biol. vég.)* 9: 149-187.

IUCN/UNEP/WWF (1987). *Madagascar, an environmental profile.* Edited by M.D. Jenkins. IUCN, Gland, Switzerland and Cambridge, U.K.

Jolly, A. (1986). Lemur Survival. In: Benirschke, K. (Ed.), *Primates: The Road to Self-Sustaining Populations.* Springer-Verlag, New York. Pp. 71-98.

Jolly, A., Oberlé, P. and Albignac, R. (Eds) (1984). *Key Environments: Madagascar.* Pergamon Press, Oxford.

Kavanagh, M., Eudey, A.A. and Mack, D. (1987). The effects of live trapping and trade on primate populations. In: Marsh, C.W. and Mittermeier, R. (Eds), *Primate Conservation in the Tropical Forest.* Alan R. Liss, Inc., New York. Pp. 147-177.

Mittermeier, R. (1986). *An Action Plan for Conservation of Biological Diversity in Madagascar.* Unpublished report.

Mittermeier, R. and Oates, J.F. (1985). Primate diversity: the world's top countries. *Primate Conservation* 5: 41-48.

Nicoll, M.E. and Langrand, O. (1989). *Revue Générale du Système d'Aires Protégées et de la Conservation à Madagascar.* Unpublished report to WWF.

Pollock, J.I. (1986). Primates and conservation priorities in Madagascar. *Oryx* 20(4): 209-216.

Rakotovao, L, Barre, V. and Sayer, J. (Eds), (1988). *L'Equilibre des Ecosystèmes Forestiers à Madagascar. Actes d'un séminaire international.* IUCN, Gland, Switzerland and Cambridge, U.K.

Sussman, R.W., Richard, A.F. and Ravelojaona, G. (1985). Madagascar: current projects and problems in conservation. *Primate Conservation* 5: 53-59.

White, F. (1983). *The Vegetation of Africa. A Descriptive Memoir to Accompany the Unesco/AETFAT/UNSO Vegetation Map of Africa.* Natural Resources Research 20, Unesco, Paris.

World Resources Institute (1988). *World Resources 1988-1989. An Assessment of the Resource Base that Supports the Global Economy.* Basic Books, Inc., New York.

THE LEMURS OF MADAGASCAR AND THEIR DEGREE OF THREAT

Family CHEIROGALEIDAE

Microcebus murinus	Grey Mouse Lemur	Abundant
Microcebus rufus	Brown Mouse Lemur	Abundant
Mirza coquereli	Coquerel's Dwarf Lemur	V
Cheirogaleus medius	Fat-tailed Dwarf Lemur	Abundant
Cheirogaleus major	Greater Dwarf Lemur	Abundant
Allocebus trichotis	Hairy-eared Dwarf Lemur	E
Phaner furcifer	Fork-marked Dwarf Lemur	R

Family MEGALADAPIDAE

Lepilemur dorsalis	Grey-backed Sportive Lemur	V
Lepilemur edwardsi	Milne-Edwards' Sportive Lemur	R
Lepilemur leucopus	White-footed Sportive Lemur	R
Lepilemur microdon	Microdon Sportive Lemur	R
Lepilemur mustelinus	Weasel Sportive Lemur	R
Lepilemur ruficaudatus	Red-tailed Sportive Lemur	R
Lepilemur septentrionalis	Northern Sportive Lemur	V

Family LEMURIDAE

Lemur catta	Ring-tailed Lemur	V
Lemur coronatus	Crowned Lemur	E
Lemur macaco	Black Lemur	
m. macaco	Black Lemur	V
m. flavifrons	Sclater's Lemur	E
Lemur mongoz	Mongoose Lemur	E
Lemur rubriventer	Red-bellied Lemur	V
Lemur fulvus	Brown lemur	
f. albifrons	White-fronted Lemur	R
f. albocollaris	White-collared Lemur	V
f. collaris	Collared Lemur	V
f. fulvus	Brown Lemur	R
f. mayottensis	Mayotte Lemur	V
f. rufus	Red-fronted Lemur	R
f. sanfordi	Sanford's Lemur	V
Varecia variegata	Ruffed Lemur	
v. variegata	Black and White Ruffed Lemur	E
v. rubra	Red-ruffed Lemur	E
Hapalemur griseus	Grey Gentle Lemur	
g. griseus	Grey Gentle Lemur	K
g. alaotrensis	Alaotran Gentle Lemur	E
g. occidentalis	Western Gentle Lemur	V
Hapalemur aureus	Golden Bamboo Lemur	E
Hapalemur simus	Greater Bamboo Gentle Lemur	E

Family INDRIIDAE

Avahi laniger	Woolly Lemur	
l. laniger	Eastern Woolly Lemur	V
l. occidentalis	Western Woolly Lemur	V
Indri indri	Indri	E
Propithecus diadema	Diademed Sifaka	
d. diadema	Diademed Sifaka	E
d. candidus	Silky Sifaka	E
d. edwardsi	Milne-Edwards' Sifaka	E
d. perrieri	Perrier's Sifaka	E

Propithecus tattersalli	Golden-crowned Sifaka	E
Propithecus verreauxi	Verreaux's Sifaka	
verreauxi	Verreaux's Sifaka	V
v. coquereli	Coquerel's Sifaka	V
v. deckeni	Decken's Sifaka	V

Family DAUBENTONIIDAE

Daubentonia madagascariensis	Aye-aye	E

LEMURS OF MADAGASCAR and the Comoros:
The IUCN Red Data Book

PROTECTED AREAS OF MADAGASCAR

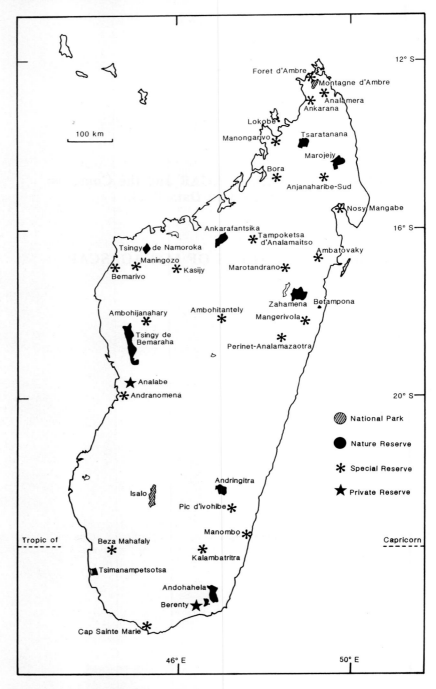

Figure 3:   Protected Areas in Madagascar

18

PROTECTED AREAS OF MADAGASCAR

Six categories of protected areas are recognised in Madagascar:

1) Strict Nature Reserves (Réserves Naturelles Intégrales)
2) National Parks (Parcs Nationaux)
3) Special Reserves (Réserves Speciales)
4) Classified Forests (Forêts Classées)
5) Reafforestation zones (Périmètres de Raboisement et de Restauration)
6) Biosphere Reserves (Réserves de la Biosphère)

The Strict Nature Reserves were created by Decree 66-242 of 1st June 1966 though the network of reserves was originally set up in 1927. Access is forbidden to everybody except officials of the Water and Forest Department and researchers who have obtained permission from the relevant Government Ministries (Ministère de la Production Animal [Elevage et Pêche] and des Eaux et Forêts). Each reserve is supervised by a headman (Chef de Réserve) and several assistants. There are 11 Nature Reserves, a twelfth (R.N.I. 2) on the Masoala Peninsula was degazetted in 1964 by Decree 64-381 and is now only a Classified Forest. The size of the Nature Reserves varies from the 740 ha of Lokobe on the small island of Nosy Bé to 152,000 ha of Bemaraha in the west. In total, approximately 569,500 hectares are protected as Strict Nature Reserves.

Decrees 58-07 of 28/10/58 and 62-371 of 19/7/62 contain the legislation for the National Parks in Madagascar. The public may visit these areas but access is controlled. Villagers may be accorded the right of passage through the forest and to use certain forest products but there are constraints on these rights, which have to be respected. There are two National Parks at present and a third, at Ranomafana, is in the process of being gazetted. The two existing parks total around 99,700 hectares.

The Special Reserves have been created by a number of different decrees, in general they are set up to protect one particular species of plant or animal. In theory, permission is needed to enter the Special Reserves but, in fact, traditional rights of use are allowed. Grazing of livestock, collection of plants or the introduction of animals or plants into the area is forbidden. Fishing is also forbidden, except in two of the reserves. There are 23 Special Reserves but only some of them are guarded by officials of the Water and Forest department. It is this Department which is responsible for the administration of the reserves. The smallest of the Special Reserves is the island of Nosy Mangabe at 520 ha, while only one (Ambatovaky) is over 50,000 hectares. Total area protected as Special Reserves is approximately 365,500 hectares.

Classified Forests are created by individual ministerial decrees, but local authorities are also involved. They are forest reserves but their function is, essentially, economic. Exploitation is forbidden, except for certain traditional forest products. In several Classified Forests concessions have been granted to allow charcoal making and collection of timber. Protection of the areas is not necessarily permanent. In 1989 there were 158 Classified Forests, with a total area of around 2,671,000 hectares.

The creation of Reafforestation Zones is not necessarily directly concerned with the maintenance of biological diversity. They are established to protect water basins and to protect against erosion. There is, however, a plan to create a Reafforestation Zone to protect particular species of palm in the north-east. 77 Reafforestation Zones exist, covering an area of approximately 824,000 hectares.

The first Biosphere Reserve in Madagascar was being established in 1989. It is in the north-east in the area of Mananara and will contain a strict conservation zone, with the status of a

National Park, surrounded by a buffer zone. A World Heritage Site is also planned for the west, in the region of Antsalova.

The administration of the protected areas is the responsibility of the Service de la Protection de la Nature de la Direction des Eaux et Forêts, Ministère de la Production Animale (Elevage et Pêche) et des Eaux et Forêts. The Department of Water and Forests (Direction des Eaux et Forêts) is also responsible for all the forests.

In addition to the official reserves, there are two private reserves in Madagascar owned by M. Jean de Heaulme. The smaller of these, Berenty near Taolanaro (Fort Dauphin), is a comparatively well known tourist attraction.

Details of all the Nature Reserves, the two National Parks, over half the Special Reserves, both Private Reserves and some other areas of biological importance, which it is hoped may become protected areas, can be found in an IUCN/UNEP/WWF publication (1987) and also in WWF Project 3746 "Amenagement des Aires Protegees" by Martin Nicoll and Olivier Langrand. The following list of which lemurs are present in each protected area is taken mostly from these two publications.

National Parks:

P.N.1 **Montagne d'Ambre** (18,200 ha) Upland tropical moist forest
Microcebus rufus   *Lemur coronatus*
Cheirogaleus major   *Lemur fulvus sanfordi*
Phaner furcifer   *Daubentonia madagascariensis*
Lepilemur septentrionalis

P.N.2 **Isalo** (81,540 ha) Dry deciduous forest
Lemur fulvus   *Propithecus verreauxi verreauxi,*
Lemur catta

Nature Reserves:

R.N.I.1 **Betampona** (2,228 ha) Lowland dense evergreen rain forest
Microcebus rufus   *Varecia variegata variegata*
Cheirogaleus major   *Propithecus diadema* (possibly)
Lepilemur mustelinus   *Indri indri*
Hapalemur griseus   *Avahi laniger*
Lemur fulvus albifrons   *D. madagascariensis* (probably)

R.N.I.3 **Zahamena** (73,160ha) Tropical evergreen forest
Microcebus rufus   *Varecia variegata*
Cheirogaleus major   *Propithecus diadema diadema*
Lepilemur mustelinus   *Indri indri*
Hapalemur griseus   *Avahi laniger*
Lemur fulvus albifrons   *Daubentonia madagascariensis*
Lemur rubriventer

R.N.I.4 **Tsaratanana** (48,622 ha) Tropical evergreen forest
Cheirogaleus major   *Lemur fulvus*
Phaner furcifer   *Lemur macaco*
Hapalemur griseus   *Lemur rubriventer*
Lepilemur mustelinus

R.N.I.5 Andringitra (31,160 ha) Rain forest and some dry forest
Microcebus rufus   *Lemur fulvus fulvus*
Lepilemur microdon   *Varecia variegata variegata*
Lemur catta   *Avahi laniger laniger*

R.N.I.6 Lokobe (740 ha) Humid forest
Microcebus rufus   *Lemur macaco macaco*
Lepilemur dorsalis

R.N.I.7 Ankarafantsika (60,520 ha) Dry western forest
Microcebus murinus   *Lemur mongoz*
Cheirogaleus medius   *Propithecus verreauxi coquereli*
Lepilemur edwardsi   *Avahi laniger occidentalis*
Lemur fulvus fulvus

R.N.I.8 Namoroka (21,742 ha) Dense dry forest
Microcebus murinus   *Lemur fulvus rufus*
Lepilemur edwardsi   *Propithecus verreauxi deckeni*

R.N.I.9 Bemaraha (152,000 ha) Dense dry forest
Microcebus murinus   *Hapalemur griseus occidentalis*
Phaner furcifer   *Lemur fulvus rufus*
Mirza coquereli   *Propithecus verreauxi deckeni*
Lepilemur edwardsi

R.N.I.10 Tsimanampetsotsa (43,200 ha) Dry Didiereaceae brush
Microcebus murinus   *Lepilemur leucopus* (probably)
Lemur catta   *Propithecus verreauxi verreauxi*

R.N.I.11 Andohahela (76,020 ha) Eastern rain forest and spiny forest
Microcebus murinus   *Hapalemur griseus*
Microcebus rufus   *Lemur fulvus collaris*
Cheirogaleus medius   *Lemur catta*
Cheirogaleus major   *Propithecus verreauxi verreauxi*
Lepilemur leucopus   *Propithecus diadema*
Lepilemur mustelinus (microdon)   *Avahi laniger laniger*
Phaner furcifer   *Daubentonia madagascariensis*

R.N.I.12 Marojejy (60,150 ha) Rain forest
Microcebus rufus   *Lemur rubriventer*
Cheirogaleus major   *Varecia variegata* (reported)
Lepilemur mustelinus   *Propithecus diadema candidus*
Hapalemur griseus   *Avahi laniger laniger*
Lemur fulvus   *Daubentonia madagascariensis*

Special Reserves:

Ambohijanahary (24,750 ha) Dry western forest
Propithecus verreauxi deckeni (possibly others, the fauna is unknown)

Ambohitantely (5,600 ha) Rain forest in the central plateau
Microcebus rufus   *Lemur fulvus fulvus*

Analamazaotra (Perinet) (810 ha) Eastern rain forest
Microcebus rufus   *Varecia variegata variegata* (sometimes)
Cheirogaleus major   *Propithecus diadema diadema*
Lepilemur microdon   *Indri indri*
Hapalemur griseus   *Avahi laniger laniger*
Lemur fulvus fulvus   *Daubentonia madagascariensis*
Lemur rubriventer

Analamera (34,700 ha) Mostly dry, but some rain forest
Microcebus sp. (probably *rufus*)   *Lemur coronatus*
Lepilemur septentrionalis   *Propithecus diadema perrieri*
Lemur fulvus sanfordi   *Daubentonia madagascariensis*

Andranomena (6,420 ha) Dry western forest
Microcebus murinus   *Lepilemur ruficaudatus*
Cheirogaleus medius   *Lemur fulvus rufus*
Mirza coquereli   *Propithecus verreauxi verreauxi*
Phaner furcifer

Anjanaharibe-Sud (32,100 ha) Eastern rain forest
Microcebus rufus   *Propithecus diadema candidus*
Hapalemur griseus   *Avahi laniger laniger*
Lemur fulvus   *Indri indri*

Ankarana (18,220 ha) Dry western forest
Microcebus sp. (maybe *rufus*)   *Lemur fulvus sanfordi*
Cheirogaleus medius   *Lemur coronatus*
Phaner furcifer   *Propithecus diadema perrieri*
Lepilemur septentrionalis   *Daubentonia madagascariensis*
Hapalemur griseus

Beza Mahafaly (600 ha) Spiny forest and gallery forest
Microcebus murinus   *Lemur catta*
Cheirogaleus medius   *Propithecus verreauxi verreauxi*
Lepilemur leucopus

Bora (4,780 ha) Dry western forest
Lemur fulvus   *Propithecus verreauxi*

Forêt d'Ambre (4,810 ha) Rain forest
Microcebus rufus   *Lemur fulvus sanfordi*
Cheirogaleus major   *Lemur coronatus*
Phaner furcifer   *Daubentonia madagascariensis*
Lepilemur septentrionalis.

Kalambatritra (28,250 ha) Rain forest
Lemur fulvus rufus (and others)

Manongarivo (34,250 ha) Lowland to Montane rain forest
Microcebus rufus   *Lemur fulvus*
Cheirogaleus major   *Lemur macaco*
Phaner furcifer   *Avahi laniger occidentalis*
Hapalemur griseus occidentalis   *Daubentonia madagascariensis*
Lepilemur dorsalis

Manombo (5,020 ha) Lowland eastern rain forest
Hapalemur griseus
Lemur fulvus albocollaris   *Daubentonia madagascariensis*

Nosy Mangabe (520 ha) Lowland eastern rain forest
Microcebus rufus   *Varecia variegata variegata*
Lemur fulvus albifrons   *Daubentonia madagascariensis*

Private Reserves:

Analabe Dry western forest
Microcebus murinus   *Lepilemur ruficaudatus*
Cheirogaleus medius   *Lemur fulvus rufus,*
Mirza coquereli   *Propithecus verreauxi verreauxi*
Phaner furcifer.

Berenty (200 ha) Spiny and gallery forest
Microcebus murinus   *Lemur fulvus collaris* (introduced)
Cheirogaleus medius   *Lemur catta*
Lepilemur leucopus   *Propithecus verreauxi verreauxi*
Lemur fulvus rufus (introduced)

There are other protected areas shown on the map but not mentioned above. This is because no information has been found on the lemur species within those areas.

REFERENCES

Andriamampianina, J. (1972). Les réserves naturelles intégrales de Madagascar. In: *Comptes rendus de la Conférence internationale sur la Conservation de la Nature et de ses Ressources à Madagascar. Tananarive, Madagascar 7-11 October. Publication IUCN Nouvelle Series Document supplémentaires* No. 36. Pp.103-123

Hawkins, A. F. A., Ganzhorn, Bloxam, Q.M.C., Barlow, S.C., Tonge, S.J. and Chapman, P. (in press). A survey and assessment of the conservation status and needs of lemurs, birds, lizards and snakes in the Ankarana Special Reserve, Antseranana, Madagascar: with notes on the lemurs and birds of the nearby Analamera Special Reserve. *Biological Conservation.*

IUCN/UNEP/WWF (1987). *Madagascar, an environmental profile.* Edited by M.D. Jenkins. IUCN, Gland, Switzerland and Cambridge, U.K.

Nicoll, M. and Langrand, O. (1989). *Revue Generale d'Aires Protegees et de la Conservation à Madagascar.* Unpublished report to WWF. Project number 3746.

O'Connor, S., Pidgeon, M. and Randria, Z. (1986). Conservation Program for the Andohahela Reserve, Madagascar. *Primate Conservation* 7: 48-52.

Pollock, J. I. (1984). *Preliminary Report on a Mission to Madagascar by Dr J. I. Pollock in August and September 1984.* Unpublished report to WWF.

Raxworthy, C.J. and Rakotondraparany, F. (1988). Mammals report. In: Quansah, N. (Ed.), *Manongarivo Special Reserve (Madagascar), 1987/88 Expedition Report.* Unpublished. Pp. 122-130.

Safford, R.J., Durbin, J.C. and Duckworth, J.W. (1989). *Cambridge Madagascar Rainforest Expedition to R.N.I. 12 - Marojejy.* Unpublished preliminary report.

Now available: **Nicoll, M.E. et Langrand, O. (1989)** *Madagascar: Revue de la Conservation et des Aires Protégées.* WWF, Gland, Suisse.

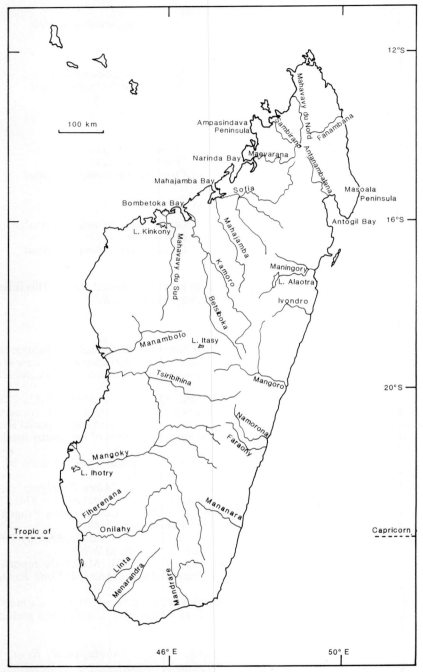

Figure 4: Map of some of Madagascar's major rivers, including most of those mentioned in the text.

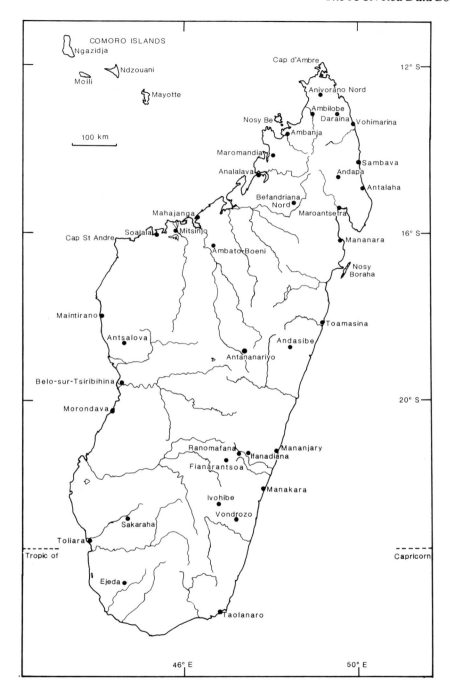

Figure 5: Map of some towns in Madagascar, including most of those mentioned in the text.

THE IUCN/SSC PRIMATE SPECIALIST GROUP

The IUCN/SSC Primate Specialist Group (PSG) has been in existence since the late 1960s and has been under the leadership of its present Chairman, Dr Russell A. Mittermeier, since 1977. The group is one of numerous specialist groups of the Species Survival Commission of IUCN and its membership has grown to nearly 200 primate scientists and conservationists from 45 different countries. The PSG is organised into six main subdivisions, corresponding to the four regions where primates occur, together with a captive breeding division and a special division for miscellaneous activities (i.e. conservation education, satellite imagery analysis, veterinary medicine, wildlife trade).

The goal of the PSG is to maintain the current diversity of the order Primates, with dual emphasis placed on:

*   ensuring the survival of threatened species wherever they occur;
*   providing effective protection for large numbers of primates in areas of high primate diversity and/or abundance.

Activities underway in many parts of the world make it inevitable that a certain portion of the world's forests and the primate species which reside in them will disappear. The role of the PSG is to minimize this loss whenever possible by:

*   setting aside special protected areas for threatened species;
*   creating large national parks and reserves in areas of high primate diversity and/or abundance;
*   maintaining parks and reserves that already exist and enforcing protective legislation in them;
*   creating public awareness of the need for primate conservation and the importance of primates as a natural heritage in the countries where they occur.

The PSG places particular emphasis on conservation of habitat and furtherance of conservation education as both these measures are considered essential and in large part inseparable. Regardless of how broadly one wishes to define conservation, long-term survival of natural populations will not be possible if habitats are not preserved and if local people in the areas where primates occur do not fully support conservation efforts. Additional measures taken by the PSG include:

*   determining ways in which man and his fellow primates can coexist in multiple use areas;
*   establishing conservation orientated captive breeding programmes for "Endangered species";
*   ending all illegal and otherwise destructive traffic in primates;
*   ensuring that research institutions using primates are aware of the conservation problems and that they are using primates as prudently as possible, without threatening the survival of any wild populations.

Among the many functions of the PSG are production of the newsletter/journal Primate Conservation (formerly the IUCN/SSC Primate Specialist Group Newsletter), edited by Isabel Constable, which is a major means of communication among the world's primate conservationists and is distributed free of charge to PSG members. The PSG is also responsible for the production of Action Plans for Primate Conservation, which update the original Global Strategy for Primate Conservation, produced in 1977. These Action Plans are intended to determine priorities in global primate conservation, to estimate the costs of conserving the world's primate fauna and to serve as tools in the fundraising efforts to make these projects possible. The first two regional Action Plans, the Action Plan for African Primate Conservation 1986-1990 by John Oates and the Action Plan for Asian Primate Conservation 1987-1991 by Ardith Eudey, have already been published. Action Plans for Madagascar and the Neotropical region are in preparation.

For further information on the IUCN/SSC Primate Specialist Group, please contact:

Dr. Russell A. Mittermeier
Conservation International
1015 Eighteenth Street, N.W.
Washington D.C. 20036
U.S.A.
Tel (202) 429-5660, Fax (202) 887-5188.

DATA SHEETS

The organisation of the data sheets

Each data sheet refers to one species and, if relevant, the subspecies within it. There are eight sections (summary, distribution, population, habitat and ecology, threats, conservation measures, captive breeding and remarks) within each sheet, which may be repeated for the subspecies, followed by a reference list for that species. The distribution maps have been adapted from those in Petter *et al* (1977), Petter and Petter Rousseaux (1979) and Tattersall (1982) with some additional information of new sightings from other reports. It is not, of course, suggested that the species concerned occurs throughout the relevant shaded part of the map. If that were the case, there would probably be no cause for concern about the status of the lemurs. Each is found in the, probably, small patches of suitable habitat within the range shown. Population numbers and/or densities and information as to whether the species is declining is given in the section on population. The habitat and ecology section has been expanded to make it more detailed than in previous Red Data Books. It is hoped that this will make it a useful reference for anybody attempting a study of the lemurs. The threats to each species are essentially similar throughout Madagascar, more so than when a species is found in many different countries. Similarly for the conservation measures. Information on captive breeding has come mainly from ISIS sheets, which mostly list only USA institutions, and from Wilde *et al* (1988) who have reported on only European institutions. Obviously this information is, as a result, probably far from complete, but it should at least give an idea of what numbers of each species are held and which breed well in captivity. The remarks section contains brief information on taxonomy, a short description of the species (size and colour) and its Malagasy name.

Request for further information

Information such as that presented here needs to be continually revised and updated. While the data sheets are as accurate as possible they do rely on information from those in the field. It is hoped that anybody in the position to provide the required data will do so, preferably to both IUCN, at the address and in the format of the sample inventory sheet given in Appendix A, and to Ian Tattersall as requested in Appendix B. This help will be greatly appreciated.

The taxonomic classification followed

The taxonomy of the lemurs is a constantly changing and much debated subject. There is no level of classification of this group that is accepted by all authors. The system followed here for all levels above the species is that of Schwartz and Tattersall (1985). The most controversial aspect of this classification is, undoubtedly, the positioning of *Lepilemur* in the family Megaladapidae. For species and subspecies, Jenkins (1987) is mostly followed except in the case of subspecies of *Propithecus verreauxi* and *P. diadema* where Tattersall (1986, in litt) is used. There have been two new species discovered since the publication of Jenkin's catalogue and the descriptions of these follow Meier *et al,* (1987) for *Hapalemur aureus* and Simons (1988) for *Propithecus tattersalli*.

Taxonomy References

Jenkins, P.D. (1987). *Catalogue of Primates in the British Museum (Natural History) and elsewhere in the British Isles. Part IV: Suborder Strepsirrhini, including the subfossil Madagascan lemurs and Family Tarsiidae.* British Museum (Natural History), London.

Meier, B., Albignac, R., Peyriéras, Rumpler, Y. and Wright, P. (1987). A new species of *Hapalemur* (Primates) from south east Madagascar. *Folia Primatologica* 48: 211-215.

Schwartz, J.H. and Tattersall, I. (1985). Evolutionary relationships of the living lemurs and lorises (Mammalia, Primates) and their potential affinities with European Eocene Adapidae. *Anthropological Papers of the American Museum of Natural History* 60 (1): 1-100.

Simons, E.L. (1988). A new species of *Propithecus* (Primates) from northeast Madagascar. *Folia Primatologica* 50: 143-151.

LEMURS OF MADAGASCAR and the Comoros: The IUCN Red Data Book

DATA SHEETS OF THREATENED LEMURS OF MADAGASCAR

The Grey Mouse Lemur, *Microcebus murinus*, is a tiny nocturnal species found in Madagascar's dry western forests. It is common in secondary vegetation.
Photo by Mark Pidgeon.

GREY or LESSER MOUSE LEMUR

ABUNDANT

Microcebus murinus **(J. F. Miller. 1777)**

Order PRIMATES

Family CHEIROGALEIDAE

SUMMARY The small, nocturnal Grey Mouse Lemur is found throughout the dry deciduous forest of the west and south of Madagascar. It is common in secondary forest, possibly more so than in undisturbed areas. It can reach high population densities and appears unlikely to be severely threatened at present. However, destruction of its habitat is occurring and it is probable that its numbers are declining. It has been the subject of several short term studies. It is usually seen alone while foraging at night but sleeps in groups during the day, the composition of which depends on the season. *M. murinus* is an omnivore, its diet includes fruit, insects, flowers, seeds, gums and leaves. There are over 370 animals in captivity and most were bred there. It occurs in most of the protected areas in the west and south, from Andohahela to Analamera. Listed in Appendix 1 of CITES, Class A of the African Convention and is protected by Malagasy law.

DISTRIBUTION Occurs throughout the dry deciduous forested areas of western and southern Madagascar from Taolanaro (Fort Dauphin) to, at least, the Sambirano River, though its precise northern limit is not known (Tattersall, 1982). It has recently been reported in Ankarana Special Reserve (Fowler *et al*, 1989), but other authors are not sure which species of Mouse Lemur is present in either Ankarana or Analamera Special Reserves (Hawkins *et al*, in press; Nicoll and Langrand, 1989; Ganzhorn, *in litt.*). It appears to be replaced by *M. rufus* in the Sambirano Region as it is this species that is reported in Manongarivo Special Reserve (Raxworthy and Rakotondraparany, 1988; Nicoll and Langrand, 1989). *M. murinus* is found in drier areas of Andohahela Special Reserve (M. Pidgeon, *in litt.*) and in the littoral forest in the area around Taolanaro (Martin, 1972).

POPULATION Population numbers are unknown, but the Grey Mouse Lemur must be one of the most numerous of the lemurs. However, Richard *et al* (1985) suspect that its numbers are "probably" declining. Population density has been estimated by Petter (1978) and Hladik *et al* (1980) in Marosalaza Forest, north of Morondava; the former estimated 3-4 individuals per ha (i.e. 300-400 per sq. km) and the latter, 400 animals per sq. km. Ganzhorn (1988) found much lower densities at Ampijoroa in Ankarafantsika Forest, only 42 ± 19 (mean and 95% confidence limits) individuals per sq. km. However, Martin's (1972) observations that this species occurs in "population nuclei" implies that it would be difficult to estimate accurate densities when extrapolating from a small to a large area. In addition, Grey Mouse Lemurs can be very difficult to find at some times of the year, particularly during long dry periods, and this causes another problem in estimating densities (M. Pidgeon, *in litt.*).

HABITAT AND ECOLOGY Grey Mouse Lemurs are reported to be far more common in secondary forest than in primary forest; they were even found in gardens and in patches of waste land round the port at Taolanaro (Martin, 1973) and have been seen in very degraded roadside bush and scrub habitat (M. Pidgeon, *in litt.*). They occupy the "fine branch" niche and, as a result, the height at which they are seen depends on the height at which fine branches, lianes and dense foliage are found (Martin, 1972, 1973). In secondary forest and along paths they are generally observed at 0-10m above the ground, whereas they are found at 15-30m in the canopy of primary forest (Martin, 1973). *M. murinus* is found in the spiny forest parcels of Andohahela Special Reserve and is more numerous in this habitat than in the gallery forest (M. Pidgeon, *in litt.*). In the area around Taolanaro, Martin (1972) found

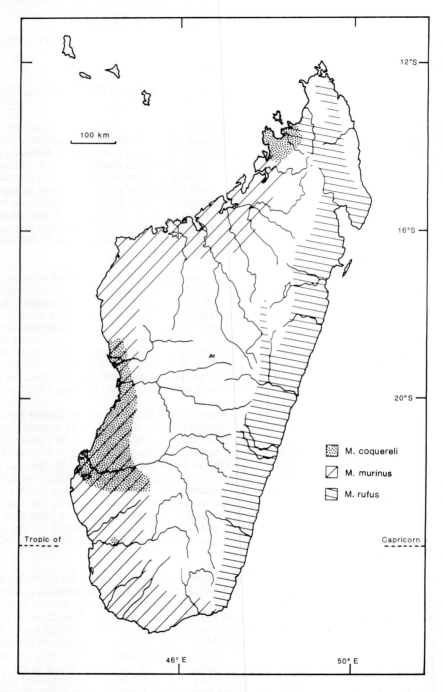

100 km

12°S

16°S

20°S

M. coquereli

M. murinus

M. rufus

Tropic of

Capricorn

46° E

50° E

Figure 6: Distribution of *Mirza* and both species of *Microcebus*. Shaded areas represent approximate limits of ranges.

this species in the drier, littoral forest, while the very similar Brown Mouse Lemur was in the inland, rain forest area.

The Grey Mouse Lemur is omnivorous; invertebrates and fruit appear to be the most important components of its diet, but it has also been seen eating flowers, nectar, leaves (*Uapaca* sp), sap and gum (from *Euphorbia* and *Terminalia* trees), secretions from Homopteran larvae, and small vertebrates such as tree frogs, geckos and chameleons (Martin, 1972, 1973; Petter, 1978; Hladik, 1979; Barre *et al*, 1988). Its insect prey was frequently caught on the ground (Martin, 1972, 1973). Though there is no period of dormancy, as there is in *Cheirogaleus* spp, the Mouse Lemur does lay down some fat in its tail (its volume varies from 5 to 20 cu cm through the year) and under its skin and this is probably used to make up for the reduced food available in the dry season from June to September (Martin, 1972; Petter, 1978; Hladik, 1979; Petter-Rousseaux, 1980). Grey Mouse Lemurs are most often seen alone at night, but, during the day, they are frequently seen asleep in groups. Their nests are either spherical constructions made from leaves or are in tree hollows, it appears that the latter are preferred (Martin, 1972, 1973). The minimum external diameter of trees in which Mouse Lemur nests were found was 5 cm and the median was 13 cm; it may be that trees of this size are a necessary part of a healthy habitat for *M. murinus*. (Martin, 1973). In the non-mating season in Mandena, males were always found either singly or in pairs at nest sites while females were in groups of 1-15 (with a median of four), the sexes were usually separate (Martin, 1972). However, group composition was very different during the mating season at the same study site; mixed sex groups were common, frequently a single male was found sharing a nest site with between three and seven females, though single females were also found with between one and three males (Martin, 1973). During a brief radio-tracking study in Ankarafantsika Forest, Pagès-Feuillade (1989) confirmed that male Grey Mouse Lemurs usually sleep alone, whereas females are often in groups. Martin (1972, 1973) found that, in apparently homogenous belts of forest, Grey Mouse Lemurs tended to occur in localised concentrations ("population nuclei"). In his study, the sex ratio was biased towards females (three or four females to one large male) in the population nucleus core, while smaller, adult males were found on the periphery. Marked individuals were found no more than 50m from their original sighting point, which suggested that home ranges were quite small (Martin, 1972, 1973). Two brief radio-tracking studies in Ankarafantsika Forest found that males tended to have bigger home ranges than females and that the males travelled further during the night (Barre *et al*, 1988; Pagès-Feuillade, 1989). During a six week study, Pagès-Feuillade (1989) found that her four radio collared males had home ranges of 3.2 $\pm$ 0.22 ha, while those of four females were 1.8 $\pm$ 0.24 ha (Pagès-Feuillade, 1989). The ranges of nine individuals overlapped, occupying a total of 7 ha, with the central portion being shared by all (Pagès-Feuillade, 1989). There was 66% overlap in the males' ranges and 44% overlap between females' ranges (Pagès-Feuillade, 1989). Neither of the studies in Ankarafantsika found any sign of a biased sex ratio, as Martin had done (1972, 1973), nor were central and peripheral males found (Barre *et al*, 1988; Pagès-Feuillade, 1989).

In Mandena, mating of the Grey Mouse Lemurs begins around mid-September and infants are born in November (Martin, 1972). Gestation period is 59-62 days (Petter-Rousseaux, 1964). The infants are born in a leaf nest or in a tree hole, litter size is usually two although singletons, triplets or, very occasionally, quadruplets can be produced (Petter-Rousseaux, 1964, 1988). Offspring up to three weeks of age (in captivity) are carried in their mother's mouth, rather than clinging to her fur (Petter-Rousseaux, 1964; Martin, 1972). Within two months, the young are behaving much like adult Mouse Lemurs, females are sexually mature within a year but, in captivity, they were at least 18 months old before they gave birth (Petter-Rousseaux, 1964).

THREATS The Grey Mouse Lemur is very small and nocturnal, it exists in areas of secondary forest and brush and, therefore, it seems unlikely that it could be severely threatened. However, Richard *et al* (1985) suspect that its numbers are "probably" declining as a result of habitat destruction. Sussman and Richard (1986) point out that since this species is dependent upon areas of dense undergrowth, it is possible that the extensive grazing by cattle and goats in southern Madagascar is destroying some of its optimal habitat. Martin (1972, 1973) also notes that trees of a certain age and size containing hollows of appropriate dimensions may be necessary for the long-term maintenance of a thriving Mouse Lemur population. Heavy tree-felling occurred in Martin's study area between 1968 and 1970 and he found that this was having an effect on *M. murinus*. For instance, individuals tended to be lighter in 1970, they were using smaller trees as nesting sites and the maximum female nesting group size was only seven as opposed to 15 in the earlier study (Martin, 1973).

CONSERVATION MEASURES Found in Andohahela, Ankarafantsika, Namoroka, Bemaraha and Tsimanampetsotsa Nature Reserves, in Andranomena and Beza Mahafaly Special Reserves, in Berenty and Analabe Private Reserves and may be in Analamera and Ankarana Special Reserves (Nicoll and Langrand, 1989)

At present, no specific measures are needed to conserve this Mouse Lemur. However, a range wide survey to determine which Mouse Lemur is where would be useful. These could be done in conjunction with surveys of more threatened species.

All species of Cheirogaleidae are listed in Appendix 1 of the 1973 Convention on International Trade in Endangered Species of Wild Fauna and Flora. Trade in them, or their products, is subject to strict regulation and may not be carried out for primarily commercial purposes.

All Lemuroidea are listed in Class A of the African Convention, 1969. They may not, therefore, be hunted, killed, captured or collected without the authorization of the highest competent authority, and then only if required in the national interest or for scientific purposes.

Malagasy law protects all lemurs from unauthorised capture and from hunting.

CAPTIVE BREEDING The Grey Mouse Lemur breeds well in captivity, though it is not as common in zoos as the larger lemurs, presumably because it is small, grey, nocturnal and generally not so interesting as an exhibit. ISIS (June 1989) lists 171 individuals (their *M. murinus* [no subspecies] and *M. m. murinus*) in 14 institutes. Over 97% of these Mouse Lemurs are captive born. The largest single colony is at Duke Primate Center. Over 97% of these Mouse Lemurs are captive born. Wilde *et al* (1988) list 172 individuals in 15 European institutes that are not included in ISIS lists and there are a further 30 animals at Paris Zoo (J.-J. Petter, *in litt.*)

REMARKS The Grey Mouse Lemur is one of the smallest primates, its mean body weight is 60g , though there are considerable seasonal fluctuations in this (Martin, 1972). Fur on its back is grey to grey-brown and greyish-white below. It has large membranous ears. For a more detailed description see Tattersall (1982), Jenkins (1987) or Petter *et al* (1977). The Malagasy names of this species are tsidy, pondiky, vakiandri, titilivaha and koitsiky (Paulian, 1981; Tattersall, 1982).

REFERENCES

Barre, V., Lebac, A., Petter, J.-J. and Albignac, R.(1988). Etude du Microcèbe par radiotracking dans la forêt de l'Ankarafantsika. In: Rakotovao, L., Barre, V. and Sayer, J. (Eds), *L'Equilibre des Ecosystèmes forestiers à Madagascar:* Actes d'un séminaire international. IUCN, Gland and Cambridge. Pp. 61-71.

Fowler, S.V., Chapman, P., Hurd, S., McHale, M., Ramangason, G.-S., Randriamsy, J.-E., Stewart, P., Walters, R. and Wilson, J.M. (1989). Survey and management proposals for a tropical deciduous forest reserve at Ankarana in northern Madagascar. *Biological Conservation* 47: 297-313.

Ganzhorn, J. U. (1988). Food partitioning among Malagasy primates. *Oecologia* (Berlin) 75: 436-450.

Hawkins, A.F.A., Ganzhorn, J.U., Bloxam, Q.M.C., Barlow, S.C., Tonge, S.J., and Chapman, P. (in press). A survey and assessment of the conservation status and needs of lemurs, birds, lizards and snakes in the Ankarana Special Reserve, Antseranana, Madagascar: with notes on the lemurs and birds of the nearby Analamera Special Reserve. *Biological Conservation*.

Hladik, C.M. (1979). Diet and ecology of prosimians. In: Doyle, G.A. and Martin, R.D. (Eds), *The Study of Prosimian Behavior*. Academic Press, New York. Pp. 307-357.

Hladik, C.M., Charles-Dominique, P. and Petter, J.-J. (1980). Feeding strategies of five nocturnal prosimians in the dry forest of the west coast of Madagascar. In: Charles-Dominique, P., Cooper, H.M., Hladik, A., Hladik, C.M., Pagès, E., Pariente, G.F., Petter-Rousseaux, A., Petter, J.-J. and Schilling, A. (Eds), *Nocturnal Malagasy Primates: Ecology, Physiology and Behavior*. Academic Press, New York. Pp. 41-73.

ISIS (1989). *ISIS Species Distribution Report Abstract for Mammals,* 30 June 1989. International Species Information System, 12101 Johnny Cake Ridge Road, Apple Valley, MN, U.S.A.

Jenkins, P.D. (1987). *Catalogue of Primates in the British Museum (Natural History) and elsewhere in the British Isles. Part IV: Suborder Strepsirrhini, including the Subfossil Madagascan Lemurs and Family Tarsiidae.* British Museum (Natural History), London.

Martin, R.D. (1972). A preliminary field study of the lesser mouse lemur (*Microcebus murinus* J. F. Miller 1777). *Zeitschrift für Tierpsychologie,* Supplement 9: 43-89.

Martin, R.D. (1973). A review of the behaviour and ecology of the lesser mouse lemur (*Microcebus murinus* J.F. Miller 1777). In: Michael, R.P. and Crook, J.H. (Eds),*Comparative Ecology and Behaviour of Primates*. Academic Press, London. Pp. 1-68.

Nicoll, M.E. and Langrand, O. (1989). *Revue Générale du Système d'Aires Protégées et de la Conservation à Madagascar*. Unpublished report to WWF.

Pagès-Feuillade, E. (1989). Modalités de l'occupation de l'espace et relations interindividuelles chez un prosimien nocturne malagache (*Microcebus murinus*). *Folia Primatologica* 50 (3/4): 204-220.

Paulian, R. (1981). Les mammifères: vestiges d'un monde disparu. In: Oberlé, P. (Ed.), *Madagascar, Une Sanctuaire de la Nature*. Le Chevalier, Paris. Pp. 75-94.

Petter, J-J., Albignac, R. and Rumpler, Y. (1977). Mammifères lémuriens (Primates prosimiens). *Faune de Madagascar* No. 44. ORSTOM-CNRS, Paris.

Petter, J.-J. (1978). Ecological and physiological adaptations of five sympatric nocturnal lemurs to seasonal variation in food production. In: Chivers, D.J. and Herbert, J. (Eds), *Recent Advances in Primatology 1: Behaviour*. Academic Press, London. Pp.211-223.

Petter-Rousseaux, A. (1964). Reproductive physiology and behavior of the Lemuroidae. In: Buettner-Janusch, J. (Ed.), *Evolution and Genetic Biology of the Primates.*. Academic Press, New York. Pp. 91-132.

Petter-Rousseaux, A. (1980). Seasonal activity rhythms, reproduction, and body weight variations in five sympatric nocturnal prosimians, in simulated light and climatic conditions. In: Charles-Dominique, P., Cooper, H.M., Hladik, A., Hladik, C.M., Pagès, E., Pariente, G.F., Petter-Rousseaux, A., Petter, J.-J. and Schilling, A. (Eds), *Nocturnal Malagasy Primates: Ecology, Physiology and Behavior*. Academic Press, New York. Pp.137-152.

Petter-Rousseaux, A. (1988). Photopériode et réproduction de *Microcebus murinus.* In: Rakotovao, L., Barre, V. and Sayer, J. (Eds), *L'Equilibre des Ecosystèmes forestiers à Madagascar: Actes d'un séminaire international.* IUCN, Gland, Switzerland and Cambridge, UK. Pp. 72-77.

Raxworthy, C.J. and Rakotondraparany, F. (1988). Mammals report. In: Quansah, N. (Ed.), *Manongarivo Special Reserve (Madagascar), 1987/88 Expedition Report.* Unpublished report, Madagascar Environmental Research Group, U.K.

Richard, A.F., Sussman, R.W. and Ravelojaona, G. (1985). Madagascar: current projects and problems in conservation. *Primate Conservation* 5: 53-59.

Susman, R.W. and Richard, A.F. (1986). Lemur conservation in Madagascar: the status of lemurs in the south. *Primate Conservation* 7: 86-92.

Tattersall, I. (1982). *The Primates of Madagascar.* Columbia University Press, New York.

Wilde, J., Schwibbe, M.H. and Arsene, A. (1988). A census for captive primates in Europe. *Primate Report* 21: 1-120.

The Brown Mouse Lemur, *Microcebus rufus*, is the smallest of the lemurs. It is found in the eastern rain forests where it can survive in scrub secondary vegetation.
Photo by Mark Pidgeon.

BROWN or RUFOUS MOUSE LEMUR

ABUNDANT

Microcebus rufus (Lesson, 1840)

Order **PRIMATES**   Family **CHEIROGALEIDAE**

SUMMARY The smallest of the Malagasy primates, the Brown Mouse Lemur is found throughout the eastern rain forest and across to the Sambirano Region in the north-west of Madagascar. It is found in primary forest but is more common in secondary forest. Though it is vulnerable to habitat destruction and its numbers are probably declining, it is unlikely to be severely threatened. *M. rufus* has not been studied in any detail. It is a nocturnal, mostly solitary species which feeds principally on fruit and insects. There are very few individuals in captivity. It is found in several reserves. Listed in Appendix 1 of CITES, Class A of the African Convention and is protected by Malagasy law.

DISTRIBUTION Brown Mouse Lemurs are found throughout the rain forest of eastern Madagascar from Taolanaro (Fort Dauphin) to Montagne d'Ambre and across to the Sambirano Region and Nosy Bé (Tattersall, 1982; Petter and Petter-Rousseaux, 1979; Petter *et al*, 1977). A Brown Mouse Lemur (its specific status is unclear) also exists south of the Sambirano River, though it occurs only sparsely there; specimens have been collected near Morondava and have been reported from Ankarafantsika where they are sympatric with the Grey Mouse Lemur (Petter *et al,* 1971; Petter *et al,* 1977; Tattersall, 1982; Petter and Andriatsarafara, 1987).

POPULATION Population numbers are not known but Sussman *et al* (1985) report that its numbers are "probably" declining. Density has been estimated in Analamazaotra Forest (Perinet) as 110 ± 34 individuals per sq. km (mean and 95% confidence limits) (Ganzhorn, 1988). However, the apparent population density in Analamazaotra was five times lower in 1985/86 than in 1984 (mean 0.11 per 100m compared to 0.52 per 100m respectively) and Ganzhorn suggests this was due to the availability of fruiting shrubs and trees (Ganzhorn, 1987, 1988). This implies that, for *M. rufus* at least, figures for population density which are based on transect walks can be very misleading. Petter and Petter-Rousseaux (1964) found 250-262 individuals per sq. km at Mahambo on the east coast.

HABITAT AND ECOLOGY There are few, other than incidental, observations on this species. It, like the Grey Mouse Lemur, appears to be more common in secondary vegetation than in primary forest. During a short trapping study near Ranomafana in south-eastern Madagascar, the Brown Mouse Lemur was seen most frequently in an old plantation of the introduced Chinese guava, *Psidium cattleyanum*. Here an 80m trap line with ten traps caught 24 individuals, while seven other traps spaced over 110m in a much less disturbed area of primary forest caught only four individuals (Harcourt, 1987 and unpubl. data). At Analamazaotra (Perinet) *M. rufus* can be found in old eucalyptus plantations, though at greatly reduced densities compared to those in "natural" forest (Ganzhorn, 1987).

The diet of this species seems to be very similar to that of the Grey Mouse Lemur, they have been seen eating fruit, insects and flowers (Martin, 1972; Harcourt, 1987) and, very occasionally, young leaves (Ganzhorn, 1988). They are normally seen eating in shrubs and little trees but they have also been seen in the tops of the tallest trees in Analamazaotra Forest (Ganzhorn, 1988). They appear to be much less prone to storing fat in their tail than the Grey Mouse Lemur, and this is probably related to the less marked seasonal differences in food availability (Martin, 1972).

Little is known about the Brown Mouse Lemurs' social organisation, they are mostly seen alone during the night. During a brief study at Ranomafana 23 males and only five females were caught, but this biased sex ratio could not be explained (Harcourt, 1987). *M. rufus* sleeps in tree holes and leaf nests in the daytime (Martin, 1972) and has been seen using old birds' nests as well (Pollock, 1979). There are no reports as to the sex or numbers of animals sleeping together during the day.

THREATS There are no recognised threats specific to the Brown Mouse Lemur, but all Madagascar's primates are declining to a greater or lesser degree due to habitat destruction. However, this small, nocturnal species must be one of the least threatened, especially as it appears to thrive in secondary vegetation providing that fruit and insects are available there.

CONSERVATION MEASURES *M. rufus* is probably present in most of the protected areas throughout its range. It is reported in Montagne d'Ambre National Park, in Marojejy, Zahamena, Betampona, Andringitra and Andohahela Nature Reserves and in Manongarivo, Analamazaotra, Anjanaharibe-Sud and Nosy Mangabe Special Reserves (Pollock, 1984; Safford *et al*, 1989; Nicoll and Langrand, 1989; O'Connor *et al*, 1986; Raxworthy and Rakotondraparany, 1988; Constable *et al*, 1985). Mouse Lemurs have been reported in Ankarana and Analamera Special Reserves but it is not clear whether these are the Grey or Brown species (Nicoll and Langrand, 1989; Ganzhorn, *in litt.*).

There are no conservation measures suggested specifically for the Brown Mouse Lemur, but a range wide survey, to determine which Mouse Lemur is where, would be useful.

All species of Cheirogaleidae are listed in Appendix 1 of the 1973 Convention on International Trade in Endangered Species of Wild Fauna and Flora. Trade in them, or their products, is subject to strict regulation and may not be carried out for primarily commercial purposes.

All Lemuroidea are listed in Class A of the African Convention, 1969. They may not, therefore, be hunted, killed, captured or collected without the authorization of the highest competent authority, and then only if required in the national interest or for scientific purposes.

All lemurs are protected from unauthorised capture and from hunting by Malagasy law.

CAPTIVE BREEDING ISIS (June 1989) does not list any of this species in captivity. Wilde *et al* (1988) report 18 individuals in Rotterdam Zoo and there is one pair at Tsimbazaza in Madagascar (G. Rakotoarisoa and M. Pidgeon, *in litt.*). In captivity, they do not breed as well as *M. murinus* (E. Simons, *in litt.*).

REMARKS This species is even smaller than the Grey Mouse Lemur, average weight is around 50 g (Harcourt, 1987). It is distinguished from *M. murinus* by its slightly smaller ears and the red tinge to its coat. For a more detailed description see Petter *et al* (1977), Tattersall (1982) and Jenkins (1987). The taxonomic status of the Brown Mouse Lemurs south of the Sambirano River is unclear (Tattersall, 1982). The Malagasy names of this species are tsidy and tsitsihy or tsitsidy (Paulian, 1981; Tattersall, 1982).

REFERENCES

Constable, I.D., Mittermeier, R.A., Pollock, J.I., Ratsirarson, J. and Simons, H. (1985). Sightings of aye-ayes and red ruffed lemurs on Nosy Mangabe and the Masoala Peninsula. *Primate Conservation* 5: 59-62.

Ganzhorn, J.U. (1987). A possible role of plantations for primate conservation in Madagascar. *American Journal of Primatology* 12: 205-215.

Ganzhorn, J.U. (1988). Food partitioning among Malagasy primates. *Oecologia* (Berlin) 75: 436-450.

Harcourt, C.S. (1987). Brief trap/retrap study of the brown mouse lemur (*Microcebus rufus*). *Folia Primatologica* 49: 209-211.

ISIS (1989). *ISIS Species Distribution Report Abstract for Mammals,* 30 June 1989. International Species Information System, 12101 Johnny Cake Ridge Road, Apple Valley, MN, U.S.A. Pp 17-22.

Jenkins, P.D. (1987). *Catalogue of Primates in the British Museum (Natural History) and elsewhere in the British Isles. Part IV: Suborder Strepsirrhini, including the Subfossil Madagascan Lemurs and Family Tarsiidae.* British Museum (Natural History), London.

Martin, R.D. (1972). A preliminary field study of the lesser mouse lemur (*Microcebus murinus* J. F. Miller 1777). *Zeitschrift für Tierpsychologie,* Supplement 9: 43-89.

Nicoll, M.E. and Langrand, O. (1989). *Revue Générale du Système d'Aires Protégées et de la Conservation à Madagascar.* Unpublished report to WWF.

O'Connor, S., Pidgeon, M. and Randria, Z. (1986). Conservation program for the Andohahela Reserve, Madagascar. *Primate Conservation* 7: 48-52.

Paulian, R. (1981). Les mammifères: vestiges d'un monde disparu. In: Oberlé, P. (Ed.), *Madagascar, Une Sanctuaire de la Nature.* Le Chevalier, Paris. Pp. 75-94.

Petter, J-J., Albignac, R. and Rumpler, Y. (1977). Mammifères lémuriens (Primates prosimiens). *Faune de Madagascar* No. 44. ORSTOM-CNRS, Paris.

Petter, J.-J. and Andriatsarafara, F. (1987). Conservation status and distribution of lemurs in the west and northwest of Madagascar. *Primate Conservation* 8: 169-171

Petter, J.-J. and Petter-Rousseaux, A. (1964). Première tentative d'estimation des densités de peuplement des lémuriens malagaches. *La Terre et la Vie* 18: 427-435.

Petter, J.-J., Schilling, A. and Pariente, G. (1971). Observations éco-éthologiques sur deux lemuriens malagaches nocturnes: *Phaner furcifer* et *Microcebus coquereli. La Terre et la Vie* 25: 287-327.

Pollock, J.I. (1979). Spatial distribution and ranging behavior in lemurs. In: Doyle, G.A. and Martin, R.D. (Eds), *The Study of Prosimian Behavior.* Academic Press, New York. Pp. 359-409.

Pollock, J.I. (1984). Preliminary report on a mission to Madagascar by Dr J. I. Pollock in August and September 1984. Unpublished report to WWF.

Raxworthy, C.J. and Rakotondraparany, F. (1988). Mammals report. In: Quansah, N. (Ed.), *Manongarivo Special Reserve (Madagascar), 1987/88 Expedition Report.* Unpublished report, Madagascar Environmental Research Group, U.K.

Safford, R.J., Durbin, J.C. and Duckworth, J.W. (1989). Cambridge Madagascar rainforest expedition to R.N.I. No. 12 - Marojejy. Unpublished preliminary report.

Sussman, R.W., Richard, A.F. and Ravelojaona, G. (1985). Madagascar: current projects and problems in conservation. *Primate Conservation* 5: 53-59.

Tattersall, I. (1982). *The Primates of Madagascar.* Columbia University Press, New York.

Wilde, J., Schwibbe, M.H. and Arsene, A. (1988). A census for captive primates in Europe. *Primate Report* 21: 1-120.

Coquerel's Dwarf Lemur, *Mirza coquereli*, is a nocturnal species which survives the dry season in the western forests by eating carbohydrate-rich secretions from insect larvae. Photo by Jean-Jacque Petter/WWF

COQUEREL'S DWARF LEMUR

Mirza coquereli (A. Grandidier, 1867)

Order PRIMATES

VULNERABLE

Family CHEIROGALEIDAE

SUMMARY Coquerel's Dwarf Lemur is a nocturnal species found in some areas of dry deciduous forest and in the more humid Sambirano Region in the west of Madagascar. The extent of its distribution is not clear. Population numbers are not known and estimates of density vary considerably. It appears to thrive in secondary forest, it has been reported at densities as high as 385 individuals per sq. km in an area dominated by cashew nut trees. It is, however, thought to be declining in number due to destruction of its habitat. The only studies of *M. coquereli* have been brief and more are needed, though surveys to determine its distribution would be more valuable in determining its conservation status. Its diet includes insects, flowers, fruit, small vertebrates and, particularly, the secretions from Homopteran larvae. It, like all the lemurs, is threatened by habitat destruction. This Dwarf Lemur is found in only three protected areas. A colony of about 50 individuals at Duke Primate Center breeds well, but the species is kept in few other institutes. Listed in Appendix 1 of CITES, Class A of the African Convention and is protected by Malagasy Law.

DISTRIBUTION Discontinuously distributed along the west coast of Madagascar. The maps of its range given by Petter *et al* (1977), Petter and Petter-Rousseaux (1979) and Tattersall (1982) differ quite considerably, those of the first two authors being more extensive than the latter's. Tattersall (1982) shows its range from near Ankazoabo (i.e. just south of the Mangoky River) northwards to around Antsalova and also in the Sambirano region (the Ampasindava Peninsula and Ambanja area). Petter *et al* (1977) and Petter and Petter-Rousseaux (1979) show it also extending along the west coast from around Cap St André to Narinda` Bay. However, in their text, Petter *et al* (1977) say that it only probably exists in this stretch of west coast. M. Pidgeon (*in litt.*) reports seeing an individual of this species as far south as the north bank of the Onilahy River, about 40 km due east from the coast. His sighting was confirmed by M. Nicoll (*in litt.* from M. Pidgeon).

POPULATION Numbers are unknown and cannot be estimated until the range of Coquerel's Dwarf Lemur is much better known. Petter *et al* (1971) estimated densities of 50 individuals per sq. km in Marosalaza Forest (50 km north of Morondava), but they recorded as many as 210 per sq. km when counting in a strip of forest 5 m in width along either side of a river in the region. In the same forest, Hladik *et al* (1980) estimated that there were 30 individuals per sq. km. The density (and biomass) of this species is the lowest of the five nocturnal lemurs found in Marosalaza Forest (Hladik *et al*, 1980). Much higher densities of *M. coquereli* have been reported from an area of secondary forest near Ambanja which was dominated by *Anacardium occidentalae* (cashew nut) trees. Here there were as many as 385 individuals per sq. km (Andrianarivo, 1981). In 1975, Richard and Sussman considered *M. coquereli* to be extremely rare and probably on the brink of extinction. Later, in 1985, Sussman *et al* recorded the species as probably declining in number due to habitat destruction.

HABITAT AND ECOLOGY Within the dry deciduous forest of western Madagascar, Coquerel's Dwarf Lemur is generally found along rivers and near semipermanent ponds, where the forest is thicker and slightly taller than in the drier areas (Petter *et al*, 1971). In Marosalaza forest, *M. coquereli* has been briefly studied using radio tracking equipment (Pages, 1978, 1980). This was done during part of the dry season (June-July) in 1974. *M. coquereli* feeds on a variety of food resources including insects, spiders, frogs, chameleons, small birds, fruits, flowers, buds, gums, and insect secretions (Pages, 1980,

Andrianarivo, 1981). During the dry season, the secretions of cochineals and homopteran larvae are particularly important (Petter *et al*, 1971; Hladik *et al,* 1980) and, during June in Marosalaza Forest these accounted for 50% of the feeding observations (Pages 1980). However, these secretions are low in protein (Hladik *et al,* 1980) and it appears that the distribution of Coquerel's Dwarf Lemur depends more on the availability of other insects than on these colonies (Pages, 1980). Andrianarivo (1981) found that in secondary forest dominated by cashew nut trees, the cashew fruits were a very important food source during the dry season. In Marosalaza, feeding usually occurred at heights between 1.5 and 3m, though *M. coquereli* may also forage on the ground (Pages, 1980).

The species is nocturnal, spending the day in a spherical nest made of interlaced lianas, branches and leaves which is usually located in the fork of a large branch or among dense lianas at a height of 2-10m (Petter *et al*, 1971; Pages 1980, Andrianarivo, 1981). In Marosalaza Forest a female and her offspring could be found sharing a nest, but males were never seen with them (Pages, 1980). This was not the case at a study site in secondary forest near Ambanja. Here, out of four occupied nests two contained an adult male and female, one contained two young individuals and in the fourth there was an adult female and a young animal (Andrianarivo, 1981). In the area near Ambanja, nests were found clustered together in "villages" of about 1 ha in size (Andrianarivo, 1981). Six to ten individuals lived in each of these "villages" and though they changed nests within the area they did not move between nesting areas (Andrianarivo, 1981). Individuals left their nests around dusk and generally spent the first half of the night feeding, self-grooming or resting, while the second half of the night was devoted more to social activities such as vocalisations, mutual grooming and play (Pages, 1978, 1980). There was also an increase in distance travelled during this second part of the night (Pages, 1978, 1980).

Pages (1978, 1980) found that the home range of adults of both sexes appeared to contain a heavily used and defended central area (1.5 ha for males and 2.5-3.0 ha for females), surrounded by a large peripheral area (a maximum of 4 ha for males and 4.5 ha for females), which was less frequently visited. There was a much greater degree of overlap in the peripheral area, however even the central core could be overlapped by an adult individual of the opposite sex or, in the case of females, by their offspring (Pages, 1980). The males generally made longer incursions into distant areas than did females (Pages, 1980). Meetings between individuals were rare, males encountered other animals only every other night on average and prolonged contact was even less frequent (Pages, 1980). Although adult males met a number of adult females, their periods of prolonged contact appeared to be restricted to just one of these females; Pages (1978, 1980) suggested a loose pair bonding social system in this species.

Mating takes place in October, gestation lasts three months (Petter-Rousseaux, 1980) and normally two infants are born (Pages, 1978). Infants initially stay in the nest, they leave this for the first time when they are about three weeks old (Pages, 1980). They, like most of the other members of the family Cheirogaleidae, do not ride on their mother, but are carried in her mouth (Pages, 1980).

THREATS *M. coquereli* may be threatened by habitat destruction though its high density in secondary forest suggests that it may survive the disappearance of its natural habitat. The forests in the Sambirano Region are being cleared for cultivation, while the dry deciduous forests are mostly being destroyed by fire. These are frequently set to encourage new grass growth for the large numbers of livestock that are kept in western Madagascar. In 1981, FAO/UNEP estimated net degradation of the western forests to be perhaps 200,000 ha since 1955.

CONSERVATION MEASURES Found in Bemaraha Nature Reserve, Andranomena Special Reserve and the Private Reserve of Analabe (Nicoll and Langrand, 1989). All three reserves would benefit from more guards with better equipment to protect them, particularly from fires. Signposting of the Reserve boundaries would be an asset, as would an education programme for the local villagers to emphasise the uniqueness of the reserves and their biota. Analabe has great tourist potential and this could be developed for the benefit of both the wildlife and the local people (Nicoll and Langrand, 1989)

Surveys are desirable to determine the actual distribution and numbers of *M. coquereli* so that an effective conservation strategy can be developed.

All species of Cheirogaleidae are listed in Appendix 1 of the 1973 Convention on International Trade in Endangered Species of Wild Fauna and Flora. Trade in them, or their products, is subject to strict regulation and may not be carried out for primarily commercial purposes.

All Lemuroidea are listed in Class A of the African Convention, 1969. They may not, therefore, be hunted, killed, captured or collected without the authorization of the highest competent authority, and then only if required in the national interest or for scientific purposes.

All lemurs are protected from unauthorised capture and from hunting by the laws of Madagascar. However, its is very difficult to enforce these regulations.

CAPTIVE BREEDING This species breed wells in captivity (Petter *et al*, 1977; E. Simons, *in litt*.), but it is not kept by many institutions. According to the ISIS records (June 1989) there are 62 individuals in captivity, most of which (45) are at Duke Primate Center; Cincinnati holds eight animals, San Francisco has six and Paris has three. It is reported that 95% of the 62 animals are captive born; all those in American insitutions are descendents of six individuals imported by Duke in 1982 (E. Simons, *in litt*.). Duke Primate Center is now coordinating a captive breeding programme for this species (E. Simons, pers. comm.).

REMARKS Tattersall (1982) puts this species in its own genus; however, it is still frequently referred to as belonging to the genus *Microcebus*. *M. coquereli*, at 300g (Pages, 1978), is considerably larger than the Mouse Lemurs. Dorsally, the fur of this species is brown or grey-brown, sometimes with rosy or yellowish tinges; ventrally the grey base colour of the downy hair shows through beneath the yellowish or slightly russet tips (Tattersall, 1982). The ears of Coquerel's Dwarf Lemur are long and hairless. For a more detailed description see Petter *et al* (1977) or Tattersall (1982). In the southern area of its range, this species is called tsiba or tilitilivaha and setohy or fitily in its northern range.

REFERENCES

Andrianarivo, A.J. (1981). Etude comparee de l'organisation sociale chez *Microcebus coquereli*. Unpublished dissertation, University of Madagascar, Antananarivo.
FAO/UNEP (1981). *Tropical Forest Resources Assessment Project. Forest Resources of Tropical Africa. Part II Country Briefs*. FAO, ROME.
Hladik, C.M., Charles-Dominique, P. and Petter, J.-J. (1980). Feeding strategies of five nocturnal prosimians in the dry forest of the west coast of Madagascar. In: Charles-Dominique, P., Cooper, H.M., Hladik, A., Hladik, C.M., Pages, E., Pariente, G.F., Petter-Rousseaux, A., Petter, J.-J. and Schilling, A. (Eds), *Nocturnal Malagasy Primates: Ecology, Physiology and Behavior*. Academic Press, New York. Pp. 41-73.
ISIS (1989). *ISIS Species Distribution Report Abstract for Mammals*, 30 June 1989. International Species Information System, 12101 Johnny Cake Ridge Road, Apple Valley, MN, U.S.A.
Nicoll, M.E. and Langrand, O. (1989). *Revue Générale du Système d'Aires Protégées de la Conservation à Madagascar*. Unpublished report to WWF.

Pages, E. (1978). Home range, behaviour and tactile communication in a nocturnal malagasy lemur *Microcebus coquereli.* In: Chivers, D.A. and Joysey, K.A. (Eds), *Recent Advances in Primatology, Vol 3.* Academic Press, London. Pp. 171-177.

Pages, E. (1980). Ethoecology of *Microcebus coquereli* during the dry season. In: Charles-Dominique, P., Cooper, H.M., Hladik, A., Hladik, C.M., Pages, E., Pariente, G.F., Petter-Rousseaux, A., Petter, J.-J. and Schilling, A. (Eds), *Nocturnal Malagasy Primates: Ecology, Physiology and Behavior.* Academic Press, New York. Pp. 97-116.

Petter, J-J., Albignac, R. and Rumpler, Y. (1977). Mammifères lémuriens (Primates prosimiens). *Faune de Madagascar* No. 44. ORSTOM-CNRS, Paris.

Petter, J.-J. and Petter-Rousseaux, A. (1979). Classification of the Prosimians In: Doyle, G.A. and Martin, R.D. (Eds), *The Study of Prosimian Behavior.* Academic Press, London. Pp. 1-44.

Petter, J.-J., Schilling, A. and Pariente, G. (1971). Observations éco-éthologiques sur deux lemuriens malagaches nocturnes: *Phaner furcifer* et *Microcebus coquereli. La Terre et la Vie* 25: 287-327.

Petter-Rousseaux, A. (1980). Seasonal activity rhythms, reproduction, and body weight variations in five sympatric nocturnal prosimians, in simulated light and climatic conditions. In: Charles-Dominique, P., Cooper, H.M., Hladik, A., Hladik, C.M., Pages, E., Pariente, G.F., Petter-Rousseaux, A., Petter, J.-J. and Schilling, A. (Eds), *Nocturnal Malagasy Primates: Ecology, Physiology and Behavior.* Academic Press, New York. Pp. 97-116.

Pages, E., Pariente, G.F., Petter-Rousseaux, A., Petter, J.-J. and Schilling, A. (Eds), *Nocturnal Malagasy Primates: Ecology, Physiology and Behavior.* Academic Press, New York. Pp. 137-152.

Richard, A.F. and Sussman, R.W. (1975). Future of the Malagasy lemurs: conservation or extinction? In: Tattersall, I. and Sussman, R.W. (Eds), *Lemur Biology,* Plenum Press, New York. Pp. 335-350.

Sussman, R.W., Richard, A.F. and Ravelojaona (1985). Madagascar: current projects and problems in conservation. *Primate Conservation* 5: 53-58.

Tattersall, I. (1982). *The Primates of Madagascar.* Columbia University Press, New York.

The Fat-tailed Dwarf Lemur, *Cheirogaleus medius*, stores fat in its tail which enables it to survive long periods of food shortage in the dry western forests.
Photo by Russell Mittermeier.

FAT-TAILED DWARF LEMUR

ABUNDANT

Cheirogaleus medius E. Geoffroy, 1812

Order **PRIMATES** Family **CHEIROGALEIDAE**

SUMMARY The Fat-tailed Dwarf Lemur is one of the smaller, nocturnal lemurs. It has a wide distribution in the dry forests, both primary and secondary, in the west and south of Madagascar. Population numbers are unknown, but the species is considered to be declining as the dry forests are being reduced in area. However, it can be found at densities as high as 300-400 per sq. km which, along with its wide distribution, suggests that it may not be severely threatened. The species has been studied briefly but little is known of its social organisation. Its diet consists of fruit, flowers and insects. The most characteristic feature of *Cheirogaleus medius* is its ability to become torpid for six to eight months in the dry season. It is found in at least seven protected areas. There is a minimum of 120 individuals in captivity and most are captive bred. Listed in Appendix 1 of CITES and Class A of the African Convention and protected by Malagasy law.

DISTRIBUTION Found in the dry forests of southern and western Madagascar from Narinda Bay to Taolanaro (Fort Dauphin) (Tattersall, 1982; Petter and Petter-Rouseaux, 1979). Locality information on museum specimens collected late last century and in 1929-1931 indicate that the Fat-tailed Dwarf Lemur was then found in eastern and northern Madagascar and in the Sambirano region, in sympatry with *C. major* (Tattersall, 1982), but there are no recent reports of its occurrence in these areas except in Ankarana, where *Cheirogaleus* sp. was seen and members of the expedition identified it provisionally as *C. medius* (Hawkins *et al*, in press).

POPULATION Numbers are unknown but the species is considered to be declining due to habitat destruction (Richard and Sussman, 1975, 1987). It is, however, found at densities as high as 300-400 animals per sq. km in deciduous forest near Morondava (Petter, 1978; Hladik, 1979), which, along with its wide distribution, suggests that it may not be severely threatened as yet. Estimates of population densities at other areas are lower, 37 individuals per sq. km at Berenty (Russell, in Jolly, 1987, 1988), and either 12 (Albignac, 1981) or 81 $\pm$ 36 individuals per sq. km (mean and 95% confidence limits based on 10 census walks along 1.7 km of trail [Ganzhorn, 1988]) at Ankarafantsika.

HABITAT AND ECOLOGY Fat-tailed Dwarf Lemurs are found in both primary and well-established secondary forest (Martin, 1984). In 1935, Rand reported that he found them in gallery forest through savanna and dry brush. The animals are active for half the year or less, they avoid the seasonal shortage of food by becoming torpid during the dry season (May-October). At this time individuals can be found alone or in groups of up to five individuals in hollow tree trunks (Petter, 1978, Hladik, 1979; Hladik *et al*, 1980). The age/sex composition of the dormant groups varies. Petter (1988) found solitary adults of both sexes; two young females; an adult male and female with two young females; an adult male and female with one young female; and a group of two adult males, one adult female and two young females during observations at his study site near Morondava. Adults can become torpid as early as March, while offspring born that year tend to become dormant slightly later, thereby suffering less competition for food (Hladik *et al*, 1980). They re-emerge in November at the beginning of the rainy season (Petter, 1978).

In Marosalaza Forest, the diet of *C. medius* includes fruit (*Operculicarya gummifera*, *Grewia glanulosa*, *Strychnos decussata* and *Diospyros aculeata*) and flowers (*Baudouina fluggeiformis*), the nectar of some flowers (e.g. *Delonix floribunda*), insects (especially beetles), a few leaf buds, gums and some small vertebrates (the skin of a chameleon was

51

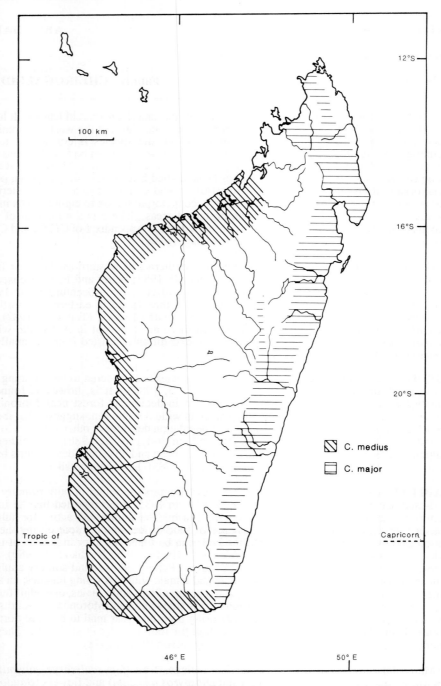

Figure 7: Distribution of both species of *Cheirogaleus*. Shaded areas represent approximate limits of ranges.

found in one faecal sample) (Hladik, 1979, Hladik *et al*, 1980). Flowers and nectar are used at the beginning of the rainy season (November), fruits and an increasing proportion of insects are taken from December to February, while from then onwards fruits are the staple food (Hladik, 1979; Hladik *et al*, 1980). During the rains, the animals lay down fat under their skin and in their tail, their body weight increases by approximately 75 g, to about 220 g, and the volume of their tail triples, from a mean of 15 cc in November to a mean of 42 cc in May (Hladik *et al*, 1980).

In a study of 31 marked individuals, *C. medius* had a home range with a maximum diameter of 200 m (about 4 ha) and the ranges of adult animals overlapped (Hladik *et al*, 1980). In captivity, adult animals of the same sex are intolerant of each other (Hladik *et al*, 1980), but there is no information available on their social organisation in the wild.

In Marosalaza Forest, mating was observed at the beginning of November and infants were born in January (Petter, 1978; Hladik *et al*, 1980). Gestation in this species is 61-64 days; litter size varies from one to four, but twins are most frequently produced (Foerg, 1982). In captivity, offspring reached adult weight between the 14th and 16th week of life and they attained sexual maturity in their first year (Foerg, 1982).

THREATS There appear to be no threats specific to *C. medius*. However, the dry forests of the west are being reduced in area every year. Even in the early 1970s few large areas of western forest remained, most persist only in small isolated residual patches (IUCN/UNEP/WWF, 1987). FAO/UNEP (1981) estimated net degradation of these forests to have been perhaps 200,000 ha since 1955. Fires are set each year to encourage new grass growth for grazing and this is the principal cause of forest destruction in the west. Similarly, the southern forests are being degraded, collection of wood for charcoal is one of the major threats. Though the Fat-tailed Dwarf Lemur has been seen in brush vegetation (Rand, 1935), it is likely that it needs hollow trees of a certain size to be able to survive the dry season. Nevertheless, the wide distribution of the species and its ability to survive in secondary forest makes it unlikely that it is severely threatened.

CONSERVATION MEASURES *C. medius* is reported in two Nature Reserves, Ankarafantsika and Andohahela, it is also found in the Special Reserves of Andranomena, Beza Mahafaly and, probably, Ankarana and the Private Reserves of Berenty and Analabe (Richard, 1975; Nicoll and Langrand, 1989; O'Connor *et al*, 1986, 1987; Andriamampianina, 1981; Hawkins *et al*, in press).

The Department of Water and Forests (Direction des Eaux et Forêts) and the World Bank are developing a management programme for Ankarafantsika Reserve and the Classified Forest of Ampijoroa (Nicoll and Langrand, 1989). More money is required for effective guarding of the Reserve and a fire break is needed around the area (Nicoll and Langrand, 1989). In addition, a reafforestation programme is necessary, to provide the local people with fuel and building material, as is education as to the importance of the forest and the protected area (Nicoll and Langrand, 1989).

The other reserves in which *C. medius* is found suffer from more or less the same problems: cattle grazing within them, fires destroying more each year, cutting and collecting of wood and some illegal hunting. Similar conservation measures are needed for each, more protection, education of the local people and development of alternatives to using the forest for fuel and building materials. If tourists can be encouraged, as has happened at Berenty, this provides money and employment for the local people.

All species of Cheirogaleidae are listed in Appendix 1 of the 1973 Convention on International Trade in Endangered Species of Wild Fauna and Flora. Trade in them, or their products, is subject to strict regulation and may not be carried out for primarily commercial purposes.

All Lemuroidea are listed in Class A of the African Convention, 1969. They may not, therefore, be hunted, killed, captured or collected without the authorization of the highest competent authority, and then only if required in the national interest or for scientific purposes.

Malagasy law protects all lemurs from unauthorised capture or killing, but this is very difficult to enforce.

CAPTIVE BREEDING Breeds well in captivity. In June 1989, there were 59 males, 45 females and 12 unsexed individuals held in nine institutes, of which 94 % were captive born (ISIS). The majority (49) are at Duke Primate Center. Wilde *et al* (1988) report another nine individuals in two institutes not included in the ISIS list. Many more could be bred, but few zoos are interested as a small, dull, nocturnal species does not make a good exhibit (E. Simons, *in litt.*).

REMARKS This species is sometimes divided into two subspecies, *C. m. medius* and *C. m. samati*, but Petter and Petter (1971), Petter *et al* (1977) and Tattersall (1982) consider this distinction unwarranted. Fur is short and dense, grey with rosy or brownish tints on the upperparts and white to light brown on the underparts (Tattersall, 1982). Body weight changes seasonally. In Marosalaza Forest, adult mean body weight varied from 142 g in November to 217g in March (Hladik *et al*, 1980), an individual can weigh as much as 400 g (Petter *et al*, 1977). See Tattersall (1982) for a more detailed description of the species. In the north-west, the Malagasy name for this species is matavirambo or matavrambo; kely beohy or kelibehohy in the Morondava region and tsidy or tsitsihy in the far south (Tattersall, 1982; Petter *et al*, 1977).

REFERENCES

Albignac, R. (1981). Lemurine social and territorial organisation in a north-western Malagasy forest (restricted area of Ampijoroa). In: Chiarelli, A.B. and Corruccini, R.S. (Eds), *Primate Behavior and Sociobiology.* Springer Verlag, Berlin. Pp. 25-29.

Andriamampianina, J. (1981). Les réserves naturelles et la protection de la nature à Madagascar. In Oberlé (Ed.), *Madagascar, un Sanctuaire de la Nature.* Pp. 105-111.

FAO/UNEP (1981). *Tropical Forest Resources Assessment Project. Forest Resources of Tropical Africa. Part II Country Briefs.* FAO, Rome.

Foerg, R. (1982). Reproduction in *Cheirogaleus medius. Folia Primatologica* 39: 49-62.

Ganzhorn, J.U. (1988). Food partitioning among Malagasy primates. *Oecologia* 75: 436-450.

Hawkins, A.F.A., Ganzhorn, J.U., Q.M.C. Bloxham, Barlow, S.C., Tonge S.J. and Chapman, P. (in press). A survey and assessment of the conservation status and needs of lemurs, birds, lizards and snakes in Ankarana Special Reserve, Antseranana, Madagascar: with notes on the lemurs and birds of the nearby Analamera Special Reserve. *Biological Conservation*

Hladik, C.M. (1979). Diet and ecology of prosimians. In: Doyle, G.A. and Martin, R.D. *The Study of Prosimian Behavior.* Academic Press, New York. Pp. 307-357.

Hladik, C.M. and Charles-Dominique, P. and Petter, J.-J. (1980). Feeding strategies of five nocturnal prosimians in the dry forest of the West coast of Madagascar. In: Charles-Dominique, P., Cooper, H. M., Hladik, A., Hladik, C. M., Pages, E., Pariente, G. F., Petter-Rousseaux, A., Petter, J.-J. and Schilling, A. (Eds), *Nocturnal Malagasy Primates: Ecology, Physiology and Behavior.* Academic Press, New York. Pp. 41-73.

ISIS (1989). *ISIS Species Distribution Report Abstract for Mammals,* 30 June 1989. International Species Information System, 12101 Johnny Cake Ridge Road, Apple Valley, MN, U.S.A.

IUCN/UNEP/WWF (1987). *Madagascar, an Environmental Profile.* Edited by M.D. Jenkins. IUCN, Gland, Switzerland and Cambridge, U.K.

Jolly, A. (1987). Priorités dans l'étude des populations de Lémuriens. In: *Priorités en Matière de Conservation des Espèces à Madagascar.* Occasional Papers of the IUCN Species Survival Commission, Number 2.

Jolly, A. (1988). Lemur survival. In: Benirschke, K. (Ed.), *Primates: The Road to Self-Sustaining Populations.* Springer-Verlag, New York. Pp. 71-98.

Martin, R.D. (1984). Dwarf and mouse lemurs. In: Macdonald, D. (Ed.), *The Encyclopaedia of Mammals:1.* George Allen and Unwin, London. P. 331.

Nicoll, M.E. and Langrand, O. (1989). *Revue Générale du Système d'Aires Protégées et de la Conservation à Madagascar.* Unpublished report to WWF.

O'Connor, S., Pidgeon, M. and Randria, Z. (1986). Conservation program for the Andohahela Reserve, Madagascar. *Primate Conservation* 7: 48-52.

O'Connor, S, Pidgeon, M. and Randria, Z. (1987). Un programme de conservation pour la Réserve d'Andohahela. In: *Priorités en Matière de Conservation des Espèces à Madagascar.* Occasional Papers of the IUCN Species Survival Commission, Number 2.

Petter, A. and Petter, J.-J. (1971). Part 3.1 Infraorder Lemuriformes. In: Meester, J. and Setzer,H.W. (Eds), *The Mammals of Africa: An Identification Manual.* Smithsonian Institution Press, City of Washington. Pp. 1-10.

Petter, J-J., Albignac, R. and Rumpler, Y. (1977). Mammifères lémuriens (Primates prosimiens). *Faune de Madagascar* No. 44. ORSTOM-CNRS, Paris.

Petter, J.-J. and Petter-Rousseaux, A. (1979). Classification of the Prosimians In: Doyle, G.A. and Martin, R.D. (Eds), *The Study of Prosimian Behavior.* Academic Press, London. Pp. 1-44.

Petter, J.-J. (1988). Contribution à l'étude du *Cheirogaleus medius* dans la fôret de Morondava. In: Rakotovao, L., Barre, V. and Sayer, J. (Eds), *L'Equilibre des Ecosystèmes forestiers à Madagascar: Actes d'un séminaire international.* IUCN Gland, Switzerland and Cambridge, U.K. Pp. 57-60.

Rand, A.L. (1935). On the habits of some Madagascar mammals. *Journal of Mammalogy*, 16: 89-104.

Raxworthy, C.J. and Rakotondraparany, F. (1988). Mammals report. In: Quansah, N. (Ed.), *Manongarivo Special Reserve (Madagascar), 1987/88 Expedition Report.* Madagascar Environmental Research Group, U.K.

Richard, A. (1975). Patterns of mating in *Propithecus verreauxi verreauxi.* In: Martin, R.D., Doyle, G.A. and Walker, A.C. (Eds), *Prosimian Biology.* Duckworth, London. Pp. 49-74.

Richard, A.F. and Sussman, R.W. (1975). Future of the Malagasy lemurs; conservation or extinction? In: Tattersall, I. and Sussman, R.W. (Eds), *Lemur Biology.* Plenum Press, New York. Pp. 335-350.

Richard, A.F. and Sussman, R.W. (1987). Framework for Primate Conservation in Madagascar. In: Marsh, C.W. and Mittermeier, R. (Eds), *Primate Conservation in the Tropical Forest.* Alan R. Liss, Inc., New York. Pp. 329-341.

Tattersall, I. (1982). *The Primates of Madagascar.* Columbia University Press, New York.

Wilde, J., Schwibbe, M.H. and Arsene, A. (1988). A census for captive primates in Europe. *Primate Report* 21: 1-120.

The nocturnal Greater Dwarf Lemur, *Cheirogaleus major*, is found in the eastern rain forests.
Photo by Phillip Coffrey/Jersey Wildlife Preservation Trust.

GREATER DWARF LEMUR

ABUNDANT

Cheirogaleus major E. Geoffroy, 1812

Order **PRIMATES**   Family **CHEIROGALEIDAE**

SUMMARY   The Greater Dwarf Lemur is a small, nocturnal species that is widely distributed in the eastern rain forest. There are no estimates of total population number, but it is reported to occur at high densities in some areas. It is possible that *Cheirogaleus major* is one of the least threatened of the lemur species but, nevertheless, it is less widespread than it was even a few decades ago. There have been no detailed studies of this species and little is known about its habitat requirements or its ecology. It is a nocturnal species, usually sighted alone at night. Its diet includes ripe fruit and invertebrates. It has a three month torpid period from July to October. It occurs in at least nine protected areas. Only three individuals, all female, are held in captivity. Listed in Appendix 1 of CITES, in Class A of the African Convention and protected by Malagasy law.

DISTRIBUTION   Found throughout the eastern rain forest, from Taolanaro (Fort Dauphin) in the south to Montagne d'Ambre in the far north and extending westwards to the Tsaratanana Massif and the Sambirano region (Tattersall, 1982). As recently as a few decades ago the range of this species extended onto the central plateau (Tattersall, 1982). Petter *et al*, (1977) and Petter and Petter-Rouseaux (1979) show a population of *C. major* on the Bongolava Massif, near the Manambolo River in the west of Madagascar. In a 1987 publication Petter and Andriatsarafara report that *C. major* have recently been caught on the Bongolava Massif but they gives no details. They also think it likely that the species is present in Ankarafantsika.

POPULATION   Numbers are unknown but Richard and Sussman (1975, 1987) report that the species is declining. It is found at high densities in some areas (Petter *et al*, 1977), as many as 75-110 per sq. km were reported at Mahambo (Petter and Petter-Rousseaux,1964), while Ganzhorn estimated 68 $\pm$ 38 individuals per sq. km (mean and 95% confidence limits based on 25 census walks along 3.2 km of trails) in Analamazaotra Forest. The wide distribution of the species suggests that total population number may be quite high.

HABITAT AND ECOLOGY   A small, nocturnal species, which lives in primary rain forest and well-established secondary forest (Martin 1984). Little is known about its social organisation but it is invariably sighted alone (Petter *et al*, 1977). During the day it may sleep in a tree hollow or a nest. Petter *et al* (1977) report finding two adults together in one nest. There are few data on ranging patterns of this species though Martin (1972) found that Dwarf Lemurs rarely descended below 3 m in the trees and that they preferred large branches to fine ones. He describes them as slow moving, essentially quadrupedal forms. The diet of the Greater Dwarf Lemur consists of ripe fruit, nectar and pollen with insects and, probably, small vertebrates also being taken, they have never been seen to eat leaves (Petter *et al*, 1977). A peculiarity of both this species and the Fat-tailed Dwarf Lemur is their ability to store fat in their tail, which enables them to survive periods of dormancy in winter. *C. major* is reported to have a three month torpid period between July and October (Petter *et al*, 1977). During this time they hide in the leaf litter at the foot of a big tree (Paulin, 1981; Petter *et al*, 1977).

Length of gestation in *C. major* is 70 days and the infants are born in January, in Madagascar's summer (Petter-Rousseaux, 1964). A litter of two or three offspring is generally produced (Petter *et al*, 1977). They cannot cling to their mother, instead she carries them in her mouth when necessary (Petter-Rousseaux, 1964). Within a month of birth the infants can follow their mother when she goes to feed (Petter-Rousseaux, 1964). Lactation lasts about 1.5 months, but the young start eating fruit at about 25 days of age (Petter-Rousseaux, 1964).

THREATS Destruction of the rain forests for timber, fuel and agricultural land is a threat to this species. However its small size and nocturnal habits will ensure that it survives longer than its larger, diurnal relatives. Its wide distribution within the rain forest suggests that it may be one of the less threatened of the lemurs, though more information on its habitat requirements is needed before its true status can be ascertained. Both E. Simons and I. Tattersall (*in litt.*) consider this species more threatened than *C. medius*, the Fat-tailed Dwarf Lemur found in the west of Madagascar. Tattersall's (1982) report that Greater Dwarf Lemurs used to be found in areas of the central plateau as recently as a few decades ago does indicate that it is susceptible to changes in its habitat. *C. major* is hunted for food by local people using long sticks to poke around in holes where it might be resting (Petter *et al*, 1977).

CONSERVATION MEASURES The Greater Dwarf Lemur occurs in a number of protected areas including the Montagne d'Ambre National Park, the Nature Reserves of Betampona, Zahamena, Tsaratanana and Andohahela and the Special Reserves of Analamazaotra, Nosy Mangabe and Manongarivo (Andriamampianina and Peyrieras, 1972; Nicoll and Langrand, 1989; Constable *et al*, 1985; O'Connor *et al*, 1986, Raxworthy and Rakotondraparany, 1988). Several new areas which contain *C. major* have been proposed for protection (Nicoll and Langrand, 1989). These are Ranomafana and Masoala (both proposed as National Parks) and Mananara (proposed as a Biosphere Reserve). All the protected areas need adequate funding and guards to ensure the survival of the lemurs within them. In addition, education projects for the local people to demonstrate the importance of the reserves would be useful, as would development programmes that provide alternatives to harmful exploitation of the protected areas.

Studies of the habitat requirements of the Greater Dwarf Lemur would help to ascertain its conservation status. E. Simons (*in litt.*) considers it important to import males to join the females at Duke Primate Center so that a captive breeding colony of this species can be established.

All species of Cheirogaleidae are listed in Appendix 1 of the 1973 Convention on International Trade in Endangered Species of Wild Fauna and Flora. Trade in them, or their products, is subject to strict regulation and may not be carried out for primarily commercial purposes.

All Lemuroidea are listed in Class A of the African Convention, 1969. They may not, therefore, be hunted, killed, captured or collected without the authorization of the highest competent authority, and then only if required in the national interest or for scientific purposes.

All lemurs are protected under Malagasy law. The national legislation is based primarily on the 1933 London Convention and on Ordonnance No. 60-126 of 3rd October 1960. It is, however, difficult to enforce the laws preventing capture or killing of the lemurs.

CAPTIVE BREEDING Three wild born individuals, all females, are held at Duke Primate Center (ISIS, June 1989). It appears that this species survives in captivity but it is difficult to breed (Petter *et al*, 1977). However, Petter *et al* (1977) reports the birth of triplets to one female and twins to two others in Paris. There are no longer any captive individuals in Paris.

REMARKS Some authors recognise two subspecies of the Greater Dwarf Lemur, *C. m. crossleyi,* with reddish fur, occurring north of the Masoala Peninsula and the browner *C.*

m. major to the south (Petter and Petter, 1971; Petter *et al*, 1977; Petter and Petter-Rousseaux, 1979; Jenkins, 1987). Tattersall (1982) considers the species variable but monotypic. Fur short and dense, grey brown to reddish above with paler underparts; dark rings around the eyes (Tattersall, 1982; Martin, 1984). Body weight varies seasonally, mean is about 450 g (Petter *et al*, 1977, Tattersall, 1982; Martin, 1984). Malagasy names for this species are tsitsihy, tsidy and hataka (Tattersall, 1982).

REFERENCES

Constable, I.D., Mittermeier, R.A., Pollock, J.I., Ratsirarson, J. and Simons, H. (1985). Sightings of aye-ayes and red-ruffed lemurs on Nosy Mangabe and the Masoala Peninsula. *Primate Conservation* 5: 59-62.

Jenkins, P.D. (1987). *Catalogue of Primates in the British Museum (Natural History) and elsewhere in the British Isles. Part IV: Suborder Strepsirrhini, including the subfossil Madagascan lemurs and family Tarsiidae.* British Museum (Natural History), London.

Martin, R.D. (1984). Dwarf and mouse lemurs. In: Macdonald, D. (Ed.), *The Encyclopaedia of Mammals:1.* George Allen and Unwin, London. P. 331.

O'Connor, S., Pidgeon, M. and Randria, Z. (1986). Conservation program for the Andohahela Reserve, Madagascar. *Primate Conservation* 7: 48-52.

Paulin, R.R. (1981). Les mammifères: vestiges d' un monde disparu. In: Oberlé, P. (Ed.), *Madagagascar un sanctuaire de la nature.* Libraire de Madagascar, Antananarivo. Pp. 75-94.

Petter, J.-J. and Andriatsarafara, F. (1987). Conservation status and distribution of lemurs in the west and northwest of Madagascar. *Primate Conservation* 8: 169-171.

Petter, A. and Petter, J.-J. (1971). Part 3.1 Infraorder Lemuriformes. In: Meester, J. and Setzer, H.W. (Eds), *The Mammals of Africa: An Identification Manual.* Smithsonian Institution Press, City of Washington. Pp. 1-10.

Petter, J-J., Albignac, R. and Rumpler, Y. (1977). Mammifères lémuriens (Primates prosimiens). *Faune de Madagascar* No. 44. ORSTOM-CNRS, Paris.

Petter, J.-J. and Petter-Rousseaux, A. (1979). Classification of the Prosimians In: Doyle, G.A. and Martin, R.D. (Eds), *The Study of Prosimain Behavior.* Academic Press, London. Pp. 1-44.

Petter, J.J. and Petter-Rousseaux, A. (1964). Première tentative d'estimation des densités de peuplement des lémuriens malagaches. *La Terre et La Vie* 18: 427-435.

Petter-Rousseaux, A. (1964). Reproductive physiology and behavior of the Lemuroidae. In: Buettner-Janusch, J. (Ed.), *Evolution and Genetic Biology of the Primates.* Academic Press, New York. Pp. 91-132.

Raxworthy, C.J. and Rakotondraparany, F. (1988). Mammals report. In: Quansah, N. (Ed.), *Manongarivo Special Reserve (Madagascar), 1987/88 Expedition Report.* Madagascar Environmental Research Group, U.K.

Richard, A.F. and Sussman, R.W. (1975). Future of the Malagasy Lemurs; Conservation or Extinction? In: Tattersall, I. and Sussman, R.W. (Eds), *Lemur Biology.* Plenum Press, New York. Pp. 335-350.

Richard, A.F. and Sussman, R.W. (1987). Framework for Primate Conservation in Madagascar. In: Marsh, C. W. and Mittermeier, R. (Eds), *Primate Conservation in the Tropical Forest.* Alan R. Liss, Inc., New York. Pp. 329-341.

Tattersall, I. (1982). *The Primates of Madagascar.* Columbia University Press, New York.

The Hairy-eared Dwarf Lemur, *Allocebus trichotis*, is possibly the least known of all the lemur species. It has been found in only one area of north-eastern Madagascar, where it was rediscovered in 1989.
Photo by Bernhard Meier.

HAIRY-EARED DWARF LEMUR   ENDANGERED

Allocebus trichotis (Günther, 1875)

Order PRIMATES   Family CHEIROGALEIDAE

SUMMARY   Until 1989 the Hairy-eared Dwarf Lemur was known from only five museum specimens, all but one of which were collected in the last century. However, it was rediscovered in 1989 in lowland forest in north-east Madagascar. Little or no information is available on its distribution or numbers, nor on any aspects of its ecology. It may be very rare or simply very cryptic, it is nocturnal. It must be threatened, however, by destruction of its habitat, the eastern rain forests. Three individuals are in captivity in Madagascar. Listed in Appendix 1 of CITES, Class A of the African Convention and is protected by Malagasy law.

DISTRIBUTION   Until its rediscovery in 1989, the Hairy-eared Dwarf Lemur was known from only five museum specimens. The holotype was collected by Crossley in 1874, but the information on its label, stating that it was collected in S. Madagascar, differs from Gunther's (1875) statement that it came from between "Tamantave" (i.e. Toamasina, on the east coast) and "Murundava" (i.e. Morondava, on the west coast) (Tattersall, 1982). The provenance of the two collected by Humblot around 1880 is unknown (Tattersall, 1982). A fourth specimen has recently been discovered in the collections of the Naturhistoriska Rijksmuseet in Stockholm by G. H. Albrecht (pers. comm. to P. Jenkins, 1987). No date is given for this specimen. Its locality is either "Nanaka" or "Namaka" (Jenkins, 1987). Jenkins suggests that this may be equivalent to Nanakara (24°17'S, 45°53'E), but as this village is not in an area of rain forest, it seems an unlikely site for the Hairy-eared Dwarf Lemur ever to have been located. Peyrieras, in 1965, captured the fifth specimen in Andranomahitsy forest, near the village of Ambavala, 16 km from the town of Mananara, which is on the east coast of Madagascar (Peyrieras pers. comm. to Meier and Albignac, in press). An expedition to the same forest in 1975 failed to find any *Allocebus trichotis* (Petter *et al*, 1977). However, it was relocated there by Bernhard Meier and Ronald Albignac early in 1989.

Meier and Albignac (in press) consider that the distribution of this species may be restricted and patchy. They report seeing a number of *Allocebus* in the area around Mananara. Meier saw one individual close to the village of Ambavala (16°12'S, 49°37'E) and one at 16°26'S, 49°38'E, 1.5 km from the Bedinta mountain, which is 34 km from Mananara. In addition, three individuals were caught near the village of Andranombazaha (16°28'S, 49°38'E).

Tattersall (1982) suggests that the species once occurred quite widely in the eastern humid forests, but the paucity of either specimens or sightings makes it difficult to confirm this.

POPULATION   Numbers are not known, but Tattersall, in 1982, considered this the rarest of the surviving lemurs and one which probably never existed at high densities. Meier and Albignac (in press) say that the population density may be very low. Its numbers are almost certainly declining as the eastern rain forests are reduced in size (Richard and Sussman, 1975, 1987). Meier and Albignac (in press) also consider that its numbers are probably declining.

HABITAT AND ECOLOGY   Comparatively little is known about this species but it appears to occur only in lowland rain forest. One of the individuals seen by Meier was in degraded primary lowland forest, while the other was in virgin primary forest (Meier and

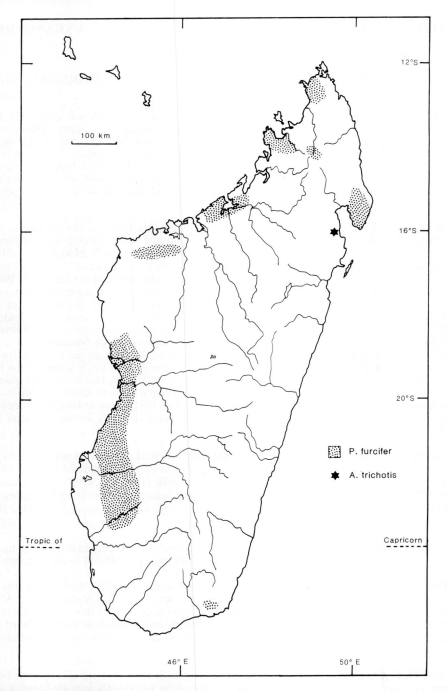

Figure 8: Distribution of *Phaner* and *Allocebus*. Shaded areas represent approximate limits of ranges.

Albignac, in press). The three captured individuals were all in primary lowland forest (Meier and Albignac, in press). It is a nocturnal species, becoming active at dusk and remaining so until the very first light of dawn (Meier and Albignac, in press). It jumps a lot, in a manner similar to *Microcebus* rather than *Cheirogaleus* (Meier and Albignac, in press). There is no information on the diet of the Hairy-eared Dwarf Lemur in the wild. Meier and Albignac (in press) suggest that this species may feed on nectar, it has a very long tongue and, in captivity, eats honey. Caged animals ate locusts, which were jumped on and caught with both hands; fruit was also eaten (Meier and Albignac, in press). In May, *Allocebus* has a considerable fat deposit which is not stored in the tail, as in *Cheirogaleus*, but is distributed all over the body (Meier and Albignac, in press). Local people reported that they did not see active Hairy-eared Dwarf Lemurs between May and September and it appears that they are in some type of hibernation during that time (Meier and Albignac, in press). In captivity, activity is drastically reduced from June to September (Meier and Albignac, in press). The animals are usually found sleeping in tree holes. One individual was caught in a hole in a small dead tree that was broken off 4 m above the ground (Meier and Albignac, in press). This was a juvenile male and there were two other individuals in the same hole. Local people reported that usually two or three individuals are found in a tree hole but that up to six animals could be together (Meier and Albignac, in press). It is possible that infants are born in January or February as some Malagasy tree cutters saw half grown individuals in March (Meier and Albignac, in press).

THREATS The main threat to this species must be destruction of the rain forest for agriculture and fuel and by timber companies. It has recently been estimated that 111,000 ha of eastern rain forest have been cleared each year between 1950 and 1985, most of this has been the lowland forest (Green and Sussman, in press). If the cutting continues, forests on only the steepest slopes will survive the next thirty-five years (Green and Sussman, in press) and this will probably mean the extinction of *Allocebus* if it does, indeed, live only in the lowland rain forest.

CONSERVATION MEASURES There are no measures suggested specifically for conserving the Hairy-eared Dwarf Lemur and, until more is known about its ecology and range, none can be made. Its chances of survival will be increased by preservation of the eastern rain forest. An area around Mananara, the only known location of *Allocebus*, has been proposed as a Biosphere Reserve (Nicoll and Langrand, 1989). It is suggested that the protected area should have the status of a National Park and that a buffer zone be set up surrounding it (Nicoll and Langrand, 1989). Extensive surveys are needed to try to locate any remaining populations of the Hairy-eared Dwarf Lemur.

All species of Cheirogaleidae are listed in Appendix 1 of the 1973 Convention on International Trade in Endangered Species of Wild Fauna and Flora. Trade in them, or their products, is subject to strict regulation and may not be carried out for primarily commercial purposes.

All Lemuroidea are listed in Class A of the African Convention, 1969. They may not, therefore, be hunted, killed, captured or collected without the authorization of the highest competent authority, and then only if required in the national interest or for scientific purposes.

Malagasy law protects all lemurs from unauthorised capture and from hunting, but this is very difficult to enforce.

CAPTIVE BREEDING Until recently, none had been kept in captivity except the one collected by Peyrieras, which he had for only a few days (Petter *et al*, 1977). Now there are three individuals, an adult pair and a juvenile, being held in captivity in Madagascar (Meier and Albignac, in press).

REMARKS The adult female of this species caught by Meier and Albignac (in press) weighed 80 g, while the adult male weighed 75 g. A juvenile of unknown sex weighed 58g Body length of the female was 145 mm, tail length was 165 mm; body length of the male was 125 mm and tail length was 195 mm. Pelage on the dorsal side was rosy brownish-grey, while the ventral fur was grey. There are narrow dark rings round the eyes. Its ears are very short and concealed in fur but long wavy hairs form the eartufts from which this lemur gets its common name. Its nails are kneeled, except on the hallux, but the apex of the nails are rounded, not pointed (Meier and Albignac, in press). For a more complete description of *Allocebus trichotis*, see Günther (1875), Petter-Rousseaux and Petter (1967), Tattersall (1982), Jenkins (1987) and Meier and Albignac (in press). The species was initially classified in the genus *Cheirogaleus* (Günther, 1875), but is now considered to be in its own genus (Petter-Rousseaux and Petter, 1967; Tattersall, 1982; Jenkins, 1987). The Malagasy name of this species is tsidy ala, meaning mouse lemur of the big forest, as opposed to tsidy savoka (*Microcebus rufus*), meaning mouse lemur of the brush (Meier and Albignac, in press).

REFERENCES

Günther, A. (1875). Notes on some mammals from Madagascar. *Proceedings of the Zoological Society, London:* 78-80.

Jenkins, P. D. (1987). *Catalogue of Primates in the British Museum (Natural History) and elsewhere in the British Isles. Part IV: Suborder Strepsirrhini, including the Subfossil Madagascan Lemurs and Family Tarsiidae.* British Museum (Natural History), London.

Meier, B. and Albignac, R. (in press). Rediscovery of *Allocebus trichotis* Günther 1875 (Primates) in North East Madagascar. *Folia Primatologica.*

Nicoll, M.E. and Langrand, O. (1989). *Revue Générale du Système d'Aires Protégés et de la Conservation à Madgascar.* Unpublished report to WWF.

Petter, J-J., Albignac, R. and Rumpler, Y. (1977). Mammifères lémuriens (Primates Prosimiens) *Faune de Madagascar* No. 44. ORSTOM-CNRS, Paris.

Petter, J.-J. and Petter-Rousseaux, A. (1979). Classification of the Prosimians. In: Doyle, G.A. and Martin, R.D. (Eds), *The Study of Prosimian Behavior.* Academic Press, London. Pp. 1-44.

Petter-Rousseaux, A. and Petter, J.-J. (1967). Contribution á la systématique des Cheirogaleinae (lémuriens malagaches). *Allocebus*, gen. nov. pour *Cheirogaleus trichotis* Günther 1875. *Mammalia* 31: 574-582.

Richard, A.F. and Sussman, R.W. (1975). Future of the Malagasy Lemurs; Conservation or Extinction? In: Tattersall, I. and Sussman, R.W. (Eds), *Lemur Biology.* Plenum Press, New York. Pp. 335-350.

Richard, A.F. and Sussman, R.W. (1987). Framework for Primate Conservation in Madagascar. In: Marsh, C.W. and Mittermeier, R. (Eds), *Primate Conservation in the Tropical Rain Forest.* Alan R. Liss, Inc., New York. Pp. 329-341.

Tattersall, I. (1982). *The Primates of Madagascar.* Columbia University Press, New York.

The nocturnal Fork-marked Lemur, *Phaner furcifer*, is found widely but patchily distributed in Madagascar. There are probably several subspecies.
Photo by Russell Mittermeier.

FORK-MARKED LEMUR **RARE**

***Phaner furcifer* (Blainville, 1839)**

Order PRIMATES **Family CHEIROGALEIDAE**

SUMMARY The Fork-marked Lemur is a small nocturnal species with a wide, but discontinuous, distribution in Madagascar. It is found in both humid and dry deciduous forests and is common in secondary forest. Several subspecies have recently been described. Population numbers are unknown but they are considered to be declining. Figures for densities vary from 850 individuals per sq. km to 50 per sq. km. *Phaner furcifer* is a territorial species and is frequently seen in pairs during the night. The main component of its diet is gum though some insects, fruit and nectar are also taken. It is found in several reserves, but is threatened by habitat destruction in most areas. Only two are recorded in captivity. Listed in Appendix 1 of CITES, in Class A of the African Convention and is protected under Malagasy law

DISTRIBUTION *Phaner* has a wide but discontinuous distribution in Madagascar. It is found mainly in the dry deciduous forest in the west of the country, where it extends from about the latitude of Toliara (Tulear) northwards to near Antsalova. Petter *et al* (1977) and Petter and Petter-Rousseaux (1979) show another portion of *Phaner*'s range from Cap St André southwards along the coast to north of the Bay of Bombetoka, whereas Tattersall (1982) shows two smaller, disjunct populations, one south of Soalala and the other around the Bay of Bombetoka. *Phaner* also occurs in the Sambirano region (on the Ampasindava Peninsula), in the far north around Montagne d'Ambre and in the eastern rain forest on the Masoala Peninsula (Tattersall, 1982, Petter *et al*, 1977; Petter and Petter-Rousseaux, 1979). Again, the range shown by Tattersall (1982) in the east is much smaller than that shown by the other authors. Petter *et al* (1977) and Petter and Petter-Rousseaux (1979) show *Phaner* extending north from the Masoala Peninsula to beyond Sambava, while Tattersall (1982) considers that it extends only as far as Antalaha. Two other populations have also been reported, one on the Tsaratanana Massif (Andriamampianina and Peyrieras, 1972) and the other in the arid Didierea bush in the south in Andohahela reserve (Russell and McGeorge, 1977). The presence of *Phaner* in parcel 2 of Andohahela Reserve is confirmed by M. Pidgeon (*in litt.*) but only in the gallery forest. The presence of the species in Bemaraha Nature Reserve has been reported (Petter and Andriatsarafara, 1987; Nicoll and Langrand, 1989).

Groves and Tattersall (in press) consider that there are the five principal populations of *Phaner* existing today and that there are four different subspecies of the Fork-marked Lemur. These are mentioned in "Remarks". They consider that reports of the presence of *Phaner* in Andohahela, Tsaratanana and around the Bay of Bombetoka need further confirmation, as does its existence between Tsiribihina River and Namoroka.

POPULATION Total numbers are unknown but they are considered to be probably declining (Richard and Sussman, 1975, 1987). Petter *et al* (1971) counted 17 *Phaner* in 2 ha of Marosalaza Forest (in the west, 50 kms north of Morondava), thereby estimating a density of 850 individuals per sq. km. In another area, near Mangoky 200 km south of Marosalaza, they estimated population densities of at least 550 individuals per sq. km. Charles-Dominique and Petter (1980) found 14 individuals in their 25 ha study area in Marosalaza Forest and, from this, estimate densities of 50-60 individuals per sq. km. They consider that the densities estimated by Petter *et al* (1971) reflect observations in small, gum rich areas and that these high numbers cannot be extrapolated to mean population densities.

HABITAT AND ECOLOGY This species is found in the humid forests of the east and the Sambirano region as well as in the dry deciduous forests of the west (Petter *et al*, 1971). It has also been reported in the Didiereaceae bush in the south (Russell and McGeorge, 1977) though more recent observations suggest that it is confined to the gallery forest there (M. Pidgeon, *in litt.*). Petter *et al* (1975), working in Marosalaza Forests, found that *P. furcifer* was most often seen in areas of secondary forest, although it appeared that this species did not occupy zones in which a continuous canopy was missing (Petter *et al*, 1975). Between March and May, gum, particularly from *Terminalia* trees, was the principal food of *Phaner* in Marosalaza Forest, but insects, sap and bud exudate were also taken (Charles-Dominique and Petter, 1980). In November, *Terminalia* gum was still providing the bulk of the Fork-marked Lemur's diet, but flowers were licked and the "syrup" from insect larvae of the family Machaerotidae was also eaten (Charles-Dominique and Petter, 1980). *Phaner* spends the day in holes, usually in large trees such as Baobabs (*Adansonia* spp), or sometimes in the abandoned nests of *Mirza coquereli* (Petter *et al*, 1971, 1975); it leaves these at nightfall and feeds most actively for the first hour of the night (Petter *et al*, 1975). Locomotion consists of rapid quadrupedal running, climbing and leaping, generally at 3-4m (where most horizontal branches occur in Marosalaza) though they were also seen on the ground and at above 10m (Petter *et al*, 1975).

Charles-Dominique and Petter (1980) found three territories, each containing one adult male and one adult female *Phaner,* though they also found a solitary male in a territory and one male with a range overlapping those of two females. Four of these territories also contained juvenile individuals. The pairs were in close proximity for about half of the night and were in almost continuous vocal contact throughout the night; in addition, they slept together during the day (Charles-Dominique and Petter, 1980). The male whose range overlapped those of two females divided his active and rest time between the two of them (Charles-Dominique and Petter, 1980). Mean size of females' territories was about 4 ha, while that of the males was 3.8 ha.; there was little overlap between the territories of same sex individuals (Charles-Dominique and Petter, 1980). The overlap zones appeared to be "meeting areas", between three and nine neighbours coming together and emitting simultaneous calls for 10-20 minutes; no aggression was seen on these occasions (Charles-Dominique and Petter, 1980). Allogrooming was frequent between males, females and juveniles (Charles-Dominique and Petter, 1980). Charles-Dominique (1978) described this social stystem as "pre-gregarious".

The Fork-marked Lemur is very vocal, a mean of 30 loud calls an hour (emitted only by the males) have been counted in a radius of about 200m in Marosalaza forest; olfactory signals appear to be much less important in this species than in other nocturnal prosimians (Charles-Dominique and Petter, 1980).

Mating occurs in June (Charles-Dominique and Petter, 1980). A single infant is born in November or December. It is initially left in a tree hole and then carried on the front of its mother, later moving to her back (Petter *et al*, 1971, 1975; Charles-Dominique and Petter, 1980).

THREATS Nothing specific recorded for this species, but its habitat is being destroyed by fires, clearing for pasture land and for crops.

CONSERVATION MEASURES Found in Ankarana, Manongarivo and Andranomena Special Reserves, the Nature Reserves of Bemaraha, Tsaratanana and Andohahela, Mt d'Ambre National Park and Analabe Private Reserve (Raxworthy and Rakotondraparany, 1988; Hawkins *et al,* in press; Nicoll and Langrand, 1989). In general, all these areas would benefit from better protection and conservation awareness programmes would help the local people understand the importance of the reserves and their wildlife (Nicoll and Langrand, 1989).

It has been proposed that a National Park is established on the Masoala Peninsula and this would protect what is probably a distinct subspecies of *Phaner*.

Surveys are needed to find out the range and numbers of this species. Without this information, the conservation status of *Phaner* cannot be assessed, nor can the populations requiring protection be identified.

All species of Cheirogaleidae are listed in Appendix 1 of the 1973 Convention on International Trade in Endangered Species of Wild Fauna and Flora. Trade in them, or their products, is subject to strict regulation and may not be carried out for primarily commercial purposes.

All Lemuroidea are listed in Class A of the African Convention, 1969. They may not, therefore, be hunted, killed, captured or collected without the authorization of the highest competent authority, and then only if required in the national interest or for scientific purposes.

Malagasy law protects all lemurs from unauthorised capture and from killing. This is, however, very difficult to enforce.

CAPTIVE BREEDING ISIS (June, 1989) does not record any *Phaner* in captivity. At least two females and one male have been kept in Brunoy, France for "several years" (Petter-Rousseaux, 1980; Cooper, 1980), but it is not clear if they ever bred there. Two individuals are now in Paris Zoo (J.-J. Petter, *in litt.*).

REMARKS A small lemur of 360-500g (Petter *et al*, 1977), characterised by a broad dorsal stripe which bifurcates on the crown, the two stripes continuing to the eyes. Fur on the back is grey-brown, underparts are white to pale brown (Tattersall, 1982). Though traditionally viewed as monotypic it was suggested in 1975 that the populations in the north and east should be regarded as distinct subspecies (Petter *et al*, 1975) and four subspecies have now been described by Groves and Tattersall (in press). These are: *P. f. furcifer*, found on the Masoala Peninsula; *P. f. pallescens* found in western Madagascar from just south of Fiherenana River to the region of Soalala (though the authors consider it absent between the Tsiribihina River and Namoroka); *P. f. parienti* in the Sambirano region; and *P. f. electromontis* found in the area of Mt d'Ambre. Malagasy names for *P. furcifer* are tanta, tantaraolana, vakiandrina and vakivoho (Petter *et al*, 1977; Tattersall, 1982; Paulian, 1981).

REFERENCES

Charles-Dominique, P. (1978). Solitary and gregarious prosimians: evolution of social structure in primates. In: Chivers, D.J. and Joysey, K.A. (Eds), *Recent Advances in Primatology, Volume 3: Evolution*. Academic Press, London. Pp. 139-149.

Charles-Dominique, P. and Petter, J.-J. (1980). Ecology and Social life of *Phaner furcifer*. In: Charles-Dominique, P., Cooper, H.M., Hladik, A., Hladik, C.M., Pages, E., Pariente, G.F., Petter-Rousseaux, A., Petter, J.-J. and Schilling, A. (Eds), *Nocturnal Malagasy Primates: Ecology, Physiology and Behavior*. Academic Press, New York. Pp. 75-95.

Cooper, H.M. (1980). Ecological correlates of visual learning in nocturnal prosimians. In: Charles-Dominique, P., Cooper, H.M., Hladik, A., Hladik, C.M., Pages, E., Pariente, G.F., Petter-Rousseaux, A., Petter, J.-J. and Schilling, A. (Eds), *Nocturnal Malagasy Primates: Ecology, Physiology and Behavior*. Academic Press, New York. Pp. 191-203.

Groves, C.P. and Tattersall, I. (in press). Geographical variation in the Fork-marked lemur *Phaner furcifer* (Mammalia, Primates). *Folia primatologica*.

ISIS (1989). *ISIS Species Distribution Report Abstract for Mammals,* 30 June 1989. International Species Information System, 12101 Johnny Cake Ridge Road, Apple Valley, MN, U.S.A. Pp. 17-22.

Nicoll, M.E. and Langrand, O. (1989). *Revue Générale du Système d'Aires Protégées et de la Conservation à Madagascar.* Unpublished report to WWF.

Paulian, R.R. (1981). Les mammifères: Vestiges d'un monde disparu. In: Oberlé, P. (Ed.), *Madagascar un Sanctuaire de la Nature.* La Societe Malagache d'Edition, Antananarivo. Pp. 75-94.

Petter, J-J., Albignac, R. and Rumpler, Y. (1977). Mammifères lémuriens (Primates prosimiens). *Faune de Madagascar* No. 44. ORSTOM-CNRS, Paris.

Petter, J.-J. and Andriatsarafara, F. (1987). Conservation status and distribution of lemurs in the west and northwest of Madagascar. *Primate Conservation* 8: 169-171.

Petter, J.-J. and Petter-Rousseaux, A. (1979). Classification of the Prosimians In: Doyle, G.A. and Martin, R.D. (Eds), *The Study of Prosimian Behavior.* Academic Press, London. Pp. 1-44.

Petter, J.-J., Schilling, A. and Pariente, G. (1975). Observations on behavior and ecology of *Phaner furcifer.* In: Tattersall, I. and Sussman, R.W. (Eds), *Lemur Biology.* Plenum Press, New York. Pp. 209-218.

Petter, J.-J., Schilling, A. and Pariente, G. (1971). Observations éco-éthologiques sur deux lémuriens malagaches nocturnes: *Phaner furcifer* et *Microcebus coquereli. La Terre et la Vie* 3: 287-327.

Petter-Rousseaux, A. (1980). Seasonal activity rhythms, reproduction, and body weight variations in five sympatric nocturnal prosimians, in simulated light and climatic conditions. In: Charles-Dominique, P., Cooper, H.M., Hladik, A., Hladik, C.M., Pages, E., Pariente, G.F., Petter-Rousseaux, A., Petter, J.-J. and Schilling, A. (Eds), *Nocturnal Malagasy Primates: Ecology, Physiology and Behavior.* Academic Press, New York. Pp. 137-152.

Richard, A.F. and Sussman, R.W. (1975). Future of the Malagasy lemurs; conservation or extinction? In: Tattersall, I. and Sussman, R.W. (Eds), *Lemur Biology,* Plenum Press, New York. Pp. 335-350.

Richard, A.F. and Sussman, R.W. (1987). Framework for Primate Conservation in Madagascar. In: Marsh, C.W. and Mittermeier, R. (Eds), *Primate Conservation in the Tropical Rain Forest,* Alan R. Liss Inc., New York. Pp. 329-341.

Russell, R.J. and McGeorge, L.W. (1977). Distribution of *Phaner* (Primates, Lemuriformes, Cheirogaleidae, Phanerinae) in southeast Madagascar. *Journal of Biogeography* 4: 169-170.

Tattersall, I. (1982). *The Primates of Madagascar.* Columbia University Press, New York.

The Grey-backed Sportive Lemur, *Lepilemur dorsalis,* has a very limited distribution in north-western Madagascar. It is threatened by destruction of its habitat.
Photo by Chris Raxworthy.

GREY-BACKED or NOSY BÉ SPORTIVE LEMUR   VULNERABLE

Lepilemur dorsalis Gray, 1871

Order PRIMATES   Family MEGALADAPIDAE

SUMMARY The Grey-backed Sportive Lemur is one of the least widely distributed of the Sportive Lemurs. It is found only in the Sambirano Region of north-west Madagascar and on the island of Nosy-Bé. Population numbers are unknown. Only very brief studies have been made of this species and little is known of its ecology and social organisation. It is a solitary, nocturnal species which feeds principally on leaves, though fruit and bark are also taken. *Lepilemur dorsalis* is certainly threatened by habitat destruction. It is found in two Reserves, Manongarivo on the mainland and Lokobe on Nosy Bé, neither of which is safe from encroachment. None is in captivity. Listed in Appendix 1 of CITES, Class A of the African Convention and is protected under Malagasy law.

DISTRIBUTION Inhabits the Sambirano Region on the north-west coast of Madagascar and the island of Nosy Bé (Tattersall, 1982; Petter *et al*, 1977; Petter and Petter-Rousseaux, 1979). The latter two authors show a more northerly extension to the range of the Grey-backed Sportive Lemur than does Tattersall.

POPULATION Population numbers are unknown but the limited distribution of this species suggest that it must be one of the least common of the Sportive Lemurs. Numbers are declining as the forest is being cleared throughout its range.

HABITAT AND ECOLOGY The forests on Nosy Bé and in the Sambirano Region where this species occurs are humid forests quite similar in structure, though not in floristic composition, to those in the east. On Nosy Bé, the nocturnal *L. dorsalis* apparently does not sleep in tree holes instead it spends the day curled up in foliage (Petter and Petter, 1971). However, it has been observed in Manongarivo Reserve asleep in tree holes (Raxworthy and Rakotondraparany, 1988). It feeds on leaves, fruit and bark (Petter and Petter, 1971). One infant is born between September and November (Petter and Petter, 1971).

THREATS The main threat to this species is habitat destruction due to agricultural encroachment and clearance for settlement. Most of the forests on the coast have been destroyed and the remainder are patchy in distribution. Even the protected areas are not safe from this encroachment. An expedition to Manongarivo Special Reserve in 1988 found that a large area of the reserve had already been cleared and that this was continuing. The disturbance extended to about 6 km into the reserve (Quansah, 1988). In the Nature Reserve on Nosy Bé where *L.dorsalis* is also found, the main threat is illegal exploitation of the forest, trees are cut for making into canoes and for building material and the land is cleared for coffee and rice plantations (Nicoll and Langrand, 1989).

CONSERVATION MEASURES Found in Manongarivo Special Reserve (Raxworthy and Rakotondraparany, 1988) and in Lokobe Nature Reserve on Nosy Bé (Petter *et al*, 1977).

Neither of the reserves in which this species is found is adequetely protected from encroachment. Conservation awareness programmes would be helpful so that the local people could learn about the existence and the importance of the reserves. Around Manongarivo, slash and burn clearing of the forest will cease only if alternative agricultural practices are developed so that the land already cleared can produce enough food on a sustainable basis to support the villagers (Quansah, 1988). The reserve on Nosy Bé could

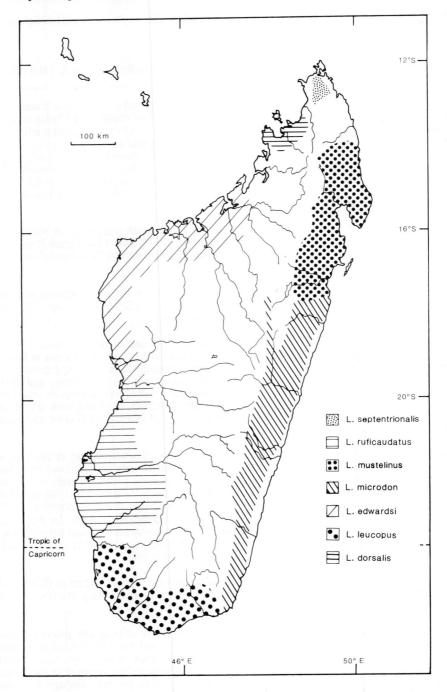

100 km

12°S

16°S

20°S

Tropic of
Capricorn

46° E

50° E

L. septentrionalis

L. ruficaudatus

L. mustelinus

L. microdon

L. edwardsi

L. leucopus

L. dorsalis

Figure 9: Distribution of all species of *Lepilemur*. Shaded areas represent approximate
limits of ranges.

74

be developed as a tourist attraction, this would provide some employment and income to the islanders (Nicoll and Langrand, 1989).

All species of Lemuridae (which is taken to include the genus *Lepilemur*) are listed in Appendix 1 of the 1973 Convention on International Trade in Endangered Species of Wild Fauna and Flora.

Trade in them, or their products, is subject to strict regulation and may not be carried out for primarily commercial purposes.

All Lemuroidea are listed in Class A of the African Convention, 1969. They may not, therefore, be hunted, killed, captured or collected without the authorization of the highest competent authority, and then only if required in the national interest or for scientific purposes.

Malagasy law protects all lemurs from unauthorised capture and from hunting. It is, however, very difficult to enforce this.

CAPTIVE BREEDING None is known to occur in captivity. Breeding of all the Sportive Lemurs appears to be difficult (Rumpler, 1975, Petter *et al*, 1977).

REMARKS The Grey-backed Sportive Lemur is one of the smaller species within the genus. Its head and body measure 250-260 mm (Tattersall, 1982) and it probably weighs around 500 g. Upperparts are medium to dark brown and underparts are also brown, only a little paler than the dorsum (Tattersall, 1982). See Jenkins (1987) and Tattersall (1982) for more measurements of this species.

The taxonomy of this group is very confused. It is common for all the types to be considered as subspecies of *L. mustelinus* (e.g. Tattersall, 1982; Richard, 1984), while the names and numbers of the forms vary with the author. Tattersall (*in litt.*) now considers that the genus should contain several species. The Grey-backed Sportive Lemur was described as a distinct species by Rumpler (1975) on the basis of karyotype studies. There is also considerable disagreement over which family the genus should be in. It is traditionally put in Lemuridae, now it is commonly placed in Lepilemuridae but Schwartz and Tattersall (1985) have placed it in Megaladapidae, along with some of the extinct lemurs. More details of the taxonomy can be found in Tattersall (1982) and Jenkins (1987). The Malagasy name for this species is apongy (Tattersall, 1982).

REFERENCES

Jenkins, P. D. (1987). *Catalogue of Primates in the British Museum (Natural History) and elsewhere in the British Isles. Part IV: Suborder Strepsirrhini, including the Subfossil Madagascan Lemurs and the Family Tarsiidae.* British Museum (Natural History), London.
Nicoll, M.E. and Langrand, O. (1989). *Revue Générale du Système d'Aires Protégées de la Conservation à Madagascar.* Unpublished report to WWF.
Petter, A. and Petter, J.J. (1971). Part 3.1 Infraorder Lemuriformes. In: Meester, J. and Setzer, H.W. (Eds), *The Mammals of Africa: An Identification Manual.* Smithsonian Institution Press, City of Washington.
Petter, J-J., Albignac, R. and Rumpler, Y. (1977). Mammifères lémuriens (Primates prosimiens). *Faune de Madagascar* No. 44. ORSTOM-CNRS, Paris.
Petter, J.-J. and Petter-Rousseaux, A. (1979). Classification of the Prosimians. In: Doyle, G.A. and Martin, R.D. (Eds), *The Study of Prosimian Behavior.* Academic Press, London. Pp. 1-44.

Quansah, N. (Ed.), (1988). Conclusions and Recommendations. *Manongarivo Special Reserve (Madagascar): 1987/88 Expedition Report.* Madagascar Environmental Research Group, U.K.

Raxworthy, C.J. and Rakotondraparany, F. (1988). Mammals report. In: Quansah, N. (Ed.), *Manongarivo Special Reserve (Madagascar): 1987/88 Expedition Report.* Madagascar Environmental Research Group, U.K.

Richard, A.F. (1984). Lemurs. In: Macdonald, D. (Ed.), *The Encyclopaedia of Mammals:1.* George Allen and Unwin, London. Pp. 330-331.

Rumpler, Y. (1975). The significance of chromosomal studies in the systematics of the Malagasy lemurs. In: Tattersall, I. and Sussman, R.W. (Eds), *Lemur Biology.* Plenum Press, New York. Pp. 25-40.

Schwartz, J.H. and Tattersall, I. (1985). Evolutionary relationships of the living lemurs and lorises (Mammalia, Primates) and their potential affinities with European Eocene Adapidae. *Anthropological Papers of the American Museum of Natural History* 60 (1): 1-100.

Tattersall, I. (1982). *The Primates of Madagascar.* Columbia University Press, New York.

Milne-Edwards' Sportive Lemur, *Lepilemur edwardsi*, is found in the dry, deciduous forests of western Madagascar. Its main diet is leaves.
Photo by Russell Mittermeier.

MILNE-EDWARDS' SPORTIVE LEMUR   RARE

Lepilemur edwardsi Major, 1894

Order PRIMATES   Family MEGALADAPIDAE

SUMMARY Milne-Edward's Sportive Lemur is found in the dry deciduous forests of western Madagascar but its precise distibution is not known. There are no estimates of population number but the species may be found at high densities in some areas. *Lepilemur edwardsi* has been studied only briefly and there is little information available on its ecology and social organisation. It is a solitary, nocturnal species and its main diet is leaves. Probably threatened by habitat destruction. The species is found in at least three protected areas. None occurs in captivity. Listed in Appendix 1 of CITES, Class A of the African Convention and is protected by Malagasy law.

DISTRIBUTION This species is found in the dry deciduous forests of western Madagascar. Petter and Petter-Rousseaux (1979) show a very discontinuous distribution from approximately 14°40'S to just north of Manambolo River (this discontinuity appears to be largely a function of mapping its occurrence in the remaining forests in the west, whereas it is usual to show more approximate ranges, including whole areas rather than particular habitats). Petter *et al* (1977) show two large populations, a southern one between Manambolo and Manambao Rivers, and a more northerly one from approximately 17°S to 15°S, with a small disjunct population between them. Tattersall (1982) gives the distribution from the Bay of Mahajamba south to at least Antsalova, and possibly as far as Tsiribihina River.

POPULATION No estimations of population numbers have been made, though Albignac (1981) suggests that they can exist at quite high densities; he caught 25 individuals in a 16 ha study site at Ampijoroa in Ankarafantsika Forest. However, Ganzhorn (1988) reports densities of only 57± 22 individuals per sq. km (mean and 95% confidence limits, based on 10 census walks along 1.7 km of trail) at Ampijoroa.

HABITAT AND ECOLOGY Two or three individuals (males and females) sleep together in tree holes but they generally move separately at night (Albignac, 1981; Petter *et al*, 1977). The home range of this species is reported to be about 1 ha, with the ranges of "certain males" being larger (Albignac, 1981). Overlap of the ranges can be quite extensive (Albignac, 1981). *L.edwardsi* has aggresive auditory territorial behaviours involving howling and shaking of branches (Albignac, 1981). The main diet of this sportive lemur is leaves, including mature ones, but it also takes fruit, flowers and fleshy seeds (Razanahoera-Rakotomalala, 1981; Albignac, 1981; Ganzhorn, 1988).

THREATS No specific information, but habitat loss must be a threat. Fires, set each year to encourage new grass growth for domestic stock, are the main cause of the destruction of the dry deciduous forests. For instance, 500 ha of forest in Namoroka Nature Reserve was burnt in 1984 (Nicoll and Langrand, 1989). In 1981, FAO/UNEP estimated net degradation of of the western forests to have been perhaps 200,000 ha since 1955. The map in Petter and Petter-Rousseaux (1979) suggests that the populations are becoming increasingly small and isolated as the forest disappears.

CONSERVATION MEASURES Milne-Edwards' Sportive Lemur is found in the Nature Reserves of Ankarafantsika, Namoroka and Bemaraha and it may also be in some of the Special Reserves that are in its range.

More guards with better equipment would be an asset in all the reserves in the west as it is essential that the fires are controlled (Nicoll and Langrand, 1989). Education projects that demonstrate the danger of the fires and the benefits of the reserves to the local people would be helpful for the conservation of the protected areas. In addition, notices on the boundaries of the reserves could be used to inform people that hunting and tree cutting is illegal (Nicoll and Langrand, 1989). The Department of Water and Forests, with the World Bank, is developing a management programme for Ankarafantsika and this will benefit by the inclusion of a reafforestation plan to provide wood for fuel and building material (Nicoll and Langrand, 1989).

All species of Lemuridae (which is taken to include the genus *Lepilemur*) are listed in Appendix 1 of the 1973 Convention on International Trade in Endangered Species of Wild Fauna and Flora. Trade in them, or their products, is subject to strict regulation and may not be carried out for primarily commercial purposes.

All Lemuroidea are listed in Class A of the African Convention, 1969. They may not, therefore, be hunted, killed, captured or collected without the authorization of the highest competent authority, and then only if required in the national interest or for scientific purposes.

Malagasy law protects all lemurs from hunting or unauthorised capture, but it is difficult to enforce this.

CAPTIVE BREEDING None is known to be held in captivity. Members of the genus *Lepilemur* do not survive well in captivity (Petter *et al*, 1977).

REMARKS The dimensions of this species are quite similar to those of *L. ruficaudatus* (Tattersall, 1982; Jenkins, 1987), it weighs between 800 and 1000 g (Razanahoera, 1988). Its dorsal fur is grey-brown with a red-brown wash, while its underparts are grey, flecked with cream (Tattersall, 1982; Jenkins, 1987).

The taxonomy of *Lepilemur* is very confused. It is common for all the forms within the genus to be considered as subspecies of *L. mustelinus* (e.g. Tattersall, 1982; Richard, 1984) and the number and names of the types vary with the author. Though, Tattersall (*in litt.*) now considers that the genus does contain several species, he remains unconvinced that *edwardsi* warrants separation from *ruficaudatus*, the species found in the dry forests to the south of the range of *edwardsi*. There is also considerable disagreement over which family the genus should be in. Traditionally it is put in Lemuridae, now it is commonly placed in Lepilemuridae but Schwartz and Tattersall (1985) have placed it in Megaladapidae, along with some of the extinct lemurs. Further details of the taxonomy of this group can be found in Tattersall (1982) and Jenkins (1987). In Ankarafantsika and north of there, the Malagasy name for this species is repahaka; south of Ankarafantsika, it is called boenga (Tattersall, 1982).

REFERENCES

Albignac, R. (1981). Lemurine social and territorial organisation in a north-western Malagasy Forest (restricted area of Ampijoroa). In: Chiarelli, A.B. and Corruccini, R.S. (Eds), *Primate Behavior and Sociobiology.* Springer Verlag, Berlin. Pp. 25-29.

FAO/UNEP (1981). *Tropical Forest Resources Assessment Project. Forest Resources of Tropical Africa. Part II Country Briefs.* FAO, Rome.

Ganzhorn, J. (1988). Food partitioning among Malagasy primates. *Oecologia* (Berlin) 75: 436-450.

Jenkins, P.D. (1987). *Catalogue of Primates in the British Museum (Natural History) and elsewhere in the British Isles. Part IV: Suborder Strepsirrhini, including the Subfossil Madagascan Lemurs and the Family Tarsiidae.* British Museum (Natural History), London.

Nicoll, M.E. and Langrand, O. (1989). *Revue Générale du Système d'Aires Protégées de la Conservation à Madagascar.* Unpublished report to WWF.

Petter, J-J., Albignac, R. and Rumpler, Y. (1977). Mammifères lémuriens (Primates prosimiens). *Faune de Madagascar* No. 44. ORSTOM-CNRS, Paris.

Petter, J.-J. and Petter-Rousseaux, A. (1979). Classification of the Prosimians. In: Doyle, G.A. and Martin, R.D. (Eds), *The Study of Prosimian Behavior.* Academic Press, London. Pp. 1-44.

Razanahoera-Rakotomalala, M. (1981). Les adaptations alimentaires comparés de deux lémuriens folivores sympatriques: *Avahi* Jourdan, 1934 - *Lepilemur* I. Geoffroy, 1851. Unpublished PhD thesis, University of Madagascar, Antananarivo.

Razanahoera, M.R. (1988). Comportement alimentaire de deux espèces sympatriques dans la forêt d'Ankarafantsika (nord-ouest de Madagascar): *Lepilemur edwardsi* et *Avahi laniger* (Lémuriens Nocturnes). In: Rakotovao, L., Barre, V. and Sayer, J. (Eds), *L'Equilibre des Ecosystèmes Forestiers à Madagascar Actes d'un séminaire international.* IUCN, Gland, Switzerland and Cambridge, U.K. Pp. 96-99.

Schwartz, J.H. and Tattersall, I. (1985). Evolutionary relationships of the living lemurs and lorises (Mammalia, Primates) and their potential affinities with European Eocene Adapidae. *Anthropological Papers of the American Museum of Natural History* 60 (1): 1-100.

Tattersall, I. (1982). *The Primates of Madagascar.* Columbia University Press, New York.

The White-footed Sportive Lemur, *Lepilemur leucopus*, is found in southern Madagascar.
Its numbers are probably declining as the forests there are being reduced in area.
Photo by Chris Raxworthy.

WHITE-FOOTED SPORTIVE LEMUR   RARE

Lepilemur leucopus **Major, 1894**

Order **PRIMATES**   Family   **MEGALADAPIDAE**

SUMMARY The White-footed Sportive Lemur is found only in the primary Didiereaceae forest and the remaining gallery forests of southern Madagascar. Its precise distribution is not known. Overall population figures are unknown, but it is reported to occur at very high densities in some habitats, as many as 810 individuals per sq. km. It is a nocturnal, mainly solitary, folivore. There have been at least two brief studies of *Lepilemur leucopus* but their findings are contradictory. Its numbers are probably declining as the dry forests are being reduced in area. It is present in four reserves. None is in captivity. Listed in Appendix 1 of CITES, Class A of the African Convention and protected by Malagasy law.

DISTRIBUTION Found in the primary Didiereaceae and gallery forests of southern Madagascar (Sussman and Richard,1986) from Taolanaro (Fort-Dauphin) westwards to Onilahy River (Petter and Petter-Rousseaux, 1979; Petter *et al*, 1977). Tattersall (1982) considers its westwards range to be at least as far as Ejeda, and only possibly to Onilahy River.

POPULATION Total population figures are not known, but numbers as high as 810 individuals per sq. km have been reported in dense areas of gallery forest bordering the river in Berenty Private Reserve (Charles-Dominique and Hladik, 1971). Density throughout the gallery forest at Berenty was calculated to be 450 individuals per sq. km (Charles-Dominique and Hladik, 1971; Hladik and Charles Dominique, 1974). The densities were estimated to be somewhat lower in the Didiereaceae bush in the same area, here there were 200-350 individuals per sq. km (Charles-Dominique and Hladik, 1971; Hladik and Charles-Dominique, 1974).

HABITAT AND ECOLOGY This medium sized nocturnal lemur has been studied briefly by Charles-Dominique and Hladik (1971, 1974) in *Didierea* bush near Berenty. In the dry months of September and October, the diet of the White-footed Sportive Lemur was primarily the tough foliage of *Alluaudia procera* and *A. ascendens* (Charles-Dominique and Hladik, 1971; Hladik and Charles-Dominique, 1974). At the driest time of the year, when no leaves were available, the White-footed Sportive Lemur survived on a diet of *Alluaudia* flowers (Charles-Dominique and Hladik, 1971; Hladik and Charles-Dominique, 1974). These authors report that the Sportive Lemur injests its faeces (caecotrophy), thereby gaining extra nutrition from its poor quality, folivorous diet.

White-footed Sportive Lemurs live in small territories. Mean range size of adult females was 0.18 ha (between 0.15 and 0.32 ha), adult males had bigger ranges, of 0.3 ha (between 0.20 and 0.46 ha), and juvenile females ranged over 0.19 ha (0.18-0.20 ha) (Hladik and Charles-Dominque, 1974). There was little range sharing within the sexes, but males' territories overlapped those of females (Hladik and Charles-Dominique, 1974). The territory of one male (the largest) overlapped the ranges of five females, while those of the three other males overlapped two, one and one females (Hladik and Charles-Dominique, 1974). Females shared their ranges with their immature offspring and it was possible that adult daughters remained in their natal range (Charles-Dominique and Hladik, 1971). Territories were defended by mutual surveillance, especially between males, by vocalisations and by displays rather than by olfactory cues (Hladik and Charles-Dominique, 1974).

Males and females slept separately, either in a tree hole or on a bundle of lianes or other vegetation (Hladik and Charles-Dominique, 1974). They emerged, frequently after a bout of calling (pers. obs.), when the sun set, but their activity throughout the night was minimal, one male *Lepilemur* travelled only 270m during a full night's follow (Charles-Dominique and Hladik, 1971). Mode of locomotion is principally vertical clinging and leaping.

A later study by Russell (1980) at the same site produced results contradictory to those of Hladik and Charles-Dominique. He suggests that *Lepilemur leucopus* is as active as other lemurs, spending only 13% of the night at rest, and travelling an average of 400m a night. He also found that male/female or female/female pairs often shared most or all of a range and these were rarely defended by vocalisations or surveillance behaviour (Russell, 1977 in Tattersall, 1982). Russell (1980) found no evidence of caecotrophy.

Mating occurs between May and July and after a gestation period of about four and a half months, females give birth to a single infant in September to November (Petter *et al*, 1977). Sexual maturity is attained at 18 months (Richard, 1984) and females can probably have one offspring each year thereafter (Petter *et al*, 1977).

THREATS The dry forest in the south is being destroyed by fire, over grazing and poor land use and this is probably a threat to *L. leucopus*. However, no specific information is available. Though the two small reserves in which it is found, Beza-Mahafaly Special Reserve and Berenty Private Reserve, are well demarcated, fenced and guarded, this is not so for the Natural Reserves of Andohahela and Tsimanampetsotsa (Sussman *et al*, 1987). The principal threat to the forests in the south is probably the collection of wood for conversion into charcoal (M. Pidgeon, *in litt.*).

CONSERVATION MEASURES The White-footed Sportive Lemur is found in two Nature Reserves, Andohahela (O'Connor *et al*, 1986,1987) and Tsimanampetsotsa (Andriamampianina and Peyrieras, 1972) and in the Special Reserve of Beza-Mahafaly as well as in the Private Reserve of Berenty (Sussman and Richard, 1986; Sussman *et al*, 1987).

The Department of Water and Forests, the University of Madagascar, WWF and USAID have jointly proposed and financed a management plan for Andohahela Nature Reseve (Nicoll and Langrand, 1989). Under this plan it is suggested that more guards with better equipment are employed to protect the area from illegal tree felling, agricultural encroachment, overgrazing by domestic stock and hunting. In addition, it would be useful to clearly mark the boundaries of the Reserve and to patrol them. The needs of the local people for food, fuel and building material have to be satisfied without encroaching on the protected area. Education programmes could be started so that the villagers understood the importance of the reserve and what they could do to protect it. Similar measures are required to protect Tsimanampetsotsa Nature Reserve.

Surveys of the remaining vegetation and the condition of all the forests within the range of this species need to be carried out. A census of the distribution and numbers of the White-footed Sportive Lemur is needed so that its conservation status can be assessed so that any necessary protective measures can be taken.

All species of Lemuridae (which is taken to include the genus *Lepilemur*) are listed in Appendix 1 of the 1973 Convention on International Trade in Endangered Species of Wild Fauna and Flora. Trade in them, or their products, is subject to strict regulation and may not be carried out for primarily commercial purposes.

All Lemuroidea are listed in Class A of the African Convention, 1969. They may not, therefore, be hunted, killed, captured or collected without the authorization of the highest competent authority, and then only if required in the national interest or for scientific purposes.

In Madagascar, all lemurs are legally protected from killing or unauthorised capture. This is, however, impossible to enforce.

CAPTIVE BREEDING None is recorded in captivity (ISIS, June 1989). Members of this genus are generally difficult to keep alive in captivity for very long (Petter *et al*, 1977).

REMARKS *L. leucopus* is possibly the smallest of the *Lepilemur* species, it weighs about 550 g. Upper parts are medium to light grey, underparts are very pale grey or white. Its tail is very light brown. The Malagasy name of the White-footed Sportive Lemur is songiky (Tattersall, 1982).

The taxonomy of this group is very confused. It is common for all the types, the names and numbers of which depend on the writer, to be considered as subspecies of *L. mustelinus* (e.g. Tattersall, 1982; Richard, 1984). Contrary to his earlier work, Tattersall (*in litt.*) now considers that the genus should contain several species. There is also considerable disagreement over which family the genus should be in. It is traditionally put in Lemuridae, now it is commonly placed in Lepilemuridae but Schwartz and Tattersall (1985) have placed it in Megaladapidae, along with some of the extinct lemurs. For a more detailed description of this species and its taxonomy see Tattersall (1982) or Jenkins (1987).

REFERENCES

Andriamampianina, J. and Peyrieras, A. (1972). Les réserves naturelles intégrales de Madagascar. In: *Comptes Rendus de la Conférence Internationale sur la Conservation de la Nature et de ses Ressources à Madagascar, Tananarive, Madagascar 7-11 Octobre 1970.* IUCN Gland, Switzerland and Cambridge, U.K. Pp. 103-123.

Charles-Dominique, P. and Hladik, C.M. (1971). Le *Lepilemur* du sud de Madagascar: écologie, alimentation et vie sociale. *La Terre et la Vie* 25: 3-66.

Hladik, C.M. and Charles-Dominique, P. (1974). The behavior and ecology of the sportive lemur (*Lepilemur mustelinus*) in relation to its dietary peculiarities. In: Martin, R.D., Doyle, G.A. and Walker, A.C. (Eds), *Prosimian Biology.* Duckworth, London. Pp. 23-37.

Hladik, C.M., Charles-Dominique, P. and Petter, J.-J. (1980). Feeding strategies of five nocturnal prosimians in the dry forest of the west coast of Madagascar. In: Charles-Dominique, P., Cooper, H.M., Hladik, A., Hladik, C.M., Pages, E., Pariente, G.F., Petter-Rousseaux, A., Petter, J.J. and Schilling, A. (Eds), *Nocturnal Malagasy Primates: Ecology, Physiology and Behavior.* Academic Press, New York. Pp. 41-73.

ISIS (1989). *ISIS Species Distribution Report Abstract for Mammals,* 30 June 1989. International Species Information System, 12101 Johnny Cake Ridge Road, Apple Valley, MN, U.S.A. Pp. 17-22.

Jenkins, P. D. (1987). *Catalogue of Primates in the British Museum (Natural History) and elsewhere in the British Isles. Part IV: Suborder Strepsirrhini, including the Subfossil Madagascan Lemurs and the Family Tarsiidae.* British Museum (Natural History), London.

Nicoll, M.E. and Langrand, O. (1989). *Revue Générale du Système d'Aires Protégées et de la Conservation à Madagascar.* Unpublished report to WWF.

O'Connor, S., Pidgeon, M. and Randria, Z. (1986). Lemur conservation in Andohahela Reserve, Madagascar. *Primate Conservation* 7: 48-52.

O'Connor, S., Pidgeon, M. and Randria, Z. (1987). Un programme de conservation pour la Réserve d'Andohahela. In: *Priorités en Matière de Conservation des Espèces à Madagascar.* Occasional Papers of the IUCN Species Survival Commission, Number 2.

Petter, J-J., Albignac, R. and Rumpler, Y. (1977). Mammifères lémuriens (Primates prosimiens). *Faune de Madagascar* No. 44. ORSTOM-CNRS, Paris.

Petter, J.-J. and Petter-Rousseaux, A. (1979). Classification of the Prosimians. In: Doyle, G.A. and Martin, R.D. (Eds), *The Study of Prosimian Behavior*. Academic Press, London. Pp. 1-44.

Richard, A.F. (1984). Lemurs. In: Macdonald, D, (Ed.), *The Encyclopaedia of Mammals*: 1. George Allen and Unwin, London. Pp. 330-331.

Russell, R.J. (1980). The environmental physiology and ecology of *Lepilemur ruficaudatus* (=*L. leucopus*) in arid southern Madagascar. *American Journal of Physical Anthropology* 52: 273-274.

Schwartz, J.H. and Tattersall, I. (1985). Evolutionary relationships of living lemurs and lorises (Mammalia, Primates) and their potential affinities with European Eocene Adapidae. *Anthropological Papers of the American Museum of Natural History* 60(1): 1-100.

Sussman, R.W. and Richard, A.F. (1986). Lemur conservation in Madagascar: the status of lemurs in the south. *Primate Conservation* 7: 85-92.

Sussman, R.W., Richard, A.F. and Rakotomanga, P. (1987). La conservation des lémuriens à Madagascar: leur statut dans le sud. In: *Priorités en Matière de Conservation des spèces à Madagascar*. Occasional Papers of the IUCN Species Survival Commission, Number 2.

Tattersall, I. (1982). *The Primates of Madagascar*. Columbia University Press, New York.

The small-toothed Sportive Lemur, *Lepilemur microdon*, occurs in the eastern rain forests. Photo by Olivier Langrand/BIOS

SMALL-TOOTHED SPORTIVE LEMUR

RARE

Lepilemur microdon Major, 1894

Order PRIMATES

Family MEGALADAPIDAE

SUMMARY The Small-toothed Sportive Lemur is probably the most widely distributed of the sportive lemurs. It is found in the south and central areas of the eastern rain forest. Some authors do not distinguish between this species and *Lepilemur mustelinus,* which is found in the rain forest north of the range of *L. microdon* and overlaps with it in some areas. There are no estimates of population number. *L. microdon* has not been studied in any detail and there is very little information on its ecology or social organisation. It is nocturnal, mainly solitary and it eats leaves, fruit and flowers. Found in several reserves. None is in captivity. Protected by Malagasy law and listed in Appendix 1 of CITES and Class A of the African Convention.

DISTRIBUTION In the eastern forests from just south of Toamasina (Tamatave) at around 18°S, to near Taolanaro (Fort-Dauphin) (Petter *et al,* 1977; Petter and Petter-Rousseaux, 1979; Jenkins, 1987). It is sympatric with *L. mustelinus* in the north of its range.

POPULATION Population numbers unknown but densities at Analamazaotra (Perinet) were estimated to be about 100 per sq. km (Charles-Dominique and Hladik, 1971). These authors did not distinguish between *Lepilemur* and *Avahi* in their nocturnal surveys, but found combined densities of 200 individuals per sq. km and they considered that approximately half of these were *Lepilemur* (Charles-Dominique and Hladik, 1971). The figure estimated by Ganzhorn (1988) in the same forest is considerably lower, only 13 ± 9 individuals per sq. km (mean and 95% confidence limits based on 25 census walks along 3.2 km of trails). The species is probably declining in number as the rain forest decreases in area.

HABITAT AND ECOLOGY Little information exists on the ecology of this species. It eats leaves, fruit and flowers and is mainly solitary (Ganzhorn, 1988).

THREATS No specific threats have been found, but the eastern rain forest, where this species occurs, is disappearing. The principal agent of destruction of this forest is slash and burn cultivation. FAO/UNEP (1981) gave a figure of 40,000 ha of previously undisturbed closed forest cleared per year for the years 1976-1980, and they estimated 35,000 ha per year for the years 1981-1985; the great majority of this is expected to be in the eastern forests (IUCN/UNEP/WWF, 1987).

CONSERVATION MEASURES Found in Andohahela (listed as *L. m. mustelinus,* O'Connor *et al,* 1987) and Analamazaotra (Perinet) Nature Reserves (Nicoll and Langrand, 1989).

Better protection is needed for the eastern forest reserves to save at least some of the area from destruction. This will succeed best if combined with education programmes and development of alternative resources to replace those supplied by the forest at the moment. Some of the protected areas could be developed as tourist attractions which would provide some employment and income for Malagasy in the area. Analamazaotra, for instance, is already comparatively easy of access and tourists do visit there.

All species of Lemuridae (which is taken to include the genus *Lepilemur*) are listed in Appendix 1 of the 1973 Convention on International Trade in Endangered Species of Wild

Fauna and Flora. Trade in them, or their products, is subject to strict regulation and may not be carried out for primarily commercial purposes.

All Lemuroidea are listed in Class A of the African Convention, 1969. They may not, therefore, be hunted, killed, captured or collected without the authorization of the highest competent authority, and then only if required in the national interest or for scientific purposes.

All lemurs are protected from killing or unauthorised capture by Malagasy law, but this is difficult to enforce.

CAPTIVE BREEDING None is known to be in captivity (ISIS, June 1989). Members of this genus generally do not survive for long in captivity (Petter *et al*, 1977).

REMARKS The Small-toothed Sportive Lemur was recognised by Major (1894) on the basis of the small size of its molars and pelage colour. It has been synonymised with *mustelinus* by some authors (e.g. Tattersall, 1982; Richard, 1984), but others identify it as a distinct species (Petter *et al*, 1977; Petter and Petter-Rousseaux, 1979). Jenkins (1987) has re-examined Major's specimens and considers that two distinct forms do occur. Though Tattersall (*in litt.*) now (in contrast to his 1982 publication) considers that the genus should contain several species (six), he still does not separate *mustelinus* and *microdon*. Jenkins (1987) describes *L. microdon* as red-brown on its upperparts, generally with a dark mid-dorsal line and a yellowish-buff wash laterally and ventrally. Its underparts are grey and its tail is distally dark brown. Its head and body length is given as 300-350 mm (Jenkins, 1987) and it probably weighs about 1 kg. Malagasy names of the eastern rain forest *Lepilemur* are trangalavaka, kotrika, fitiliky, hataka, varikosy (Tattersall, 1982), but the two species, *microdon* and *mustelinus* are not distinguished.

The taxonomy of the genus *Lepilemur* is very confused, greater details can be found in Tattersall (1982) and Jenkins (1987). Briefly, it is common for all the species to be considered as subspecies of *L. mustelinus* and the numbers and names of the subspecies vary. There is also considerable disagreement over which family the genus should be in. It is traditionally put in Lemuridae, now it is commonly placed in Lepilemuridae but Schwartz and Tattersall (1985) have placed it in Megaladapidae, along with some of the extinct lemurs.

REFERENCES

Charles-Dominique, P. and Hladik, C.M. (1971). Le *Lepilemur* du sud de Madagascar: écologie, alimentation et vie sociale. *La Terre et La Vie* 25: 3-66.

FAO/UNEP (1981). *Tropical Forest Resources Assessment Project. Forest Resources of Tropical Africa. Part II Country Briefs.* FAO, Rome.

Ganzhorn, J.U. (1988). Food partitioning among Malagasy primates. *Oecologia* 75: 436-450.

ISIS (1989). *ISIS Species Distribution Report Abstract for Mammals,* 30 June 1989. International Species Information System, 12101 Johnny Cake Ridge Road, Apple Valley, MN. U.S.A. Pp. 17-22.

IUCN/UNEP/WWF (1987). *Madagascar, an Environmental Profile.* Edited by M.D. Jenkins. IUCN, Gland, Switzerland and Cambridge, U.K.

Jenkins, P. D. (1987). *Catalogue of Primates in the British Museum (Natural History) and elsewhere in the British Isles. Part IV: Suborder Strepsirrhini, including the Subfossil Madagascan Lemurs and the Family Tarsiidae.* British Museum (Natural History), London.

Nicoll, M.E. and Langrand, O. (1989). *Revue Générale du Système d'Aires Protégées de la Conservation à Madagascar.* Unpublished report to WWF.

O'Connor, S, Pidgeon, M. and Randria, Z. (1987). Un programme de conservation pour la Réserve d'Andohahela. In: *Priorités en Matière de Conservation des Espèces à Madagascar.* Occasional Papers of the IUCN Species Survival Commission, Number 2.

Petter, J-J., Albignac, R. and Rumpler, Y. (1977). Mammifères lémuriens (Primates prosimiens). *Faune de Madagascar* No. 44. ORSTOM-CNRS, Paris.

Petter, J.-J. and Petter-Rousseaux, A. (1979). Classification of the Prosimians. In: Doyle, G.A. and Martin, R.D. (Eds), *The Study of Prosimian Behavior.* Academic Press, London. Pp. 1-44.

Richard, A. (1984). Lemurs. In: Macdonald, D. (Ed.), *Encyclopaedia of Mammals: 1.* George Allen and Unwin, London. Pp. 330-331.

Schwartz, J.H. and Tattersall, I. (1985). Evolutionary relationships of the living lemurs and lorises (Mammalia, Primates) and their potential affinities with European Eocene Adapidae. *Anthropological Papers of the American Museum of Natural History* 60 (1): 1-100.

Tattersall, I. (1982). *The Primates of Madagascar.* Columbia University Press, New York.

WEASEL SPORTIVE LEMUR

RARE

Lepilemur mustelinus I. Geoffroy, 1851

Order PRIMATES

Family MEGALADAPIDAE

SUMMARY The Weasel Sportive Lemur is a comparatively widely distributed, nocturnal species found in the eastern rain forest. Some authors do not distinguish between this species and *Lepilemur microdon*, which is found in the rain forest south of the range of *L. mustelinus*. The numbers of the Weasel Lemur are unknown, nor are there any estimates of population density. The species is, however, likely to be declining as the rain forest is destroyed. It has been studied only very briefly. Assuming that it is similar to the one species in this genus that has been studied in more detail, it is principally a folivore with little social interaction between adults. It occurs in several reserves. None is in captivity. Listed in Appendix 1 of CITES, Class A of the African Convention and is protected by Malagasy law.

DISTRIBUTION Found in the eastern rain forest from the Tsaratanana/Andapa region at around 14°S to just south of Toamasina (Tamatave) at approximately 18°25'S (map in Petter and Petter-Rouseaux, 1979), but specimens in the British Museum of Natural History extend the range of this species to 20°S (Jenkins, 1987). An area of sympatry with *L. microdon* occurs south of Tamatave to Ampitambé Forest (Jenkins, 1987; Petter and Petter-Rousseaux, 1979). A single collecting record suggests that this species used to occur futher north, as far as Vohimarina, which is beyond the range of the humid forest (Tattersall, 1982).

POPULATION There are no data on population numbers or densities of this species. They were, however, seen only rarely in Marojejy Natural Reserve (W. Duckworth, pers. comm.). Numbers are likely be declining as the rain forest decreases in area.

HABITAT AND ECOLOGY Ratsirarson and Rumpler (1988) found that this species of *Lepilemur* had a comparatively large territory of 1.5 ha. It slept in tree holes 6-12m above the ground during the dry season but on bunches of leaves and lianes in the rainy season (Ratsirarson and Rumpler, 1988). Leaping was its common mode of progression and it was never seen on the ground (Ratsirarson and Rumpler, 1988). Grooming was seen between a female and her offspring but never between adults (Ratsirarson and Rumpler, 1988).

THREATS None are known specifically for this species, but destruction of its habitat is occurring over large areas. The principal agent of destruction in the eastern rain forest is slash and burn cultivation. FAO/UNEP (1981) gave a figure of 40,000 ha of previously undisturbed closed forest cleared per year for the years 1976-1980, and estimated 35,000 ha per year for the years 1981-1985; the great majority of this is expected to be in the eastern forests (IUCN/UNEP/WWF, 1987).

CONSERVATION MEASURES Found in Marojejy and Tsaratanana Nature Reserves (Nicoll and Langrand, 1989; Safford *et al*, 1989) and may be in Zahamena, the *Lepilemur* species there was not identified (Raxworthy, 1986). It is not clear which species is present in Analamazaotra Special Reserve, it has been identified as *L. m. mustelinus* by Ganzhorn (1988), but he does not distinguish between this species and *L. microdon* (Ganzhorn, *in litt.*), either or both could be present.

Three new protected areas, in the range of this species, have been proposed; one just north of Analamazaotra (Mantady), one near Mananara and one on the Masoala Peninsula (Nicoll and Langrand, 1989). All Reserves in the east would benefit from better protection, while conservation education programmes for the local people would also help safeguard the reserves. Development plans are essential to provide alternatives to using the forest for agricultural land, fuel and building materials.

All species of Lemuridae (which is taken to include the genus *Lepilemur*) are listed in Appendix 1 of the 1973 Convention on International Trade in Endangered Species of Wild Fauna and Flora. Trade in them, or their products, is subject to strict regulation and may not be carried out for primarily commercial purposes.

All Lemuroidea are listed in Class A of the African Convention, 1969. They may not, therefore, be hunted, killed, captured or collected without the authorization of the highest competent authority, and then only if required in the national interest or for scientific purposes.

Malagasy law protects all lemurs from being killed or captured without authorisation. This is, however, very difficult to enforce.

CAPTIVE BREEDING None are recorded in captivity by ISIS (June 1989). They are reported to be very difficult to keep in captivity for any length of time (Petter *et al*, 1977).

REMARKS This species is one of the larger ones in the genus *Lepilemur*; its head and body length is 300-350 mm (Jenkins, 1987) and it probably weighs about 1 kg. Dorsally it is brown, often with a grey head, while its underparts are grey-brown (Jenkins, 1987). For a more detailed description of the species see Petter *et al*, 1977 and Jenkins, 1987. Malagasy names of the eastern rain forest *Lepilemur* are trangalavaka, kotrika, fitiliky, hataka, varikosy (Tattersall, 1982), but the two species are not distinguished.

The taxonomy of this group is very confused, greater details can be found in Tattersall (1982) and Jenkins (1987). It is common for all the Sportive Lemurs to be considered as subspecies of *L. mustelinus* and, even when this is done, some authors (e.g. Tattersall, 1982; Richard, 1984), do not distinguish between *L. m. mustelinus* and *L. m. microdon*. Though Tattersall (*in litt.*) now considers that the genus should contain several species (six), he still does not separate *mustelinus* and *microdon*. There is also considerable disagreement over which family the genus should be in. It is traditionally put in Lemuridae, now it is commonly placed in Lepilemuridae but Schwartz and Tattersall (1985) have placed it in Megaladapidae, along with some of the extinct lemurs.

REFERENCES

FAO/UNEP (1981). *Tropical Forest Resources Assessment Project. Forest Resources of Tropical Africa. Part II Country Briefs.* FAO, Rome.
Ganzhorn, J.U. (1988). Food partitioning among Malagasy primates. *Oecologia* 75: 436-450.
ISIS (1989). *ISIS Species Distribution Report Abstract for Mammals,* 30 June 1989. International Species Information System, 12101 Johnny Cake Ridge Road, Apple Valley, MN, U.S.A. Pp. 17-22.
IUCN/UNEP/WWF, (1987). *Madagascar, an environmental profile.* Edited by M.D. Jenkins. IUCN, Gland, Switzerland and Cambridge, U.K.
Jenkins, P. D. (1987). *Catalogue of Primates in the British Museum (Natural History) and elsewhere in the British Isles. Part IV: Suborder Strepsirrhini, including the subfossil Madagascan Lemurs and the Family Tarsiidae.* British Museum (Natural History), London.
Nicoll, M.E. and Langrand, O. (1989). *Revue Générale du Système d'Aires Protégées de la Conservation à Madagascar.* Unpublished report to WWF.
Petter, J-J., Albignac, R. and Rumpler, Y. (1977). Mammifères lémuriens (Primates prosimiens). *Faune de Madagascar* No. 44. ORSTOM-CNRS, Paris.

Petter, J.-J. and Petter-Rousseaux, A. (1979). Classification of the Prosimians In: Doyle, G.A. and Martin, R.D. (Eds), *The Study of Prosimian Behavior.* Academic Press, London. Pp. 1-44.

Ratsirarson, J. and Rumpler, Y. (1988). Contribution à l'etude comparée de l'eco-ethologie de deux espèces de lémuriens, *Lepilemur mustelinus* (I. Geoffroy 1850), *Lepilemur septentrionalis* (Rumpler and Albignac 1975). In: Rakotovao, L., Barre, V. and Sayer, J. (Eds), *L'Equilibre des Ecosystèmes forestiers à Madagascar, Actes d'un séminaire international.* IUCN Gland, Switzerland and Cambridge, U.K. Pp. 100-102.

Raxworthy, C. (1986). The Lemurs of Zahamena Reserve. *Primate Conservation* 7: 46-47.

Richard, A. (1984). Lemurs. In: Macdonald, D. (Ed.), *Encyclopaedia of Mammals: 1.* George Allen and Unwin, London. Pp. 330-331.

Safford, R.J., Durbin, J.C. and Duckworth, J.W. (1989). *Cambridge Madagascar Rainforest Expedition 1988 to RNI No. 12 - Marojejy.* Unpublished preliminary report.

Schwartz, J.H. and Tattersall, I. (1985). Evolutionary relationships of the living lemurs and lorises (Mammalia, Primates) and their potential affinities with European Eocene Adapidae. *Anthropological Papers of the American Museum of Natural History* 60 (1): 1-100.

Tattersall, I. (1982). *The Primates of Madagascar.* Columbia University Press, New York.

RED-TAILED SPORTIVE LEMUR

RARE

Lepilemur ruficaudatus   A. Grandidier, 1867

Order PRIMATES

Family MEGALADAPIDAE

SUMMARY The Red-tailed Sportive Lemur is endemic to the dry forests in parts of western Madagascar, but the limits of its range are not well known. Population numbers are unknown but the species can occur at densities as high as several hundred individuals per sq. km. There have been some brief studies of *Lepilemur ruficaudatus* . It is nocturnal and mostly solitary. Its diet is mainly leaves but some fruit is also eaten. There are now, in 1989, only two individuals in captivity, both of which were born there. The species occurs in two protected areas. Listed in Appendix 1 of CITES, Class A of the African Convention and is protected by Malagasy law.

DISTRIBUTION Petter and Petter-Rousseaux (1979) show this species as occurring in the western forests south of Tsiribihina River (at around 19°45'S) to approximately 23°S, with a second, small, isolated population just north of the Onilahy River. Petter *et al* (1977) and Tattersall (1982) show the Red-tailed Sportive Lemur occurring between Tsiribihina and Onilahy Rivers, but Tattersall points out that its limits are ill defined and that it may extend as far south as Ejeda.

POPULATION Total numbers are not known. Petter *et al* (1971) estimate densities of *Lepilemur* at their study site in Marosalaza Forest, 50 km north of Morondava, to be 350 individuals per sq. km in an area of tall trees and to be around 180 individuals per sq. km in an area of smaller, denser trees. Another count by these authors on a tributary of the Mangoky River gave a density of 260 individuals per sq. km (Petter *et al*, 1975). Numbers are almost certainly declining due to habitat destruction.

HABITAT AND ECOLOGY Inhabiting the dry forests of western Madagascar, the Red-tailed Sportive Lemur has to adapt to considerable seasonal variations in climate and food supply. It is principally a folivore, but fruits, especially *Diospyros* spp, are also eaten in summer (Hladik *et al*, 1980). Caecotrophy has been seen in this species in captivity (Hladik *et al*, 1980).

Mating occurs from May to July and, after a gestation period of 4-5 months, a single infant is born between September and November (Petter-Rousseaux, 1980, Petter *et al*, 1977). The infant is transported by its mother in her mouth for the first few weeks of life, but later is carried clinging to her fur (Petter-Rousseaux, 1964). Initially, the female leaves her infant on a branch or in a tree hollow while foraging (Petter-Rousseaux, 1964). Lactation continues for at least four months and the offspring stay with their mother for about a year, apparently they leave before a second infant is born (Petter-Rousseaux, 1964).

THREATS Habitat destruction is likely to be the biggest threat to this species. Forest fires are particularly common in the west and the forest is rapidly decreasing in area. Woodcutters are reported to hunt *Lepilemur* (Petter *et al*, 1977).

CONSERVATION MEASURES Occurs in Analabe Private Reserve and Andranomena Special Reserve.

A management plan is needed for all the forests between Morondava and Tsiribihina River. If this included development of a better irrigation system for the rice growing areas, it would not be necessary to clear the forests for more agricultural land (Nicoll and Langrand, 1989).

Conservation education projects for the local people would enable them to learn how important the forests are for the maintenance of their well-being.

Nicoll and Langrand (1989) have recommended that both Analabe and Andranomena Reserves would benefit from a greater number of guards with better equipment who could then patrol the areas more efficiently to prevent fires and illegal clearing of the forest. Teams looking for oil have opened paths into the reserves and these allow easy access to hunters and tree fellers (Nicoll and Langrand, 1989). If barriers were put up across the paths and notices installed informing people that they were in a reserve, this would ensure that the integrity of the areas is respected. Analabe has great potential as a tourist attraction and this could be developed (Nicoll and Langrand, 1989).

All species of Lemuridae (which is taken to include the genus *Lepilemur*) are listed in Appendix 1 of the 1973 Convention on International Trade in Endangered Species of Wild Fauna and Flora. Trade in them, or their products, is subject to strict regulation and may not be carried out for primarily commercial purposes.

All Lemuroidea are listed in Class A of the African Convention, 1969. They may not, therefore, be hunted, killed, captured or collected without the authorization of the highest competent authority, and then only if required in the national interest or for scientific purposes.

Malagasy law protects all lemurs from being killed or captured without authorisation. However, this is difficult to enforce.

CAPTIVE BREEDING This species has been kept in captivity in Brunoy, France and at least one birth has occurred there (Petter-Rousseaux, 1980). It is unclear how long any individuals survived. ISIS (June, 1989) records one captive born female in Paris Zoo and this is confirmed by Petter (*in litt.*). This genus is generally difficult to maintain in captivity (Petter *et al*, 1977).

REMARKS *L. ruficaudatus* is one of the bigger species within the genus, it weighs 600-900g (Petter *et al*, 1977). Dorsally it is light grey-brown with a red-brown wash anteriorly. It is light grey or white on its underparts (Jenkins, 1987). See Tattersall (1982) or Jenkins (1987) for morphological measurements of this species. The Malagasy name of this species is boenga (Tattersall, 1982).

The taxonomy of *Lepilemur* is very confused. It is common for all the forms within the genus to be considered as subspecies of *L. mustelinus* (e.g. Tattersall, 1982; Richard, 1984) and the number and names of the forms vary with the author. Though, Tattersall (*in litt.*) now considers that the genus does contain several species, he remains unconvinced that *ruficaudatus* and *edwardsi* (the species found in the dry forests north of the range of *ruficaudatus*) warrant separation. There is also considerable disagreement over which family the genus should be in. Traditionally it is put in Lemuridae, now it is commonly placed in Lepilemuridae but Schwartz and Tattersall (1985) have placed it in Megaladapidae, along with some of the extinct lemurs. Greater details of the taxonomy of this group can be found in Tattersall (1982) and Jenkins (1987).

REFERENCES

Hladik, C.M., Charles-Dominique, P. and Petter, J.-J. (1980). Feeding strategies of five nocturnal prosimians in the dry forest of the west coast of Madagascar. In: Charles-Dominique, P., Cooper, H.M., Hladik, A., Hladik, C.M., Pages, E., Pariente, G.F., Petter-Rousseaux, A., Petter, J.-J. and Schilling, A. (Eds), *Nocturnal Malagasy Primates: Ecology, Physiology and Behavior*. Academic Press, New York. Pp. 41-73.

ISIS (1989). *ISIS Species Distribution Report Abstract for Mammals,* 30 June 1989. International Species Information System, 12101 Johnny Cake Ridge Road, Apple Valley, MN, U.S.A. Pp. 17-22.

Jenkins, P. D. (1987). *Catalogue of Primates in the British Museum (Natural History) and elsewhere in the British Isles. Part IV: Suborder Strepsirrhini, including the Subfossil Madagascan Lemurs and the Family Tarsiidae.* British Museum (Natural History), London.

Nicoll, M.E. and Langrand, O. (1989). *Revue Générale du Système d'Aires Protégées de la Conservation à Madagascar.* Unpublished report to WWF.

Petter, J-J., Albignac, R. and Rumpler, Y. (1977). Mammifères lémuriens (Primates prosimiens) *Faune de Madagascar* No 44. ORSTOM-CNRS, Paris.

Petter, J-J., Schilling, A. and Pariente, G. (1971). Observations éco-éthologiques sur deux lémuriens malgaches nocturnes: *Phaner furcifer* and *Microcebus coquereli. La Terre et la Vie* 3: 287-327.

Petter, J-J., Schilling, A. and Pariente, G. (1975). Observations on Behavior and Ecology of *Phaner furcifer.* In: Tattersall, I. and Sussman, R.W. (Eds), *Lemur Biology.* Plenum Press, New York. Pp. 209-218.

Petter, J.-J. and Petter-Rousseaux, A. (1979). Classification of the Prosimians. In: Doyle, G.A. and Martin, R.D. (Eds), *The Study of Prosimian Behavior.* Academic Press, London. Pp. 1-44.

Petter-Rousseaux, A. (1964). Reproductive physiology and behavior of the Lemuroidea. In: Buettner-Janusch, J. (Ed.), *Evolutionary and Genetic Biology of Primates,* Volume 2. Academic Press, New York. Pp. 91-132.

Petter-Rousseaux, A. (1980). Seasonal activity rhythms, reproduction, and body weight variations in five sympatric nocturnal prosimians, in simulated light and climatic conditions. In: Charles-Dominique, P., Cooper, H.M., Hladik, A., Hladik, C.M., Pages, E., Pariente, G.F., Petter-Rousseaux, A., Petter, J.-J. and Schilling, A. (Eds), *Nocturnal Malagasy Primates: Ecology, Physiology and Behavior.* Academic Press, New York. Pp. 137-152.

Richard, A.F. (1984). Lemurs. In: Macdonald, D. (Ed.), *The Encyclopaedia of Mammals: 1.* George Allen and Unwin, London. Pp. 330-331.

Schwartz, J.H. and Tattersall, I. (1985). Evolutionary relationships of the living lemurs and lorises (Mammalia, Primates) and their potential affinities with European Eocene Adapidae. *Anthropological Papers of the American Museum of Natural History* 60 (1): 1-100.

Tattersall, I. (1982). *The Primates of Madagascar.* Columbia University Press, New York.

The Northern Sportive Lemur, *Lepilemur septentrionalis*, has a very restricted distribution. It is one of the most threatened of the genus *Lepilemur*.
Photo by Jane Wilson.

NORTHERN SPORTIVE LEMUR   VULNERABLE

Lepilemur septentrionalis **Rumpler and Albignac, 1975**

Order **PRIMATES**   Family **MEGALADAPIDAE**

SUMMARY The Northern Sportive Lemur is found in the deciduous forests in the extreme north of Madagascar. It has a very restricted distribution, which suggests it could be one of the most threatened of the Sportive Lemurs. Population numbers are unknown but it can be found at very high densities in some areas. There is very little known about the ecology and social organisation of this species. It is a nocturnal lemur, solitary and essentially folivorous, as are the other species in this genus. *Lepilemur septentrionalis* is found in three reserves. None is in captivity. Listed in Appendix 1 of CITES, Class A of the African Convention and protected by Malagasy law.

DISTRIBUTION Found in the extreme north of Madagascar, north of Ambilobé and to the south and east of Montagne d'Ambre (Tattersall, 1982, Petter *et al*, 1977; Petter and Petter-Rousseaux, 1979). Its southernmost limit is to the left (west) of the Ambilobé-Vohimarina (Vohemar) road from Betsiaka to Maromokotora and on the left (west) bank of the Lokoho River (See map in Ratsirarson *et al*, 1987).

POPULATION Total numbers are not known but this species is reported at densities as high as 564 ± 493 individuals per sq. km (mean and 95% confidence limits) in the closed canopy forests of Ankarana Special Reserve (Hawkins *et al*, in press). It was present at lower densities in the dry forest of Ankarana, 163 ± 68 individuals per sq. km and at similar densities (146 ± 48 individuals per sq. km) in Analamera Special Reserve (Hawkins *et al*, in press). Meyers (*in litt.*) estimates lower densities, 60 individuals per sq. km, in the dry forests of Analalmera

HABITAT AND ECOLOGY The forests in which this species live are mostly dry and deciduous, though there are some more humid evergreen forests in Ankarana and it is in these that the densities of *L. septentrionalis* are highest (Hawkins *et al*, in press). Territory size in this species has been reported as 1 ha (Ratsirarson and Rumpler, 1988). Adults rarely associated at night but mothers and their young were seen together (Ratsirarson and Rumpler, 1988). Tree holes or bundles of foliage were used as daytime resting places (Ratsirarson and Rumpler, 1988). The tree holes were generally six to eight metres above the ground in small, living trees (Ratsirarson and Rumpler, 1988). This species, like the others in the genus, is a folivore.

THREATS Destruction of the forests in which the Northern Sportive Lemur is found is quite widespread, even within the protected areas. Bush fires threaten the edges of Montagne d'Ambre National Park and there is illegal forestry within it (Nicoll and Langrand, 1989). Analamera Reserve is being destroyed by logging, burning and over grazing (Hawkins *et al*, in press). Lemurs are hunted in both these areas, though this is probably more of a threat to the diurnal lemurs than the smaller, nocturnal Sportive Lemur. Ankarana Reserve had been relatively undisturbed until recently but there is now a considerable amount of logging occurring within the Reserve (Wilson *et al*, 1989).

As the forests in the range of the Northern Sportive Lemur become smaller and more isolated interchange between the populations will become increasingly difficult, thereby reducing the genetic diversity of each population. It is estimated that the distance between the forests of Ankarana and those of Montagne d'Ambre has increased from 10 km in 1982 to 30 km in 1988 (Wilson *et al*, 1988, 1989).

CONSERVATION MEASURES Found in Ankarana and Analamera Special Reserves (Hawkins, *et al*, in press), and in Mt d'Ambre National Park (Nicoll and Langrand, 1989). All three reserves would benefit from increased protection. More detailed ecological studies of *L. septentrionalis* are needed to enable areas of suitable habitat to be identified.

All species of Lemuridae (which is taken to include the genus *Lepilemur*) are listed in Appendix 1 of the 1973 Convention on International Trade in Endangered Species of Wild Fauna and Flora. Trade in them, or their products, is subject to strict regulation and may not be carried out for primarily commercial purposes.

All Lemuroidea are listed in Class A of the African Convention, 1969. They may not, therefore, be hunted, killed, captured or collected without the authorization of the highest competent authority, and then only if required in the national interest or for scientific purposes.

Malagasy law protects all lemurs from hunting and unauthorised capture, but this is difficult to enforce.

CAPTIVE BREEDING None is known to occur in captivity. Members of the genus *Lepilemur* are very difficult to maintain in captivity (Petter *et al*, 1977).

REMARKS The Northern Sportive Lemur is a medium sized member of its genus. The head and body measurement of a single specimen is given as 278 mm (Tattersall, 1982), it probably weighs in the region of 700-800g. The upper parts of this species are grey, darkest on the crown, becoming lighter caudally to pale grey rump and hindlimbs (Tattersall, 1982). There tends to be a darker median stripe along its crown and back (Tattersall, 1982). Underparts are grey (Tattersall, 1982). Further measurements of *L. septentrionalis* can be found in Tattersall (1982) and Jenkins (1987). The Malagasy names of the Northern Sportive Lemur are mahiabeala and songiky (Tattersall, 1982).

The taxonomy of the genus *Lepilemur* is very confused. It is common for all the forms to be considered as subspecies of *L. mustelinus* (e.g. Tattersall, 1982; Richard, 1984), the names and numbers of which depend on the author. Tattersall (*in litt.*) now considers that the genus should contain several species. *L. septentrionalis* was described as a result of karyotype analysis by Rumpler and Albignac (1975). They also described four subspecies on the basis of their different karyotypes, but as there are no significant morphological or colour differences between the forms, and there are wild caught hybrids, Tattersall (1982) considers that they must all belong to a single, interbreeding population. This view is supported by Jenkins (1987). There is also considerable disagreement over which family the genus should be in. It is traditionally put in Lemuridae, now it is commonly placed in Lepilemuridae but Schwartz and Tattersall (1985) have placed it in Megaladapidae, along with some of the extinct lemurs. Further details of the taxonomy can be found in Tattersall (1982), Jenkins (1987) and Rumpler and Albignac (1978).

REFERENCES

Hawkins, A.F.A., Ganzhorn, J.U., Bloxham, Q.M.C., Barlow, S.C., Tonge, S.J. and Chapman, P. (in press). A survey and assessment of the conservation status and needs of the lemurs, birds, lizards and snakes in the Ankarana Special Reserve, Antseranana, Madagascar: with notes on the lemurs and birds of the nearby Analalmera Special Reserve. *Biological Conservation.*

Jenkins, P. D. (1987). *Catalogue of Primates in the British Museum (Natural History) and elsewhere in the British Isles. Part IV: Suborder Strepsirrhini, including the Subfossil Madagascan Lemurs and the Family Tarsiidae.* British Museum (Natural History), London.

Nicoll, M.E. and Langrand, O. (1989). *Revue Générale du Système d'Aires Protégées de la Conservation à Madagascar.* Unpublished report to WWF.

Petter, J-J., Albignac, R. and Rumpler, Y. (1977). Mammifères lémuriens (Primates prosimiens). *Faune de Madagascar* No. 44. ORSTOM-CNRS, Paris.

Petter, J.-J. and Petter-Rousseaux, A. (1979). Classification of the Prosimians. In: Doyle, G.A. and Martin, R.D. (Eds), *The Study of Prosimian Behavior.* Academic Press, London. Pp.1-44.

Ratsirarson, J. and Rumpler, Y. (1988). Contribution à l'etude comparée de l'éco-éthologie de deux espèces de lémuriens, *Lepilemur mustelinus* (I. Geoffroy 1850), et *Lepilemur septentrionalis* (Rumpler and Albignac, 1975). In: Rakotovao, L., Barre, V. and Sayer, J. (Eds), *L'Equilibre des Ecosystèmes Forestiers à Madagascar: Actes d'un séminaire international.* IUCN Gland, Switzerland and Cambridge, U.K. Pp. 100-102.

Ratsirarson, J., Anderson, J., Warter, S. and Rumpler, Y. (1987). Notes on the distribution of *Lepilemur septentrionalis* and *L. mustelinus* in northern Madgascar. *Primates* 28(1): 119-122.

Richard, A.F. (1984). Lemurs. In: Macdonald, D. (Ed.), *The Encyclopaedia of Mammals:1.* George Allen and Unwin, London. Pp. 330-331.

Rumpler, Y. and Albignac, R. (1975). Intraspecific chromosome variability in a lemur from the north of Madagascar: *Lepilemur septentrionalis*, species nova. *American Journal of Physical Anthropology* 42: 425-429.

Rumpler, Y. and Albignac, R. (1978). Chromosome studies of the *Lepilemur*, an endemic Malagasy genus of lemurs: contribution of the cytogenetics to their taxonomy. *Journal of Human Evolution* 7(3): 191-196.

Schwartz, J.H. and Tattersall, I. (1985). Evolutionary relationships of the living lemurs and lorises (Mammalia, Primates) and their potential affinities with European Eocene Adapidae. *Anthropological Papers of the American Museum of Natural History* 60 (1): 1-100.

Tattersall, I. (1982). *The Primates of Madagascar.* Columbia University Press, New York.

Wilson, J.M., Stewart, P.D. and Fowler, S.V. (1988). Ankarana - a rediscovered nature reserve in northern Madagascar. *Oryx* 22: 163-171.

Wilson, J.M., Stewart, P.D., Ramangason, G.-S., Denning, A.M. and Hutchings, M.S. (1989). Ecology and conservation of the crowned lemur, *Lemur coronatus,* at Ankarana, N. Madagascar, with notes on Sanford's lemur, other sympatric and subfossil lemurs. *Folia Primatologica* 52: 1-26.

The Ring-tailed Lemur, *Lemur catta*, is a diurnal group-living species. It is the most terrestrial of the lemurs. Although it is the most common of the lemurs in captivity, it is threatened by habitat destruction in Madagascar.
Photo by Mark Pidgeon.

RING-TAILED LEMUR   VULNERABLE

Lemur catta Linnaeus, 1758

Order PRIMATES   Family LEMURIDAE

SUMMARY The Ring-tailed Lemur is found in the dry forests and bush of south and south-western Madagascar. Population numbers are not known and estimates of density vary from 17 to 350 individuals per sq. km. Though previously considered not threatened, recent reports suggest this may no longer be the case. *Lemur catta* is one of the most studied of the lemurs. It is a medium-sized diurnal species which spends more time on the ground than any of the other lemurs. It is found in groups, containing several adults of both sexes, of up to 24 individuals. It's diet is principally fruit, leaves and flowers. It is the most common lemur in zoos, over 950 individuals are reported to be held in captivity. It is found in six protected areas. Listed in Appendix 1 of CITES, Class A of the African Convention and is protected by Malagasy law.

DISTRIBUTION Found patchily distributed in the dry forests and bush of south and south-western Madagascar. The northern limit to the range of *L. catta* is the forest of Mahababoky (at 20°44'S, 44°0'E), in Kirindy reserve about 45 km south of Morondava River (Sussman, 1977a). The eastern limit of its range is around 46°48'E, or, approximately, along a line joining Fianarantsoa and Taolanaro (Fort Dauphin) (Sussman, 1977a; Tattersall, 1982). The Ring-tailed Lemur ranges into the interior highlands further than does any other lemur (Tattersall, 1982).

POPULATION No figures are available for total population number. There have been a variety of density estimates for this species, mostly at Berenty (near Taolanaro). Counts of 153 and 152 individuals in 94 hectares (167 individuals per sq. km) of the reserve were made in 1972/73 by Budnitz and Dainis (1975); an earlier estimate by Jolly (1966), extrapolating from her 10 ha study site, gave figures of 350 individuals per sq. km; while Sussman (1974), on the basis of group size and home range, calculated 250 individuals per sq. km at Berenty; estimates for 1983-1985 were 115.3 individuals per sq. km when infants were excluded and 143.7 when they were not (O'Connor, 1987). In the south-west at Antserananomby, Sussman (1974) estimated that there were 215 individuals per sq. km. In the disturbed forest of Bealoka on the Mandrare River, near Berenty, density of *L. catta* was estimated at only 17.4 individuals per sq. km (O'Connor, 1987). Population numbers are probably declining (Richard and Sussman, 1987).

HABITAT AND ECOLOGY A diurnal species that lives in brush and scrub forests and in closed canopy deciduous forests, it is also found in the dry, rocky and mountainous areas in the southern portion of the central plateau where patches of deciduous forest remain (Sussman, 1977a, 1977b). The ranging and foraging patterns of *L. catta* may be related to its ability to cope with these semi-arid environments in which resources are sparse and unevenly distributed (Sussman, 1977b). They probably cannot, however, survive year round in sub-desert vegetation where there is no forest (Budnitz, 1978; M. Pidgeon, *in litt.*). There have been several sightings of the species in very dry areas away from any forest and it is possible that they migrate into these areas during the rainy season or, alternatively, there may be water available there for some months of the year; *L. catta* apparently does need to drink at least ocassionally (M. Pidgeon, *in litt.*).

Most of the studies of this species have been in Berenty, a Private Reserve near Taolanaro (Fort Dauphin), which is owned by the de Heaulme family (Jolly, 1966, 1972; Klopfer and Jolly, 1970; Budnitz and Dainis, 1975; Sussman, 1974, 1977c; Mertl-Millhollen *et al*, 1979; Jolly *et al*, 1982; Jones, 1983; Howarth *et al*, 1986; O'Connor, 1987; Mertl-Millhollen, 1988). Sussman (1974, 1977b) has also done a short study at Antserananomby, just north of the Mangoky River in the west of Madagascar. A long term study of the social organisation, demography and reproductive behaviour is underway in Beza Mahafaly Special Reserve in the south-west (Sussman, 1989; Sauther, 1989).

The Ring-tailed Lemur has been seen feeding on fruit, leaves, flowers, bark and sap from at least 34 different species of plant, but particularly from *Tamarindus indica*, the kily tree (Jolly, 1966; Sussman, 1974, 1977b and c; O'Connor, 1987). At Bealoka, the lemurs raided crops and ate melons and the leaves of sweet potatoes (O'Connor, 1987). In addition, *L. catta* has been seen eating small quantities of dead wood, earth and invertebrates (O'Connor, 1987). The amount of time the lemurs spent eating each type of food varied between study sites, seasons and years. For instance, Jolly (1966) observed the Ring-tailed Lemur spending 70% of its feeding time eating fruit and 25% eating leaves (studied between February-September, 1963 and March-May 1st 1964), while at the same site in November 1970, Sussman (1974, 1977c) recorded *L. catta* eating 59% fruit, 24% leaves, 6% flowers and some herbs, bark and sap; only 23% of their feeding time was spent eating *Tamarindus indica* (mostly leaves and pods), half that recorded by Jolly. Between July and September 1970 at Antserananomby, fruit was eaten for 33.6% of the observations, leaves for 43.6%, herbs for 14.6%, and flowers for 8% (Sussman, 1974, 1977c). There were two peaks of feeding during the day, with a rest period of two hours or so around midday (Sussman, 1977c).

Ring-tailed Lemurs are active and feed in all the strata of the forest and they, more than any other lemur, spend considerable periods of time on the ground (Budnitz, 1978; Sussman, 1974, 1977b). Sussman (1977b) found that they spent over 30% of their time on the ground at both his study sites, 70% of travel was on the ground. O'Connor (1987), however, reports only 15.8% and 17.8% of time spent on the ground in Berenty and Bealoka respectively; most travel occurred there. The Ring-tailed Lemurs were outside the area of continuous canopy for over 58% of the day, although they slept in the canopy at night (Sussman, 1977c).

The size of *L. catta* groups ranges from three to 24 individuals (Budnitz and Dainis, 1975; Jolly, 1966; Sussman, 1974, 1977b, 1989; O'Connor, 1987), with sex ratios varying between 0.6 to 2.7 adult males to females (Jolly, 1966). Within the groups there is a well defined dominance hierarchy, with the females being dominant over the males (Sussman, 1977b, Jolly, 1966). This tends to give rise to subgroups and during movement the troop can be spread out over 20 to 30 m with the subordinate males lagging in the rear (Jolly, 1966; Sussman, 1977b).

The home range size of *L. catta* appears to be directly related to the abundance and distribution of resources, including water (Sussman, 1977c). For instance, Budnitz and Dainis (1975) found that a troop of Ring-tailed Lemurs living in open forest, brush and scrub had a home range of 23.1 ha, as compared to their figures of 6.0 and 8.1 ha for troops living in "richer" closed canopy forest. In the disturbed forest of Bealoka, a group of nine animals used a range of at least 34.6 ha (O'Connor, 1987). The troops studied by Jolly (1966) and Sussman (1974) had ranges of between 5.7 and 8.8 ha. Day ranges averaged 950m (Sussman, 1977b). The degree of overlap between home ranges also changed between study periods. Each group maintained almost exclusive use of its home range and boundaries overlapped only slightly at Antseranoanomby and at Berenty in 1963-64 (Jolly, 1966; Sussman, 1977b). However, at Berenty in 1970, groups shared a large portion of their home range, though they used the overlap areas at diferent times, and intergroup encounters were more frequent (Jolly 1972, Sussman, 1974, 1977b). This same situation was recorded by O'Connor (1987) during her study in Berenty from April 1984 to September 1985.

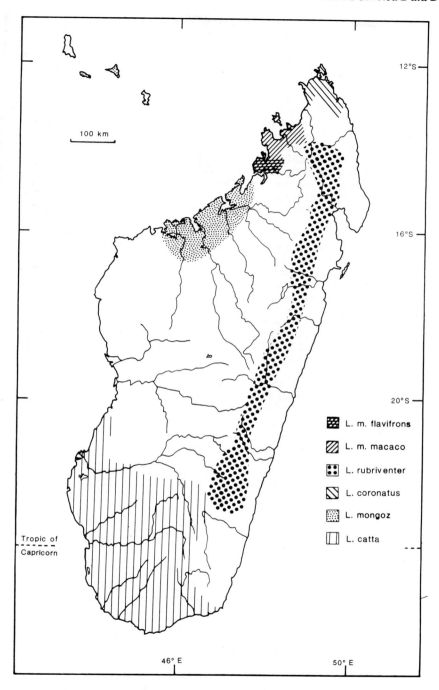

Figure 10: Distribution of all *Lemur* species except *Lemur fulvus*. Shaded areas
represent approximate limits of ranges.

L. catta begins mating in mid-April (Jolly, 1966; Budnitz and Dainis, 1975). Results from studies of *L. catta* in captivity have indicated that gestation period in this species is between 134 and 138 days (Van Horn and Eaton, 1979). In the wild, infants are born from mid-August to November, but mostly in August and September (Jolly, 1966; Budnitz and Dainis, 1975; Sussman, 1977b). Twins are produced in captivity and in the wild , but singletons are more common (Van Horn and Eaton, 1979; O'Connor, *in litt.*). The infant initially clings to its mother's front, within three days of birth it is moving around actively on its mother (Jolly, 1966, Sussman, 1977b, Klopfer and Boskoff, 1979), and by about two weeks of age it is regularly riding on her back (Sussman, 1977b). At two and a half months, although it is still carried by its mother when the troop moves, it plays with other offspring, explores its environment and climbs about in the trees and bushes tasting various foods (Sussman, 1977b). It takes two years for a female to mature, but then it seems that the majority can give birth every year (Jolly, 1972). At Beza Mahafaly it is reported that females first gave birth at three years old (Sussman, 1989). In 1987, 86% of the females there gave birth; infant mortality was 20% in the first six months of life (Sussman, 1989). Females remain in their natal area, while males transfer between troops (Jolly, 1966; Jones, 1983; Sussman, 1989).

THREATS Recent satellite surveys of the gallery forest remaining in the south of Madagascar suggest that it has diminished alarmingly (Green and Sussman, in prep). The two basic habitats of *L. catta*, the dense euphorbia bush and the riparian forest, are fairly restricted and are diminishing due to fires (set to promote grass growth), overgrazing by livestock and tree felling for making charcoal. As a result, this species may be more threatened than has been thought in the past (Sussman and Richard, 1986; A. Jolly, *in litt.*). It is hunted with dogs in some areas and it may be vulnerable to hunting pressures (Sussman and Richard, 1986). Severe hunting has almost certainly lowered the population of *L. catta* in Bealoka Forest to a critical level (O'Connor, 1987). Individuals are frequently kept as pets in Madagascar (O. Langrand, *in litt.*).

CONSERVATION MEASURES This species is found in all the protected areas within its range, namely: Isalo National Park, Tsimanampetsotsa, Andohahela and Andringitra Nature Reserves, Beza Mahafaly Special Reserve and Berenty Private Reserve (Nicoll and Langrand, 1989). Of these, Isalo and Tsimanampetsotsa are the only Government-run Reserves which do not have management and development plans either already underway or in the process of being formed (Nicoll and Langrand, 1989).

This is one of the few species that has been studied for more than a few months. In 1987, a long term study, involving individual marking of all the *L. catta* in the site, was begun in Beza-Mahafaly (Sussman, 1989).

Surveys are needed to determine the distribution and population numbers of the remaining Ring-tailed Lemurs and whether gallery forests and/or water are essential for its survival (Sussman and Richard, 1986; M. Pidgeon, *in litt.*).

All species of Lemuridae are listed in Appendix 1 of the 1973 Convention on International Trade in Endangered Species of Wild Fauna and Flora. Trade in them, or their products, is subject to strict regulation and may not be carried out for primarily commercial purposes.

All Lemuroidea are listed in Class A of the African Convention, 1969. They may not, therefore, be hunted, killed, captured or collected without the authorization of the highest competent authority, and then only if required in the national interest or for scientific purposes.

The laws of Madagascar protect all lemurs from unauthorised capture and from hunting. These are, however, difficult to enforce.

CAPTIVE BREEDING The Ring-tailed Lemur breeds very well in captivity. Females frequently bear and raise twins and there have been three cases of triplets being successfully raised at Duke Primate Center (E. Simons, *in litt.*). It is the most common lemur in captivity. ISIS (June, 1989) lists 784 individuals (95% captive born) in 93 institutes. Wilde *et al* (1988) list a further 212 individuals in European institutes that are not included in the ISIS lists. In Madagascar, there are four individuals at Ivoloina and 13 in Parc Tsimbazaza (A. Katz, M. Pidgeon, G. Rakotoarisoa, *in litt.*).

REMARKS *L. catta* is probably the most familar of the lemurs because of its comparatively frequent occurrence in zoos. It is a medium-sized species, weighing around 2.3-3.5 kg. There are no pelage differences between the sexes. Fur on the back is usually brown-grey, rump and limbs are light grey. Underparts are white or cream. Forehead, cheeks, ears, and throat are white. There are black rings round the eyes and the muzzle is black; the tail is banded black and white. For a more detailed description see Tattersall (1982) and Petter *et al*, (1977). Malagasy names are maki and hira (Tattersall, 1982).

REFERENCES

Budnitz, N. (1978). Feeding behavior of *Lemur catta* in different habitats. In: Bateson, P.P.G. and Klopfer, P.H. (Eds), *Perspectives in Ethology 3*. Plenum Press, London. Pp. 85-108.

Budnitz, N. and Dainis, K. (1975). *Lemur catta*: Ecology and behaviour. In: Tattersall, I. and Sussman, R.W. (Eds), *Lemur Biology*. Plenum Press, New York. Pp. 219-235.

Howarth, C.J., Wilson, J.M., Adamson, A.P., Wilson, M.E. and Boase, M.J. (1986). Population ecology of the ringtailed lemur, *Lemur catta,* and the white sifaka, *Propithecus verreauxi verreauxi,* at Berenty, Madagascar. *Folia Primatologica* 47: 39-48.

ISIS (1989). *ISIS Species Distribution Report Abstract for Mammals,* 30 June 1989. International Species Information System, 12101 Johnny Cake Ridge Road, Apple Valley, MN, U.S.A. Pp. 17-22.

Jolly, A. (1966). *Lemur Behavior*. University of Chicago Press, Chicago.

Jolly, A. (1972). Troop continuity and troop spacing in *Propithecus verreauxi* and *Lemur catta* at Berenty (Madagascar). *Folia Primatologica* 17: 335-362.

Jolly, A., Oliver, W.L.R., and O'Connor, S.M. (1982). Population and troop ranges of *Lemur catta* and *Lemur fulvus* at Berenty, Madagascar: 1980 census. *Folia Primatologica* 39: 115-123.

Jones, K.C. (1983). Inter-troop transfer of *Lemur catta* males at Berenty, Madagascar. *Folia Primatologica* 40: 145-160.

Klopfer, P.H. and Boskoff, K.J. (1979). Maternal behavior in prosimians. In: Doyle, G.A. and Martin, R.D. (Eds), *The Study of Prosimian Behavior*. Academic Press, New York. Pp. 123-156.

Klopfer, P.H. and Jolly, A. (1970). The stability of territorial boundaries in a lemur troop. *Folia Primatologica* 12: 199-208.

Mertl-Millhollen, A.S. (1988). Olfactory demarcation of territorial but not home range boundaries by *Lemur catta. Folia Primatologica* 50: 175-187.

Mertl-Millhollen, A.S., Gustafson, H.L., Budnitz, N., Dainis, K. and Jolly, A. (1979). Population and territory stability of the *Lemur catta* at Berenty, Madagascar. *Folia Primatologica* 31: 106-122.

Nicoll, M.E. and Langrand, O. (1989). *Revue Générale du Système d'Aires Protégées et de la Conservation à Madagascar*. Unpublished report to WWF.

O'Connor, S.M. (1987). *The Effect of Human Impact on Vegetation and the Consequences to Primates in two Riverine Forests, Southern Madagascar*. Unpublished PhD thesis, University of Cambridge, Cambridge.

Petter, J-J., Albignac, R. and Rumpler, Y. (1977). Mammifères lémuriens (Primates prosimiens). *Faune de Madagascar* No. 44. ORSTOM-CNRS, Paris.

Richard, A.F. and Sussman, R.W. (1987). Framework for primate conservation in Madagascar. In: Marsh, C.W. and Mittermeier, R. (Eds), *Primate Conservation in the Tropical Forest.* Alan R. Liss, Inc., New York. Pp. 329-341.

Sauther, M.L. (1989). Reproductive behavior of free-ranging *Lemur catta* at Beza Mahafaly Reserve. *American Journal of Physical Anthropology* 78(2): 296.

Sussman, R.W. (1974). Ecological distinctions in sympatric species of *Lemur.* In: Martin, R.D., Doyle, G.A. and Walker, A.C. (Eds), *Prosimian Biology.* Duckworth, London, Pp. 75-108.

Sussman, R.W. (1977a). Distribution of the Malagasy lemurs Part 2: *Lemur catta* and *Lemur fulvus* in southern and western Madagascar. *Annals New York Academy of Sciences* 293: 170-184.

Sussman, R.W. (1977b). Socialization, social structure, and ecology of two sympatric species of lemur. In: Chevalier-Skolnikoff, S. and Poirier, F. (Eds), *Primate Bio-Social Development.* Garland, New York. Pp. 515-528.

Sussman, R.W. (1977c). Feeding behaviour of *Lemur catta* and *Lemur fulvus.* In: Clutton-Brock, T. H. (Ed.), *Primate Ecology: Studies of feeding and ranging behaviour in lemurs, monkeys and apes.* Academic Press, London. Pp. 1-36.

Sussman, R.W. (1989). Demography of *Lemur catta* in southern Madagascar. *American Journal of Physical Anthropology* 78(2): 312.

Sussman, R. W. and Richard, A. (1986). Lemur conservation in Madagascar: The status of lemurs in the south. *Primate Conservation* 7: 85-92.

Tattersall, I. (1982). *The Primates of Madagascar.* Columbia University Press, New York.

Van Horn, R N. and Eaton, G G. (1979). Reproductive physiology and behavior in prosimians. In: Doyle, G.A. and Martin, R.D. (Eds), *The Study of Prosimian Behavior.* Academic Press, New York. Pp. 79-122.

Wilde, J., Schwibbe, M.H. and Arsene, A. (1988). A census for captive primates in Europe. *Primate Report* 21: 1-120.

The Crowned Lemur, *Lemur coronatus*, has a very restricted range in the north of Madagascar. It is hunted in some areas and is threatened by habitat destruction. This is a female.
Photo by Jane Wilson.

CROWNED LEMUR

ENDANGERED

Lemur coronatus Gray, 1842

Order **PRIMATES**

Family **LEMURIDAE**

SUMMARY The Crowned Lemur is found in the dry forests in the north and far north-east of Madagascar. It is the only lemur to occur in the dry forests of the Cap d'Ambre. Population numbers are unknown, but it can occur at densities of more than 200 individuals per sq. km. Its range is comparatively small and is shrinking due to logging, burning and cattle grazing within the forests. This species is also hunted. *L. coronatus* has been studied for several months, but much remains to be learned of its ecology and social organisation. It is mostly diurnal, though nocturnal activity is not uncommon. It has been seen in groups of up to 10 individuals with several adults of both sexes in the groups. It eats fruit and some leaves. There are about 45 individuals in captivity, many of which were bred there. Crowned Lemurs are found in the four protected areas in the north of Madagascar. Listed in Appendix 1 of CITES, Class A of the African Convention and protected by Malagasy law.

DISTRIBUTION Found in the north of Madagascar in the dry forests of Cap d'Ambre, south of this its range extends to the west as far as the Ankarana Massif, between Ambilobé and Anivorano Nord, and to the east to the Fanambana River just south of Vohimarina (Tattersall, 1982). Its range includes the slopes of Mt d'Ambre.

POPULATION Population numbers are unknown but they are considered to be probably declining (Richard and Sussman, 1987). There are a number of estimates of population density. In Analamera Special Reserve estimates of 77 ± 58 individuals per sq. km (mean and 95% confidence level) have been made, while there are reported to be as many as 221 ± 79 individuals per sq. km in the canopy forest of the *Canyon Grand* in Ankarana Special Reserve (Hawkins *et al*, in press). Even higher densities, up to 5 adults per ha (500 per sq. km) in the richest canopy forest of the Canyon Grand, have been reported (Wilson *et al*, 1989; Fowler *et al*, 1989), but the authors considered that these high densities were restricted to an area of 200 ha of selectively logged forest. Overall density throughout the *Canyon Grand* and *Canyon Forestier* was just over one individual per ha, though the density of Crowned Lemurs throughout the rest of their range was estimated to be considerably lower (Wilson *et al*, 1989). In the dry forest of Sakalava, population density of *L. coronatus* was estimated at 104 individuals per sq. km, while in the humid forest of Mt d'Ambre a density of only 49 animals per sq. km was estimated (Arbelot-Tracqui, 1983).

HABITAT AND ECOLOGY In 1935, Crowned Lemurs were reported to be very common in the dry wooded areas of the northern savanna and to occur also in the dry forest on the slopes of Mt d'Ambre, up to about 800m, but to be absent from the higher, humid forests on the summit (Rand, 1935). However, the species is now reported to occur in these humid forests and it is suggested that this is a recent extension of their range, possibly due to pressure on their preferred habitat (Petter *et al*, 1977). The species does appear to be tolerant of selective tree extraction and it is found where there is constant human disturbance (Wilson *et al*, 1988). *L. coronatus* has been studied in the dry forests of Sakalava and Ankarana and in the humid forest on Mt d'Ambre (Arbelot-Tracqui, 1983; Wilson *et al*, 1989, Fowler *et al*, 1989). In Ankarana, Crowned Lemurs were seen most frequently in the canopy forest, rather than in edge or degraded forest, though there was evidence that even the driest areas were used at times (Wilson *et al*, 1989). *L. coronatus* was observed at all levels in the forest though appeared reluctant to travel on the ground, mostly descending only to eat fallen fruit or lick earth (Arbelot-Tracqui, 1983; Wilson *et al*, 1989). In contrast, Petter *et al* (1977) found that Crowned Lemurs travelled substantial distances on the ground.

In Ankarana, the diet of the Crowned Lemur, at the end of the six month dry season, was almost exclusively made up of fruit, with leaves being taken only rarely (Wilson *et al*, 1989). The fruits that they commonly ate there included *Ficus* spp, *Strychinos* spp, *Pandanus* spp, *Diospyros* sp and *Tamarindus indica* (Wilson *et al*, 1989). It was, however, considered probable that they ate more leaves in the wet season (Wilson *et al*, 1989). The lemurs visited waterholes to drink during the dry season, some of these were deep inside caves (Wilson *et al*, 1987; 1989). In Sakalava and the humid forest on Mt d'Ambre, both fruit and leaves were eaten, though fruit seemed to be the more important component of the diet (Arbelot-Tracqui, 1983).

In Ankarana, Crowned Lemurs were generally active from first light at 04.30h until after dark at 18.15h, with a rest period from approximately 10.30h to 14.30h (Wilson *et al*, 1989). However, some groups travelled for up to two hours after nightfall and feeding and travelling was commonly noted between midnight and 02.00h. In Sakalava, activity patterns were generally similar, though in the wet season the animals tended to be more active and the midday rest period was not so prounounced (Arbelot-Tracqui, 1983). In the humid forest, activity increased, there was a short rest period early in the morning and some reduction in activity between 10.30 and 13.00 hrs (Arbelot-Tracqui, 1983). Locomotion was mostly quadrupedal but some elements of "clinging and leaping" were also observed (Wilson *et al*, 1989).

The maximum group size seen in Ankarana was nine individuals plus two infants; groups of two and three were common and solitary animals were also seen (Wilson *et al*, 1989). A typical group, however, comprised five individuals, two adult pairs and a sub-adult or juvenile (Wilson *et al*, 1989). Arbelot-Tracqui (1983) suggests that group size is reduced in the humid forests, she recorded three groups of between eight and ten individuals (mean of nine) in Sakalava and four groups of between four and six individuals (mean of five) in Mt d'Ambre. There was little spatial cohesion between the members of a group, after resting periods some individuals would frequently remain behind for an hour or more before following the departed lemurs (Wilson *et al*, 1989). Interactions between groups were rare, though smaller troops tended to leave feeding patches when approached by bigger groups (Wilson *et al*, 1989). Several aggressive interactions were observed between groups of Crowned Lemurs and Sanford's Lemurs (*Lemur fulvus sanfordi*), the latter usually displaced the Crowned Lemurs at localised resources, but male *L. coronatus* chased off Sanford's lemurs if they were approaching females with infants (Wilson *et al*, 1989). Petter *et al* (1977) report *L. coronatus* groups of between five and 10 individuals

In Ankarana, Crowned Lemurs gave birth from mid-September, thereby coinciding with the first rains, with the earliest births occuring in the richest canopy forest of the *Canyon Grand* (Wilson *et al*, 1989). Births were seen over the next five weeks, with the later ones being in the drier forests where fewer fruits were available (Wilson *et al*, 1989). Further north, in the dry forests of Sakalava and in the humid forest of Mt d'Ambre, most births occurred in the third and fourth weeks of October, (Arbelot-Tracqui, 1983). However, in Sakalava, two approximately three week old infants were seen in early February and two other infants, seen in August, were judged to be about three months old. These observations suggest further births in mid-January and mid-May respectively (Arbelot-Tracqui, 1983). The infants were initially carried on their mothers' front but then moved to ride on her back (J. Wilson, pers. comm.). One year old males were about half adult size (Wilson *et al*, 1989). In captivity, gestation length has been calculated as 125 days; age at first conception has been recorded as 20 months; a male also reached sexual maturity at this age (Kappeler, 1987). Twin and singleton births appear to be equally common (Kappeler, 1987).

THREATS Poaching of lemurs in Montagne d'Ambre National Park is reported to be widespread and increasing, both *L. coronatus* and *L. fulvus sanfordi* are shot there (Nicoll and Langrand, 1989). Bush fires threaten the edges of the Park and there is illegal forestry within it (Nicoll and Langrand, 1989). Analamera Reserve is unguarded and unmanaged, it is being destroyed by logging, burning and grazing and lemurs are hunted in this area (Hawkins *et al*, in press). Until recently, Ankarana Reserve had remained relatively undisturbed, the lemurs are not hunted there (Wilson *et al*, 1989) though boys with sling shots are reported to kill some of the animals (E. Simons, *in litt.*). A possible disaster for the lemurs in this area has now occurred. During three weeks of May 1988, one third of the forest within the *Canyon Grand* was clear felled by Kharma Sawmill Company (P. Vaucoulon, pers. comm. to Wilson, 1988). It is not known whether complete clearance of the *Canyon Grand* is planned (Wilson, 1988).

The area of suitable habitat remaining for the Crowned Lemurs is probably less than 1300 sq. km and this is continuing to shrink (Wilson *et al*, 1989). Interchange between populations of *L. coronatus* is becoming increasingly difficult as the forest patches become smaller and more isolated (Hawkins *et al*, in press; Wilson *et al*, 1989). For instance, it is estimated that the distance between the forests of Ankarana and those of Montagne d'Ambre has increased from 10 km in 1982 to 30 km in 1988 (Wilson *et al*, 1989).

CONSERVATION MEASURES The Crowned Lemur occurs in Forêt d'Ambre, Analamera and Ankarana Special Reserves and in the Montagne d'Ambre National Park (Hawkins *et al*, in press; Wilson *et al*, 1988, 1989; Nicoll and Langrand, 1989).

A management plan has been proposed for all four reserves in which the Crowned Lemur is found. This is being carried out jointly by the Department of Water and Forests, WWF, the Catholic Relief Service and US-AID (Nicoll and Langrand, 1989). The following (from Nicoll and Langrand, 1989) will be included in the plan:

Extra full-time guards, with better equipment, are necessary if the areas are to be adequately patrolled. It is suggested, for instance, that camping equipment and a motorbike are essential for a guard employed in Ankarana.

A conservation education programme for the villagers around the reserves which made them aware of the importance of the forests and the protected areas would be very productive. The reserves themselves have great educational and tourist potential and this could be developed. A visitor information centre could be set up and marked paths cut through the reserves leading to places of particular interest. If a development plan for the local people is intergrated with the management plan there is more chance that the reserves will be protected from encroachment.

Domestic animals should not be allowed into the reserve. In addition, no permits to make charcoal or exploit the trees within the reserves, should be issued and the illegal activities within the reserves has to be stopped. An alternative means of providing wood should be found. Reforestation is necessary in the places where there is severe erosion. Fire breaks are needed around the protected areas.

A French teacher, B. LeNormand has released a number of Crowned Lemurs on the small, uninhabited island of Nosy Hara (Wilson *et al*, 1988; J. Wilson, *in litt.*)

Surveys are needed to determine the remaining areas of suitable habitat for the Crowned Lemurs and their population numbers so that adequate protective measures can be taken.

All species of Lemuridae are listed in Appendix 1 of the 1973 Convention on International Trade in Endangered Species of Wild Fauna and Flora. Trade in them, or their products, is subject to strict regulation and may not be carried out for primarily commercial purposes.

All Lemuroidea are listed in Class A of the African Convention, 1969. They may not, therefore, be hunted, killed, captured or collected without the authorization of the highest

competent authority, and then only if required in the national interest or for scientific purposes.

Malagasy law protects all lemurs from unauthorised capture and from hunting, but this is impossible to enforce.

CAPTIVE BREEDING ISIS (June 1989) reports that there are 36 Crowned Lemurs in captivity (*Lemur mongoz coronatus* in their sheets), 83% of them being captive born; most of these are descendants of three individuals caught for Cologne Zoo around 1969 (E. Simons, *in litt.*). According to the ISIS lists, Cologne (Koln) Zoo holds 15 individuals, Duke Primate Center has 18, there is one pair at Los Angeles and a single animal at Touroparc. It is possible that this latter animal is *L. mongoz* and not *L. coronatus* (Lernould, *in litt.*) In addition, there is one animal in Paris Zoo (J.-J. Petter, *in litt.*), and three pairs in Mulhouse Zoo and Strasbourg Université Louis Pasteur Médecine which were imported between 1981 and 1986 and are managed as a group (J.-M. Lernould, *in litt.*). In Madagascar, there are two pairs in Tsimbazaza, which have bred successfully (M. Pidgeon, G. Rakotoarisoa, *in litt.*) and three animals at Ivoloina (A. Katz, *in litt.*). *L. coronatus* is also commonly kept as a pet in Madagascar (O. Langrand, *in litt.*)

REMARKS This species was considered to be a subspecies of *L. mongoz* until recently, but is now regarded as a distinct species. Crowned Lemurs weigh about 2kg; they are sexually dichromatic, the brown male has a triangular crown of black fur between his ears, while the female is grey with a light brown crown (Wilson *et al*, 1989). Females that are almost completely white have been reported on the slopes of Mt d'Ambre, though generally the individuals in the humid forest were darker than those in the dry forests (Arbelot-Tracqui, 1983). For a more detailed description of the species, see Tattersall (1982) or Jenkins (1987). The Malagasy names of the species are ankomba, varika and gidro (Tattersall, 1982; Petter *et al*, 1977; Paulian, 1981)

REFERENCES

Arbelot-Tracqui, V. (1983). Etude Ethoecologique de Deux Primates Prosimiens: *Lemur coronatus* Gray et *Lemur fulvus sanfordi* Archbold, Contribution a l'Étude des Mécanismes d'Isolement reproductif Intervenant dans la Spéciation. Unpublished PhD thesis, University of Rennes, France.

Fowler, S.V., Chapman, P., Hurd, S., McHale, M., Ramangason, G.-S., Randriamsy, J.- E., Stewart, P., Walters, R. and Wilson, J.M. (1989). Survey and management proposals for a tropical deciduous forest reserve at Ankarana in northern Madagascar. *Biological Conservation* 47: 297-313.

Hawkins, A.F.A., Ganzhorn, J.U., Bloxam, Q.M.C., Barlow, S.C., Tonge, S.J., and Chapman, P. (in press). A survey and assessment of the conservation status and needs of lemurs, birds, lizards and snakes in the Ankarana Special Reserve, Antseranana, Madagascar: with notes on the lemurs and birds of the nearby Analamera Special Reserve. *Biological Conservation*.

ISIS (1989). *ISIS Species Distribution Report Abstract for Mammals,* 30 June 1989. International Species Information System, 12101 Johnny Cake Ridge Road, Apple Valley, MN, U.S.A. Pp. 17-22.

Jenkins, P.D. (1987). *Catalogue of Primates in the British Museum (Natural History) and elsewhere in the British Isles Part IV: Suborder of the Strepsirrhini, including the Subfossil Madagascan Lemurs and the Family Tarsiidae.* British Museum (Natural History), London.

Kappeler, P.M. (1987). Reproduction in the crowned lemur (*Lemur coronatus*) in captivity. *American Journal of Primatology* 12: 497-503.

Nicoll, M.E. and Langrand, O. (1989). *Revue Générale du Système d'Aires Protégées et de la Conservation à Madagascar.* Unpublished report to WWF.

Paulian, R. (1981). Les mammifères: vestiges d'un monde disparu. In: Oberlé, P. (Ed.), *Madagascar, Une Sanctuaire de la Nature*. Le Chevalier, Paris. Pp. 75-94.

Petter, J-J., Albignac, R. and Rumpler, Y. (1977). Mammifères lémuriens (Primates prosimiens) *Faune de Madagascar* No. 44. ORSTOM-CNRS, Paris.

Rand, A.L. (1935). On the habits of some Madagascar animals. *Journal of Mammalogy* 16(2): 89-104.

Richard, A.F. and Sussman, R.W. (1987). Framework for Primate Conservation in Madagascar. In: Marsh, C.W. and Mittermeier, R. A. (Eds), *Primate Conservation in the Tropical Forest*. Alan R. Liss, Inc., New York. Pp. 329-341.

Tattersall, I. (1982). *The Primates of Madagascar*. Columbia University Press, New York.

Wilson, J. M. (1987). The crocodile caves of Ankarana, Madagascar. *Oryx* 21: 43-47.

Wilson, J. (Ed.) (1987). The crocodile caves of Ankarana: Expedition to northern Madagascar, 1986. *Cave Science* 14(3): 107-119.

Wilson, J.M.; Stewart, P.D. and Fowler, S.V. (1988). Ankarana - a rediscovered nature reserve in northern Madagascar. *Oryx* 22: 163-171.

Wilson, J.M. (1988). Clear-felling of more lemur forest in Madagascar. *Primate Eye* 36: 21-22.

Wilson, J.M., Stewart, P.D., Ramangason, G-S., Denning, A.M., Hutchings, M.S. (1989). Ecology and conservation of the Crowned Lemur, *Lemur coronatus*, at Ankarana, N. Madagascar: with notes on Sanford's Lemur, other sympatrics and subfossil lemurs. *Folia Primatologica* 52: 1-26.

The Black Lemur, *Lemur macaco macaco*, is the most sexually dichromatic of the lemurs. It is only the male that is black.
Photo by Josephine Andrews.

BLACK LEMUR

Lemur macaco Linnaeus, 1766

Order **PRIMATES**　　　　　　　　　　　Family **LEMURIDAE**

SUMMARY The Black Lemur is found in the evergreen forests of the Sambirano Region in north-western Madagascar and on the small islands of Nosy Bé and Nosy Komba. Two subspecies are recognised, *Lemur macaco macaco* and *L. m. flavifrons,* the former is classified as Vulnerable, the latter as Endangered. Population numbers are unknown but they may be declining due to forest destruction. However, *Lemur macaco* is reported to use plantations and secondary forest so may not be dependent on undisturbed forest. The very small range of *L. m. flavifrons* suggests that it is particularly endangered. There have been no studies of this species, though one is planned in the near future, therefore little is known about its ecology or social organisation. It is a medium-sized, group living lemur that appears to be active for part of the night as well as during the day. Its diet consists of fruit, flowers, leaves and bark. There are around 250 individuals in captivity, most of which were bred there. The species occurs in two protected areas. Listed in Appendix 1 of CITES, Class A of the African Convention and is protected by Malagasy law.

DISTRIBUTION The Black Lemur is found in the western part of northern Madagascar, but the precise limits of its range are not known (Tattersall, 1982). Its approximate range is from just south of Ambilobé southwards to Analalava and it is found on the islands of Nosy Bé and Nosy Komba (Birkel, 1987). Tattersall (1982) shows a much greater extension of its southern and eastern range than in the maps of Petter and Petter-Rousseaux (1979) or Birkel (1987). *Lemur macaco* is now considered to contain two subspecies, *L. m. macaco* and *L. m. flavifrons* (Koenders *et al*, 1985a, Birkel, 1987), the distribution of these will be considered separately.

POPULATION Population numbers are unknown. Richard and Sussman (1975, 1987) consider that they are probably declining.

HABITAT AND ECOLOGY Found in the distinctive evergreen forests of the Sambirano Region of Madagascar. There has been no long term quantitative study on *L. macaco* and very little is known about the social organisation or ecology of the species in the wild. Observations on each subspecies are given below.

THREATS As with the other lemurs, destruction of habitat is the main threat to this species. The forests in the Sambirano Region are mostly being cleared for agricultural land. Some hunting of *L. macaco* is recorded. The threats to each subspecies are considered below.

CONSERVATION MEASURES See accounts for the two subspecies.

All species of Lemuridae are listed in Appendix 1 of the 1973 Convention on International Trade in Endangered Species of Wild Fauna and Flora. Trade in them, or their products, is subject to strict regulation and may not be carried out for primarily commercial purposes.

All Lemuroidea are listed in Class A of the African Convention, 1969. They may not, therefore, be hunted, killed, captured or collected without the authorization of the highest competent authority, and then only if required in the national interest or for scientific purposes.

Malagasy law protects all lemurs from unauthorised capture and from hunting, but this is impossible to enforce.

CAPTIVE BREEDING The studbook for this species is kept by Roger Birkel of St Louis Zoological Park. In the 1987 edition 45 institutions are listed as having collections of Black Lemurs of which St Louis have the greatest numbers (17 males and 14 females). Duke Primate Center is the only other place to have over 20 individuals, they had 12 males and 8 females at the time the studbook was compiled. The total numbers in captivity are given as 116 males and 116 females from a founding stock of 20 animals (Birkel, 1987). Subspecific status is not recorded in the stud book but Duke now (February 1989) have 17 *L. m. macaco* and 7 *L. m. flavifrons* (Katz, *in litt.*). Two pairs of *L. m. flavifrons* were captured in 1984 and taken to Strasbourg Université Louis Pasteur Médecine (Koenders *et al*, 1985b) and these have given birth there (Brun and Rumpler, 1987; J.-M. Lernould, *in litt.*). A pair of *L. m. flavifrons* have been lent to Mulhouse Zoo by Strasbourg Université Louis Pasteur Médecine and these have had two infants (J.-M. Lernould, *in litt.*). In Madagascar, both subspecies are held in Ivoloina (near Toamasina) and in Tsimbazaza and have successfully bred there (A. Katz, M. Pidgeon and G. Rakotoarisoa, *in litt.*).

REMARKS This is a medium sized lemur, weighing between 2 and 3 kg (Tattersall, 1982). *L. macaco* and *L. fulvus* have been synonymised but they are now accepted as separate species by most authorities (Petter and Petter-Rousseaux, 1979; Tattersall, 1976, 1982; Jenkins, 1987). Eco-ethological studies have also shown a number of differences between the two species (Koenders, 1989).

Black Lemur   **Vulnerable**

Lemur macaco macaco **Linnaeus, 1766**

DISTRIBUTION Found in north-west Madagascar from Anivorano Nord along the coast to Maromandia and on the islands of Nosy Bé and Nosy Komba (Tattersall, 1982; Koenders *et al*, 1985; Birkel, 1987).

POPULATION Numbers are unknown. On Nosy Komba, the density of this animal was estimated at less than one animal per 2 ha (Petter *et al*, 1977).

HABITAT AND ECOLOGY This subspecies has been recorded in various habitats including undisturbed forest, secondary forest, timber plantations and secondary forest mixed with crops such as coffee and cashew nut trees (Andrews, 1989). On the islands of Nosy Bé and Nosy Komba, Black Lemurs were seen in groups of between four and 15 individuals, these were composed of several adults, typically more males than females, and two to three young (Petter, 1962). The groups maintained separate ranges during the day then joined together at night (Petter, 1962). The lemurs were active in the early morning and late afternoon and rested during the mid-day hours (Petter, 1962). Birkel (1987) visted a forest north of Ambanja and counted three groups of Black Lemurs. One contained five males and four females, a second contained four individuals of each sex and the third contained five males and one female. The groups foraged until well after nightfall and were active and feeding during the night (Birkel, 1987). It is suggested that this nocturnal foraging may be partially in response to persecution by the local people who chase the lemurs out of their crops (Andrews, *in litt.*). During a recent survey on Nosy Bé and the mainland, J. Andrews (1989) counted 27 groups of Black Lemurs, the size of these groups varied from two to twelve with average group size of seven. Neither she nor Raxworthy and Rakotondraparany (1988), working in Manongarivo Special Reserve, considered that there was a bias towards males in the groups that they saw. Black Lemurs eat fruit, leaves, bark and flowers (Petter, 1962, Petter and Petter, 1971; Petter *et al*, 1977). Females have a single young, born between September and November (Petter and Petter, 1971).

THREATS The forests, both inside and outside protected areas, are being destroyed, mostly by slash and burn agriculture. Though *L. m. macaco* is found in secondary forest, it is not clear whether some undisturbed forest is necessary for its survival. Black Lemurs are poached from the Lokobe Reserve on the island of Nosy Bé (Nicoll and Langrand, 1989). The lemurs are frequently chased and some are killed when they raid crops.

CONSERVATION MEASURES This subspecies is found in Manongarivo Special Reserve on the mainland (Raxworthy and Rakotondraparany, 1988) and in the small Nature Reserve of Lokobe on the island of Nosy Bé. They are also reported to be in Tsaratanana Nature Reserve (Nicoll and Langrand, 1989). They are a tourist attraction on the island of Nosy Komba; here the local people consider them to be sacred animals.

The Reserves in which the Black Lemur are found need better protection and conservation education programmes for the local people should be set up (Nicoll and Langrand, 1989; Quansah, 1988). Lokobe could be developed as a tourist attraction and the old paths within the Reserve should be cleared to allow easy access for the tourists (Nicoll and Langrand, 1989).

An 18 month field study, comparing the ecology of Black Lemur groups in different habitats, is planned by J. Andrews of Washington University, St Louis and University College London.

REMARKS The Black Lemur is one of the most sexually dimorphic of the lemurs. The males are a uniform black while the females' coat colour varies from light brown to a dark chestnut brown, with the crown of the head and the face ranging from chestnut to gray or black. Both sexes possess heavily tufted ears, the males' are black and the females' are white. Eye colour is yellow to reddish orange (Birkel, 1987). The Malagasy names of this species are akomba, ankomba or komba (Tattersall, 1982).

Sclater's Lemur   **Endangered**

Lemur macaco flavifrons (Gray, 1867)

DISTRIBUTION Koenders *et al* (1985a and b) consider that the northern limit of the distribution of *L. m. flavifrons* may be the Andranomalaza River and that their southern limit is around Befotaka. They report first seeing the subspecies in a forest 20 km west of Andranosamonta, 16 km north of Befotaka (Koenders *et al*, 1985a). Petter and Andriatsarafara (1987) suggest that the small Maevarano River may be the southern limit to the range of this subspecies.

POPULATION Koenders *et al* (1985a) report that *L. m. flavifrons* is abundant in the remaining patches of forest in their range, but there are no estimates of population numbers or density. They consider that Sclater's Lemur could become extinct if no protective measures are taken soon (Koenders *et al*, 1985b).

Sclater's Lemur, *Lemur macaco flavifrons,* has a very restricted distribution in north-west Madagascar. This is a female, carrying an infant on her back.
Photo by Russell Mittermeier.

HABITAT AND ECOLOGY Very little is known about the ecology or social organisation of this subspecies. It has not been studied in the wild. Koenders *et al* (1985a and b) report seeing groups of six to about 10 individuals.

THREATS *L. m flavifrons* is not found in any protected area and it is reported to be threatened with hunting, trapping and, especially, forest destruction (Koenders *et al*, 1985b). Most of the forest in its very small range has already been destroyed for agricultural land.

CONSERVATION MEASURES In 1988 a programme of conservation of *L. m. flavifrons* was jointly proposed by Strasbourg Université Louis Pasteur Médecine and Mulhouse Zoo to the Malagasy Government. This includes extension of the captive breeding programme in both Europe and Madagascar; a field study of the subspecies to discover the limits of its range and its numbers, its social structure and ecology, and the impact of the human population in the area; the investigation of the possibility of creating a reserve within the range of this subspecies; and support of a Malagasy student to work on the project (Lernould and Rumpler, 1988). Cologne Zoo, Sarrbruken Zoo and Duke Primate Center have now joined the conservation programme (Lernould, *in litt.*; E. Simons, pers. comm.).

REMARKS The males of this subspecies are also black, sometimes with a brownish tint to the fur (Birkel, 1987). The male has a crest of short, upstanding hairs on the crown of its head which is not found in *L. m. macaco* (Koenders *et al*, 1985). The females have a reddish brown coat, more orange than that of *L. m. macaco* females (Koenders *et al*, 1985a). Neither sex has ear tufts and their eyes are blue-green (Koenders *et al*, 1985a).

REFERENCES

Andrews, J. (1989). Black Lemur Survey 1988 : A survey of the distribution and habitat of black lemurs, *Lemur macaco*, in north-west Madagascar. Unpublished preliminary report.

Birkel, R. (1987). 1987 International Studbook for the Black Lemur, *Lemur macaco* Linnaeus, 1766.

Brun, B. and Rumpler, Y. (1987). Sclater's black lemur born in captivity. *Primate Conservation* 8: 54-55.

Jenkins, P. D. (1987). *Catalogue of Primates in the British Museum (Natural History) and elsewhere in the British Isles. Part IV: Suborder of the Strepsirrhini, including the Subfossil Madagascan Lemurs and the Family Tarsiidae.* British Museum (Natural History), London.

Koenders, L. (1989). An eco-ethological comparison of *Lemur fulvus* and *Lemur macaco. Human Evolution* 4 (2-3): 187-193.

Koenders, L., Rumpler, Y., and Brun, B. (1985b). Notes on the recently rediscovered Sclater's lemur (*Lemur macaco flavifrons*). *Primate Conservation* 6: 35.

Koenders, L., Rumpler, Y., Ratsirarson, J. and Peyrieras, A. (1985a). *Lemur macaco flavifrons* (Gray, 1867): a rediscovered subspecies of primates. *Folia Primatologica* 44: 210-215.

Lernould, J.-M. and Rumpler, Y. (1988). Lemurs conservation: Common captive-breeding and research programs. Abstract of poster presented at the 5th Conference on Breeding Endangered Species in Captivity, Cincinnati, October 1988.

Nicoll, M.E. and Langrand, O. (1989). *Revue Générale du Système d'Aires Protégées et de la Conservation à Madagascar.* Unpublished report to WWF.

Petter, A. and Petter, J.-J. (1971). Part 3.1 Infraorder Lemuriformes. In: Meester, J. and Setzer, H.W. (Eds), *The Mammals of Africa: An Identification Manual.* Smithsonian Institution Press, City of Washington. Pp. 1-10.

Petter, J-J., Albignac, R. and Rumpler, Y. (1977). Mammifères lémuriens (Primates prosimiens). *Faune de Madagascar* No. 44. ORSTOM-CNRS, Paris.

Petter, J.-J. (1962). Recherches sur lécologie et l'éthologie des lémuriens malgaches. *Mémoires Museum National Histoire Naturelle,* Paris (A) 27: 1-146.

Petter, J.-J. and Andriatsarafara, F. (1987). Conservation status and distribution of lemurs in the west and northwest of Madagascar. *Primate Conservation* 8: 169-171.

Petter, J.-J. and Petter-Rousseaux, A. (1979). Classification of the Prosimians. In: Doyle, G.A. and Martin, R.D. (Eds), *The Study of Prosimian Behavior.* Academic Press, London. Pp. 1-44.

Quansah, N. (Ed.) (1988). *Manongarivo Special Reserve (Madagascar): 1987/88 Expedition Report.* Madagascar Environmental Research Group, U.K.

Raxworthy, C.J. and Rakotondraparany, F. (1988). Mammal report. In: Quansah, N. (Ed.), *Manongarivo Special Reserve (Madagascar): 1987/88 Expedition Report.* Madagascar Environmental Research Group, U.K.

Richard, A.F. and Sussman, R.W. (1975). Future of the Malagasy lemurs; conservation or extinction? In: Tattersall, I. and Sussman, R.W. (Eds), *Lemur Biology.* Plenum Press, New York. Pp. 335-350.

Richard, A.F. and Sussman, R.W. (1987). Framework for Primate Conservation in Madagascar. In: Marsh, C.W. and Mittermeier, R.A. (Eds), *Primate Conservation in the Tropical Rain Forest.* Alan R. Liss, Inc., New York. Pp. 329-341.

Tattersall, I. (1982). *The Primates of Madagascar.* Columbia University Press, New York.

Tattersall, I. (1976). Notes on the status of *Lemur macaco* and *Lemur fulvus* (Primates, lemuriformes). *Anthropoplogical Papers of the American Museum of Natural History* 53(2): 257-261.

The Mongoose Lemur, *Lemur mongoz*, is a group living diurnal species found in the forests of north-west Madagascar and on Ndzouani and Moili islands in the Comoros.
Photo by Phillip Coffrey/Jersey Wildlife Preservation Trust.

MONGOOSE LEMUR

ENDANGERED

Lemur mongoz Linnaeus, 1766

Order PRIMATES

Family LEMURIDAE

SUMMARY The Mongoose Lemur is one of the two lemur species found on the Comoro Islands as well as in Madagascar; it has a very limited distribution, the exact extent of which is unknown. It is found in dry deciduous forests in Madagascar and in more humid forests in the Comoros. Neither its population numbers nor density is known but it is certainly declining in number. The species is usually seen in small family groups composed of an adult pair and associated offspring. Both nocturnal and diurnal activity have been reported. Its diet is composed mainly of flowers and nectar, though some fruit, leaves and leaf petioles are also taken. Only brief studies have been made of the species. Habitat destruction on both Madagascar and the Comoro Islands is a major threat to *L. mongoz*. It is found in only one protected area. Though many of the approximately 90 individuals of this species that are in captivity were born there, these captive bred individuals themselves generally do not breed. Listed in Appendix 1 of CITES, Class A of the African Convention and is protected by the laws of Madagascar and the Comoros.

DISTRIBUTION The precise limits of the range of this species remain to be identified. It is found in north-west Madagascar in the region of Ambato-Boéni and Ankarafantsika (Petter *et al*, 1977; Tattersall, 1982). The northern limit to its range is around Analalava on the Bay of Narinda, and it has been seen west of the Betsiboka River on the shores of Lake Kinkony near Mitsinjo (Tattersall and Sussman, 1975). It is one of the two lemur species occurring on the Comoro Islands, being found on Ndzouani (Anjouan) and Moili (Mohéli) with a few feral individuals on Ngazidja Island (Grande Comoro), which have escaped or been set free there (Tattersall, 1977b; Thorpe, 1989).

POPULATION No estimates of either population numbers or densities appear to have been made. Tattersall (*in litt.*) considers that this may be the rarest of the species in the genus *Lemur*. Sussman *et al* (1985) report that the numbers of the Mongoose Lemur are declining due to habitat destruction.

HABITAT AND ECOLOGY The Mongoose Lemur is found in dry deciduous forests in western Madagascar and in more humid forest on the Comoros. It can survive quite well in secondary vegetation (Tattersall, 1976). It has been briefly studied in the dry deciduous forest in Ankarafantsika Reserve, near the forestry station of Ampijoroa (Tattersall and Sussman, 1975; Sussman and Tattersall, 1976). Here, during the months of July and August, the study groups were exclusively nocturnal. They left their sleeping trees around 18.00 hrs and mostly fed or travelled to feeding sites between then and approximately 23.00 hrs; there was a two or three hour rest period between 22.00 and 03.00, followed by more activity until the animals returned to their sleeping sites (in dense foliage or tangled vines at the top of tall trees) around dawn (Tattersall and Sussman, 1975). Albignac (1981) found them to be predominantly crepuscular, while Petter (1962) and Harrington (1975, 1978) report diurnal activity. Harrington (1978) suggests a shift from diurnal to nocturnal activity at Ampijoroa sometime around June, which coincides with the transition from the rainy to the dry season. This change in activity patterns is confirmed by Andriatsarafara (1988). Tattersall (1976, 1977a) found that the activity patterns of the Mongoose Lemurs on Mohili and in the coastal lowlands of Anjouan were similar to those observed in the north-west of Madagascar. However, the lemurs in the central highlands were active during the day rather than at night and Tattersall (1976, 1977a) suggested that activity pattern is influenced by climatic factors.

The range of one *L. mongoz* study group was recorded as 1.15 ha but Tattersall and Sussman (1975) considered that this was probably a seasonally limited range. Distance travelled during a night ranged from 460 to 750 m and the groups used mostly the upper strata of the forest, 10-15 m above the ground (Tattersall and Sussman,1975).

In Ankarafantsika, five groups of *L. mongoz* were observed and they all contained an adult male and female and their immature offspring (Tattersall and Sussman, 1975). The groups were very cohesive during resting and travel, the adults usually sleeping in contact with each other with the offspring only 2 or 3 m away (Tattersall and Sussman, 1975). Extensive overlap was observed between group ranges, but intergroup encounters were rare and caused great agitation, vocalisations and frenetic marking by both sexes (Tattersall and Sussman, 1975). In contrast, Harrington (1978) frequently recorded *L. mongoz* groups feeding and travelling within 20 m of *L. fulvus* groups and members of the two species would even intermingle with no signs of alarm. Indeed, when the Brown Lemurs moved off, the Mongoose Lemurs generally followed and they also appeared to respond to the alarm calls of the Brown Lemurs (Harrington, 1978). Albignac (1981) records family groups, usually three or four individuals, occupying home ranges of about 100 ha in the wet lowlands of Ankarafantsika. Petter (1962) saw two groups of *L. mongoz* in Ankarafantsika, one containing six individuals and the other with eight.

Flowers, especially their nectar, were eaten most commonly in Ampijoroa, though fruit, leaves and leaf petioles were also taken (Tattersall and Sussman, 1975). Only five plant species were taken during this short study, the flowers of the kapok (*Ceiba pentandra*) accounted for 64% of feeding time (Tattersall and Sussman, 1975). Fruit was eaten more often in November and December (Andriatsarafara, 1988).

Further work by Tattersall (1976, 1977a) on the island of Ndzouani indicated that the Mongoose Lemur lived in family groups there, the one group of five individuals (two adult sized animals of each sex and a juvenile), that apparently did not fit with this social structure, was thought to be the result of twinning at the birth season before the last. However, in Mohéli, over half the 22 groups counted contained at least two apparently adult individuals of both sexes and there was even one group containing four adult sized males, two adult sized females and a juvenile, and these were not likely to be family units based on pair-bonding (Tattersall, 1976, 1977a).

Infants are probably born in mid-October both on Anjouan and on Madagascar (Tattersall, 1976). Females can give birth every year (E. Simons, *in litt;* Schmidt, 1986). On Anjouan, *L. mongoz* of 14-16 months of age had usually attained adult size and colouration but were not yet sexually mature (Tattersall, 1976).

THREATS *L. mongoz* is found in only one protected area, Ankarafantsika, and this is being encroached by clearance for pastures, by charcoal burners and, to a lesser extent, by clearing for crops (Nicoll and Langrand, 1989). The reserve is not managed and there are not enough staff to protect the area adequately (Nicoll and Langrand, 1989).

On the Comoro Islands, though the lemurs are protected by law this is not enforced (Tattersall, 1977b). The children there commonly catch infant lemurs, often by killing the mother (Tattersall, 1977b). Although local customs protect them from being hunted for food, the influx of Malagasy with a taste for lemurs may mean that they are no longer safe from hunters (Tattersall, 1983). Surveys by Tattersall in 1982 on the island of Ndzouani found that even the cloud forests, which had been relatively untouched eight years earlier, were extensively encroached and that lemurs were drastically less in evidence (Tattersall, 1983). The area of secondary habitat, in which the lemurs survived quite adequately, had also diminished to a great extent (Tattersall, 1983). Human population on Ndzouani had increased from 250 per sq. km in 1974 to 350 per sq. km in 1982, this included several thousand immigrants from Madagascar, many of whom had settled in the areas adjacent to the forest (Tattersall, 1983). In 1988, an expedition from the University of East Anglia reported that the only forest remaining in Ndzouani was on the steep peaks and valleys of the central highlands. Most of this was underplanted with bananas and grazed to varying degrees; primary forest remained in only the very steepest areas (Waters, 1989). The abundance of lemurs on Moili had also declined between 1974 and 1982 and there were considerably more areas cleared of any vegetation that could support lemurs (Tattersall, 1983). In 1982, Tattersall (1983) considered the position of the Mongoose Lemur critical on Ndzouani and becoming precarious on Moili; it is unlikely to have become anything but worse since then. Members of the 1988 UEA expedition considered that the density of lemurs on both islands had been further reduced since 1982 but they have no figures to substantiate this observation (I. Thorpe, pers. comm.). A cyclone struck the island of Moili in January 1983 and this was reported to have had a devastating effect on the vegetation, apparently extensive brush fires followed it (Tattersall, 1983; I. Thorpe, pers. comm.). This will not have improved the lemurs' chances of survival there. There appears to have been a recent increase in the frequency of cyclones hitting the Comoros and these may be more important in reducing lemur habitat than is deforestation by man (I. Thorpe, pers. comm.).

CONSERVATION MEASURES The Mongoose Lemur is found in Ankarafantsika Nature Reserve but this Reserve needs adequate protection and management. The World Bank and the Department of Water and Forests are planning a management programme for Ankarafantsika (Nicoll and Langrand, 1989). Nicoll and Langrand (1989) make the following suggestions for the protection of the Nature Reserve: the guards in the area need at least three motorbikes so that they can patrol the Reserve more effectively; the cutting of firebreaks would protect the forest from burning; reafforestation programmes would provide the local people with fuel and building material so that no more of the forest within the reserve is cut down. In addition, education of the local people about the importance of the Reserve and how the destruction of the forest will adversely affect their lives could help ensure that the area remains intact (Nicoll and Langrand, 1989).

On the Comoro Islands the lemurs are protected by law, it has been illegal to kill lemurs or keep them without a licence since 1974, and exports are restricted to a maximum of 10 females and 20 males each year (Tattersall, 1977b). In addition, destruction of the vegetation within 15 m of a watercourse is illegal (Tattersall, 1977b). Unfortunately, the authorities of the Comoros do not have the resources to enforce the laws. Education of the local people as to the importance of the forests and the interest of the lemurs would help with their protection (Tattersall, 1977b). However, the establishment of adequately guarded and managed forest reserves may be the only way to ensure the survival of the Mongoose Lemur (and *L. fulvus mayottensis*) on the Comoro Islands (Tattersall, 1983).

Surveys are needed to find the actual range of the Mongoose Lemur and estimates of population numbers should be made so that suitable and adequate conservation measures can be proposed.

All species of Lemuridae are listed in Appendix 1 of the 1973 Convention on International Trade in Endangered Species of Wild Fauna and Flora. Trade in them, or their products, is subject to strict regulation and may not be carried out for primarily commercial purposes.

All Lemuroidea are listed in Class A of the African Convention, 1969. They may not, therefore, be hunted, killed, captured or collected without the authorization of the highest competent authority, and then only if required in the national interest or for scientific purposes.

Malagasy law protects all lemurs from being killed or captured without authorisation. It is, however, very difficult to enforce this legislation.

CAPTIVE BREEDING Some of the ISIS (June, 1989) records for *L. mongoz* do not distinguish between the Mongoose Lemur and the Crowned Lemur (which they record as *L. mongoz coronatus*). However, there are at least 53 individuals recorded as *L. mongoz mongoz* and 75% of these are captive born. Duke Primate Center has the largest collection, listed as 19 males, 14 females and two unknown by ISIS and confirmed by Katz (in litt). Wilde *et al*, 1988 report 44 individuals in European Zoos (only eight of these are included in the ISIS figures). There are also four individuals in Paris Zoo (J.-J. Petter, *in litt*.) and two males at Tsimbazaza in Madagascar (M. Pidgeon and G. Rakotoarisoa, *in litt*.) which are not included in either sets of figures above. There are, therefore, around 94 individuals in captivity. Whatever the present numbers, this species has the poorest breeding record in captivity of any of the lemurs in this genus (Schaaf and Stuart, 1983; E. Simons, *in litt*.). Schmidt (1986) reports that between 1976 and 1981 only 2-9% of all captive *L. mongoz* females gave birth and only 0-2% of them had surviving young; hardly any second generation births occurred. Schaaf and Stuart (1983) failed to find any reason for the breeding failure of this species. Duke Primate Center has been most successful at breeding the Mongoose Lemur, three adult females with young were imported in 1982 and these still bear young each year (E. Simons, *in litt*.). Duke Primate Center is cocordinating a breeding programme for the Mongoose Lemur (E. Simons, pers. comm.).

REMARKS The Mongoose Lemurs on the Comoros were almost certainly taken there from Madagascar, Petter *et al* (1977) suggest that the fishermen of Mahajanga (Majunga) introduced them. *Lemur coronatus* was, until quite recently, considered to be a subspecies of *L. mongoz*, but they are now regarded as two separate species (Jenkins, 1987). *L. mongoz* weighs around 2 kg. It is sexually dichromatic. Females are generally grey-brown on their upperparts with bushy white cheeks and beard and a dark face. Males are grey with pale faces and they have bushy, reddish brown cheeks and beard. The underparts of both sexes are white to pale brown. Tattersall and Sussman (1975) have observed a darker faced, pale bearded male variant in Madagascar. For a more detailed description of the Mongoose Lemur see Petter *et al* (1977), Tattersall (1982) and Jenkins (1987). On Madagascar this species is called dredrika or gidro while it is known as komba on the Comoro Islands (Tattersall, 1982).

REFERENCES

Albignac, R. (1981). Lemurine social and territorial organisation in a north-western Malagasy forest (restricted area of Ampijoroa). In: Chiarelli, A.B. and Corruccini, R.S. (Eds), *Primate Behavior and Sociobiology.* Springer Verlag, Berlin. Pp. 25-29.

Andriatsarafara, R, (1988). Note sur les rythmes d'activité et sur le régime alimentaire de *Lemur mongoz* Linnaeus, 1766 à Ampijoroa. In: Rakotovao, L., Barre, V. and Sayer, J. (Eds), *L'Equilibre des Ecosystèmes forestiers à Madagascar: Actes d'un séminaire international.* IUCN Gland, Switzerland and Cambridge, U.K. Pp. 103-106.

Harrington, J.E. (1978). Diurnal behaviour of *Lemur mongoz* at Ampijoroa, Madagascar. *Folia Primatologica* 29: 291-302.

ISIS (1989). *ISIS Species Distribution Report Abstract for Mammals,* 30 June 1989. International Species Information System, 12101 Johnny Cake Ridge Road, Apple Valley, MN, U.S.A. Pp. 17-22.

Jenkins, P.D. (1987). *Catalogue of Primates in the British Museum (Natural History) and elsewhere in the British Isles Part IV: Suborder of the Strepsirrhini, including the Subfossil Madagascan Lemurs and the Family Tarsiidae.* British Museum (Natural History), London.

Petter, J-J., Albignac, R. and Rumpler, Y. (1977). Mammifères lémuriens (Primates prosimiens) *Faune de Madagascar* No. 44. ORSTOM-CNRS, Paris.

Petter, J.-J. (1962). Rechercher sur l'écologie et l'éthologie des lémuriens malagaches. *Mémoires Museum National Histoire Natural,* (Paris) 27: 1-146.

Schaaf, C.D. and Stuart, M.D. (1983). Reproduction of the Mongoose lemur (*Lemur mongoz*) in captivity. *Zoo Biology* 2: 23-38.

Schmidt, C.R. (1986). A review of zoo breeding programmes for primates. *International Zoo Yearbook* 24/25: 107-123.

Sussman, R.W. and Tattersall, I. (1976). Cycles of activity, group composition and diet of *Lemur mongoz mongoz* Linnaeus 1766 in Madagascar. *Folia Primatologica* 26: 270-283.

Sussman, R.W., Richard, A.F. and Ravelojaona, G. (1985). Madagascar: current projects and problems in conservation. *Primate Conservation* 5: 53-59.

Tattersall, I. (1976). Group structure and activity rhythm in *Lemur mongoz* (Primates, Lemuriformes) on Anjouan and Moheli Island, Comoro Archipelago. *Anthropological Papers of the American Museum of Natural History* 53(4): 369-380.

Tattersall, I. (1977a). Behavioural variation in *Lemur mongoz* (=*L. m. mongoz*). In: Chivers, D.J. and Joysey, K.A. (Eds), *Recent Advances in Primatology, Vol 3*. Academic Press, London. Pp.127-132.

Tattersall, I. (1977b). The lemurs of the Comoro Islands. *Oryx* 13(5): 445-448.

Tattersall, I. (1982). *The Primates of Madagascar*. Columbia University Press, New York.

Tattersall, I. (1983). Studies of the Comoro lemurs: A reappraisal. *IUCN/SSC Primate Specialist Group Newsletter* 3: 24-26.

Tattersall, I. and Sussman, R.W. (1975). Observations on the ecology and behavior of the mongoose lemur *Lemur mongoz mongoz* Linnaeus (Primates, Lemuriformes), at Ampijoroa, Madagascar. *Anthropological Papers of the American Museum of Natural History* 52(4): 195-216.

Thorpe, I. (1989). Lemurs. In: Waters, D. (Ed.), *University of East Anglia Comoro Islands Expedition 1988*. Unpublished final report. Pp. 61-62.

Waters, D. (1989). *University of East Anglia Comoro Islands Expedition 1988*. Unpublished final report.

Wilde, J., Schwibbe, M.H. and Arsene, A. (1988). A census for captive primates in Europe. *Primate Report* 21: 1-120.

The Red-bellied Lemur, *Lemur rubriventer*, is sparsely distributed throughout the eastern forests in Madagascar. This is a female carrying an infant on her back.
Photo by Olivier Langrand/WWF.

RED-BELLIED LEMUR

VULNERABLE

Lemur rubriventer I. Geoffroy, 1850

Order PRIMATES

Family LEMURIDAE

SUMMARY The Red-bellied Lemur is found, apparently sparsely distributed, throughout the eastern rain forests of Madagascar. Population numbers are unknown but this species may be the rarest of those in the genus *Lemur*. It is probably being reduced in number by the destruction of the forests throughout its range. Little is known about the ecology and social organisation of *Lemur rubriventer*, but it is currently being studied near Ranomafana in the south-east. It lives in small groups, is mostly diurnal, though some nocturnal activity has been reported, and it feeds on fruit, flowers and leaves. It has been reported in four protected areas. There are around 17 individuals in captivity, about one third of these have been born there. Listed in Appendix 1 of CITES, Class A of the African Convention and protected by Malagasy law.

DISTRIBUTION Found throughout the eastern rain forest (Petter and Petter, 1971) from Tsaratanana Massif in the north to Ivohibé, at the southern end of the Andringitra Massif (Tattersall, 1982). It is apparently confined to forests at medium and high altitudes (Petter *et al*, 1977; Tattersall, 1982). Petter and Petter-Rousseaux (1979) show the range of this species extending as far as Mananara River, somewhat further south than shown in Tattersall (1982).

POPULATION Said to be the rarest of the true lemur species (Jolly *et al*, 1984), but there are no estimates of numbers. *L. rubriventer* is reported to live at very low densities (Jolly *et al*, 1984) and Tattersall (1982) considers that they are only sparsely distributed throughout their range. The one estimate of population density, in the region around Ranomafana, was of 30 individuals per sq. km (Overdorff, 1988). Population numbers are considered to be declining due to habitat destruction (Richard and Sussman, 1975, 1987).

HABITAT AND ECOLOGY There have been three studies of this species in the rain forest near Ranomafana, in south-eastern Madgascar. One was for six months from January to June 1986 (Dague and Petter, 1988), another and was in June and July 1986 (Overdorff, 1988) and the third was from July 1986 to January 1987 (Meier, 1987). Four of seven groups censused in the south-eastern forests (at Ranomafana and Kianjavato) consisted of an adult pair of lemurs and one of these also contained a juvenile female; of the remainder, one group contained only two males and one contained three males, while the seventh was composed of an adult female and three adult sized males (Overdorff, 1988). In the longer study, groups composed of an adult pair with a juvenile were seen most commonly (32.8% n=64 observations), adult pairs were seen ten times, single males or females were observed on 11 occasions and a variety of other groups containing anything from one to three males and one to five females, with one or two young were also seen (Dague and Petter, 1988). The largest group was composed of three males, five females and one young (Dague and Petter, 1988). Meier (1987) records that *L. rubriventer* lives mostly in family groups of one female, one or two males and a subadult and/or juvenile animal. He also found groups containing two females and up to three males. Petter and Petter (1971) report group sizes of from five to ten individuals, while Pollock (1979) observed the Red-bellied Lemur in groups of two to four individuals. The relationships between the individuals in the groups are not clear.

The home range of Overdorff's (1988) study group, containing an adult pair and juvenile female, was 12-15 ha and their daily path length varied from 300 to 700m. The group travelled and fed as a unit, travelling within 5m of each other for 62% of the observation time and resting in contact 67% of the time; group progressions were mostly initiated and led by the adult female (Overdorff, 1988). Meier (1987) records one study group using a home range of 9 ha and the other using 75 ha. Dague and Petter (1988) found little evidence of territoriality in this species, when two groups met no aggresive or even avoidance behaviour was noticed.

Activity patterns were very variable between the two months of Overdorff's study. In June the group was diurnal, whereas in July it continued feeding (on *Eucalyptus* flowers) into the night until as late as 23.30, i.e. five or six hours after sunset (Overdorff, 1988). In June only fruit was eaten, mostly the introduced Chinese guava, *Psidium cattleyanum*, while in July the lemurs spent 81% of their feeding time eating the flowers of three different species, particularly those from *Eucalyptus* sp; the remaining feeding time was about equally divided between eating fruit and leaves (Overdorff, 1988). Dague and Petter (1988) also found that the diet of the Red-bellied Lemur varied with the time of the year. They were never seen to eat insects, but did take flowers, leaves and fruit, particularly the latter, from around 30 different plant species (Dague and Petter, 1988). Meier (1987) confirms that fruit is taken most often; 68 different plant species were used during his study. All forest strata, including the ground, were used when *L. rubriventer* was feeding but the outer canopy was used most frequently (Meier, 1987).

Offspring were around 4 months old in January (Dague and Petter, 1988), which means that they were born in September or October. Meier (1987) reports a birth in mid-October. They were no longer being carried on their mother's front at that age, but they did still climb on her back for short periods (Dague and Petter, 1988). It was reported to these authors that young infants were frequently carried by the male in a group, rather than by the female, and that the older infants rested with the male more often than with their mother. Singletons are probably born most frequently, but one set of twins has been born in captivity (E. Simons, *in litt.*).

THREATS The major threat to this species must be the destruction of the eastern rain forests. This is caused mainly by shifting agriculture and also by logging. FAO/UNEP (1981) gave a figure of 40,000 ha of previously undisturbed closed forest cleared per year for the years 1976-80, and projected 35,000 ha for the years 1981-85; the great majority of this is expected to be in the eastern forests (IUCN/UNEP/WWF, 1987).

CONSERVATION MEASURES The Red-bellied Lemur is found in Betampona (though it is reported to be very rare there), Tsaratanana and Marojejy Nature Reserves and in Analamazaotra Special Reserve (Andriamampianina and Peyrieras, 1972; Nicoll and Langrand, 1989; Pollock, 1984; Safford *et al*, 1989). It is also present in the area near Ranomafana, which has been proposed as a National Park (Nicoll and Langrand, 1989; Wright, 1988) A longer term study of this species is presently being undertaken by D. Overdorff, Duke University.

All the reserves in the east in which this species occurs would benefit from better protection, for this they require more guards with sufficient equipment (Nicoll and Langrand, 1989). Alternatives to using the forest for agricultural land and for fuel and building materials have to be developed if the forest is to survive and it is also important that conservation education programmes are set up to help the local people understand how important the reserves and the forest are.

All species of Lemuridae are listed in Appendix 1 of the 1973 Convention on International Trade in Endangered Species of Wild Fauna and Flora. Trade in them, or their products, is subject to strict regulation and may not be carried out for primarily commercial purposes.

All Lemuroidea are listed in Class A of the African Convention, 1969. They may not, therefore, be hunted, killed, captured or collected without the authorization of the highest

competent authority, and then only if required in the national interest or for scientific purposes.

Malagasy law protects all lemurs from unauthorised capture and from hunting, but this is difficult to enforce.

CAPTIVE BREEDING ISIS (June, 1989) lists a total of 13 Red-bellied Lemurs in captivity, seven males and six females. However, they place eight at Duke Primate Center and one at Columbus and give no location for the other four. Approximately two thirds of these are said to be captive born (ISIS, June, 1989).

Duke Primate Center reports that it has has seven individuals in captivity of which four are wild caught and three (including one pair of twins) are captive bred (E. Simons, *in litt.*). There are three individuals at Mulhouse Zoo, one of which was born in captivity, and three wild caught individuals and one captive born animal at Strasbourg Université Louis Pasteur Médecine (J.-M. Lernould, *in litt.*). In May 1989, there were three adults and one captive born infant at Tsimbazaza Zoo (M. Pidgeon and G. Rakotoarisoa, *in litt.*). This information, from sources other than ISIS, indicates that there are 17 individuals in captivity of which five are captive born.

REMARKS *L. rubriventer* is a medium sized lemur weighing about 2 kg (P. Daniels pers. comm.). Its fur is relatively long and dense, upperparts are chestnut brown, its tail is black (Tattersall, 1982). The underparts of males are dark reddish-brown while those of the females are whitish (Tattersall, 1982). For a more detailed description see Tattersall (1982), Jenkins (1987) or Petter *et al* (1977). The Malagasy names of this species are bari maso, tongona and soamiera (Paulian, 1981; Tattersall, 1982).

REFERENCES

Andriamampianina, J. and Peyrieras, A. (1972). Les réserves naturelles intégrales de Madagascar. In: *Comptes rendus de la Conférence Internationale sur la Conservation de la Nature et de ses resources à Madagascar, Tananarive, Madagascar 7-11 Octobre 1970.* IUCN, Gland, Switzerland and Cambridge, U.K.

Dague, C. and Petter, J.-J. (1988). Observations sur le *Lemur rubriventer* dans son milieu naturel. In: Rakotovao, L., Barre, V. and Sayer, J. (Eds), *L'Equilibre des Ecosystèmes forestiers à Madagascar: Actes d'un séminaire international.* IUCN, Gland, Switzerland and Cambridge, U.K. Pp. 78-89.

FAO/UNEP (1981). *Tropical Forest resources Assessment Project. Forest Resources of Tropical Africa. Part II Country Briefs.* FAO, Rome.

ISIS (1989). *ISIS Species Distribution Report Abstract for Mammals,* 30 June 1989. International Species Information System, 12101 Johnny Cake Ridge Road, Apple Valley, MN, U.S.A.

IUCN/UNEP/WWF (1987). *Madagascar, an Environmental Profile.* Edited by M.D. Jenkins. IUCN, Gland, Switzerland and Cambridge, U.K.

Jolly, A., Albignac, R. and Petter, J.-J. (1984). The lemurs. In: Jolly, A., Oberlé, P. and Albignac, R. (Eds), *Key Environments, Madagascar.* Pergamon Press, Oxford. Pp. 183-203.

Meier, B. (1987). Preliminary report of a field study on *Lemur rubriventer* and *Hapalemur simus* (nov. subspecies) in Ranomafana-Ifanadiana 312 Faritany Fianarantsoa, Madagascar, July 1986 - January 1987. Unpublished report sent to Mme Rakotovao.

Nicoll, M.E. and Langrand, O. (1989). *Revue Générale du Système d'Aires Protégées et de la Conservation à Madagascar.* Unpublished report to WWF.

Overdorff, D. (1988). Preliminary report on the activity cycle and diet of the red-bellied lemur (*Lemur rubriventer*) in Madagascar. *American Journal of Primatology* 16: 143-153.

Paulian, R.R. (1981). Les mammifères: vestiges d'un monde disparu. In: Oberlé, P. (Ed.), *Madagascar, un sanctuaire de la nature.* Le Chevalier, Paris. Pp. 75-94.

Petter, A. and Petter, J.-J. (1971). Part 3.1 Infraorder Lemuriformes. In: Meester, J. and Setzer, H.W. (Eds), *The Mammals of Africa: An Identification Manual.* Smithsonian Institution Press, City of Washington. Pp. 1-10.

Petter, J-J., Albignac, R. and Rumpler, Y. (1977). Mammifères lémuriens (Primates prosimiens). *Faune de Madagascar* No. 44. ORSTOM-CNRS, Paris.

Petter, J.-J. and Petter-Rousseaux, A. (1979). Classification of the Prosimians. In: Doyle, G.A. and Martin, R.D. (Eds), *The Study of Prosimian Behavior.* Academic Press, London. Pp. 1-44.

Pollock, J. I. (1979). Spatial distribution and ranging behavior in lemurs. In: Doyle, G.A. and Martin, R.D. (Eds), *The Study of Prosimian Behavior.* Academic Press, New York. Pp. 359-409.

Pollock, J.I. (1984). *Preliminary report on a mission to Madagascar by Dr J.I. Pollock in August and September 1984.* Unpublished report.

Richard, A.F. and Sussman, R.W. (1975). Future of the Malagasy lemurs; conservation or extinction? In: Tattersall, I. and Sussman, R.W. (Eds), *Lemur Biology.* Plenum Press, New York. Pp. 335-350.

Richard, A.F. and Sussman, R.W. (1987). Framework for Primate Conservation in Madagascar. In: Marsh, C.W. and Mittermeier, R.A. (Eds), *Primate Conservation in the Tropical Forest.* Alan R. Liss, New York. Pp. 329-341.

Safford, R.J., Durbin, J.C. and Duckworth, J.W. (1989). *Cambridge Madagascar Rainforest Expedition 1988 to R.N.I. No. 12 - Marojejy.* Unpublished preliminary report.

Tattersall, I. (1982). *The Primates of Madagascar.* Columbia University Press, New York.

Wright P. (1988). IUCN Tropical Forest Programme. Critical Sites Inventory. Report held at the World Conservation Monitoring Centre.

The Red-fronted Lemur, *Lemur fulvus rufus*, from the south-east of Madagascar. This is one of the more widely distributed of the subspecies.
Photo by Mark Pidgeon.

BROWN LEMUR

Lemur fulvus   E. Geoffroy, 1796

Order PRIMATES   Family LEMURIDAE

SUMMARY The Brown Lemur is the most widespread of the diurnal lemurs. There are six subspecies distributed throughout all the forested areas of Madagascar except the south and a seventh is present on Mayotte Island in the Comoros. An estimate of population number exists for only one subspecies; 25,000 or less of the Mayotte Lemurs remain. All subspecies are declining due, principally, to forest destruction. However, *Lemur fulvus* does survive in secondary vegetation and is a very adaptable species. *L. f. albocollaris*, *L. f. collaris*, *L.f. sanfordi* and, possibly *L. f. mayottensis* (if it is distinct from *L. f. fulvus*) are considered to be definitely threatened at present. The species has been the subject of a number of studies. It is found in groups of very variable size and composition, up to thirty animals have been seen together. Its diet consists of fruit, leaves and flowers. It breeds well in captivity and all subspecies except *L. f. albocollaris* are well represented there. *L. f. mayottensis* is the only subspecies not present in at least one protected area. Listed in Appendix 1 of CITES, in Class A of the African Convention and is protected by the laws of Madagascar.

DISTRIBUTION *L. fulvus* is widespread over Madagascar, it is present in most of the forested areas, except in the south between Taolanaro (Fort Dauphin) and the Fiherenana River (Tattersall, 1982). One subspecies, *L. f. mayottensis,* is present on Mayotte Island in the Comoros. The exact distribution of the other six subspecies is not known, maps in Tattersall (1982), Petter *et al* (1977) and Petter and Petter-Rousseaux (1979) all differ. Each subspecies is considered separately below.

POPULATION No figures are known but this is probably the most common of the diurnal lemurs. However, they are almost certainly declining in numbers as their forest habitat is destroyed (Sussman *et al,* 1985). Any estimates for population densities are given below for each subspecies.

HABITAT AND ECOLOGY The Brown Lemur is a group-living, medium-sized species. It is mostly diurnal, although can also be active at night. Its diet consists of fruit, flowers, leaves and sap. Details of ecology and social organisation will be given in the sections on each subspecies.

THREATS As for all the lemurs, habitat destruction is the main threat to the survival of the Brown Lemur. However, considering the species as a whole, it is comparatively safe from extinction at present. It is a very adaptable species, tolerant of man's activities (it will raid his crops) and it may live in quite disturbed forests (M. Pidgeon, *in litt.*). The status of and threats to the individual subspecies are considered below.

CONSERVATION MEASURES See details for the different subspecies.

All species of Lemuridae are listed in Appendix 1 of the 1973 Convention on International Trade in Endangered Species of Wild Fauna and Flora. Trade in them, or their products, is subject to strict regulation and may not be carried out for primarily commercial purposes.

All Lemuroidea are listed in Class A of the African Convention, 1969. They may not, therefore, be hunted, killed, captured or collected without the authorization of the highest competent authority, and then only if required in the national interest or for scientific purposes.

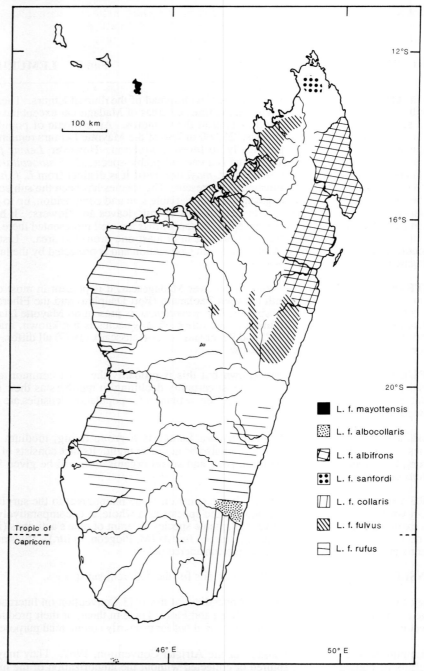

Figure 11: Distribution of all subspecies of *Lemur fulvus*. Shaded areas represent approximate limits of ranges.

Malagasy law protects all lemurs from unauthorised capture and from hunting but this is difficult or impossible to enforce at present. It is unclear what the laws are on Mayotte Island as it now has the status of a "Territorial Collectively" of France.

CAPTIVE BREEDING The Brown Lemur is the third most common lemur species in captivity, after *Lemur catta* and *Varecia variegata*. ISIS (June, 1989) lists 388 individuals in 42 institutes (they call them all subspecies of *L. macaco*). At least 80% of the individuals in each subspecies have been born in captivity (ISIS, June, 1989). According to the ISIS sheets, *L. f. albifrons* is the most common subspecies, followed by *L. f. fulvus*, *L. f. mayottensis*, *L. f. rufus*, *L. f. collaris* and, lastly, *L. f. sanfordi*; the latter two being kept only by Duke Primate Center (ISIS, June, 1989). ISIS does not record any *L. f. albocollaris* in captivity. However, Wilde *et al* (1988) list one pair at Strasbourg University, these were acquired in 1981 and bred in 1988 (J.-M. Lernould, *in litt.*). Wilde *et al* (1988) list an additional 316 individuals in European institutes that are not included in the ISIS figures, *L. f. mayottensis* make up over half of that number. The Brown Lemur is commonly kept as a pet in Madagascar and some subspecies are found and have bred in Parc Tsimbazaza and in Ivoloina, near Toamasina (A. Katz, M. Pidgeon, G. Rakotoarisoa and O. Langrand, *in litt.*).

REMARKS This species is frequently placed in synonymy with *Lemur macaco*. However, discrete populations of the Black and Brown Lemur are now known to occur together (Tattersall, 1976) and specific status is evidently warranted for each (Tattersall, 1982). Chromosomal studies support this distinction (Rumpler, 1975; Petter *et al*, 1977). *L. fulvus* is a medium-sized lemur, weighing 2-4 kg; all subspecies are sexually dichromatic. See below for brief descriptions of each subspecies and see Tattersall (1982) Jenkins (1987) and Petter *et al* (1977) for more detailed information.

White-fronted lemur   **Rare**

Lemur fulvus albifrons   E. Geoffroy, 1796

DISTRIBUTION *L. f. albifrons* is found in the eastern rain forests, but its precise limits are not known (Tattersall, 1982). Its northern limit is probably the Fanambana River (Tattersall, 1977, 1982), though Petter *et al* (1977) and Petter and Petter-Rousseaux (1979) show it extending only as far north as Sambava. Its southern limit may be around the latitude of Toamasina (Tattersall 1977, 1982; Petter *et al*, 1977) or could be the Maningory River (Petter and Petter-Rousseaux, 1979).

POPULATION Numbers have not been estimated, nor are there any figures for population densities of this subspecies. It is probably declining as the eastern forest is cleared.

HABITAT AND ECOLOGY The White-fronted Lemur occurs in the eastern rain forests. It has not been studied in the wild. They have been seen in groups of between three and six animals moving high in the canopy in Zahamena Nature Reserve (Raxworthy, 1986). In captivity, these animals showed early morning and late afternoon peaks of activity and they were active during the night (Conley, 1975).

THREATS No threats specific to *L. f. albifrons* have been identified, but more of the eastern rain forest is being destroyed every year, principally by slash and burn agriculture.

A male White-fronted lemur, *Lemur fulvus albifrons*, on Nosy Mangabe.
Photo by Caroline Harcourt.

CONSERVATION MEASURES The White-fronted Lemur occurs commonly in Zahamena Nature Reserve and is present in Marojejy and Betampona Nature Reserves (Pollock, 1984; Raxworthy, 1986; Nicoll and Langrand, 1989). Only seven groups were seen in 50 hours of searching along 100 kms of paths in Betampona (Pollock, 1984). *L. f. albifrons* was introduced to Nosy Mangabe (now a Special Reserve) in the 1930s and appears to be thriving there (J.-J. Petter, pers. comm. to Constable *et al*, 1985).

There are two more areas proposed as reserves within the range of *L. f. albifrons*: Mananara has been suggested as a Biosphere Reserve and part of the Masoala Peninsula has been proposed as a National Park. The Department of Water and Forests, MINESUP (Ministry of Higher Education), MRSTD (Ministry of Scientific Research and Technical Development) and the Missouri Botanical Garden are in the process of forming a management and development plan for the Masoala Peninsula.

There are no conservation measures suggested specifically for this subspecies though a survey to determine its distribution and numbers would be useful (St Catherine's Workshop).

CAPTIVE BREEDING ISIS (June, 1989) lists 96 animals of this subspecies in captivity. Of these, 94% are reported to be captive bred. There are also 50 individuals in European institutes that are not in the ISIS lists (Wilde *et al*, 1988). Ivoloina, near Toamasina in Madagascar holds 14 *L. f. albifrons* (A. Katz, *in litt.*). Twins have recently been born at Parc Tsimbazaza, where there are also three adult animals (M. Pidgeon, G. Rakotoarisoa, *in litt.*).

REMARKS Body weight of *L. f. albifrons* ranges from approximately 1.9 kg to 2.6 kg (Tattersall, 1982). Males of this subspecies appear to show two distinct colour phases. Most are darkish grey or grey-brown dorsally, with a black face but luxuriant white or cream forehead, crown, ears cheeks and throat. The tail is dark, the underparts pale. Some males, however, lack the white colour of the head, instead the hair here is shorter and either black or dark grey (Tattersall, 1982). In the females, the upper parts are usually grey-brown, but may be grey; some females have dark grey heads, while in others it is pale grey. Though there is substantial variation in the pelage of the females they too, essentially, fall into two groups. One resembles the *fulvus* females, while the other is closer to the *sanfordi* females (Tattersall, 1982). Malagasy names are varika and alokasy (Tattersall, 1982).

White-collared Lemur   Vulnerable

Lemur fulvus albocollaris   Rumpler, 1975

DISTRIBUTION The White-collared Lemur has a limited distribution between the Mananara and Faraony Rivers in the eastern rain forest (Tattersall, 1982). The exact extent of its range is not known, both Petter *et al* (1977) and Petter and Petter-Rousseaux (1979) show a more westerly (and more extensive) distribution than does Tattersall.

POPULATION There are no estimates of population numbers or density. Its numbers are probably declining as the eastern forests diminish in area.

HABITAT AND ECOLOGY This subspecies occurs in the rain forest. There have been no studies of it.

The White-collared Lemur, *Lemur fulvus albocollaris*, is one of the most threatened of the *fulvus* subspecies as it has only a very limited distribution.
Photo by Russell Mittermeier.

THREATS The range of *L. f. albocollaris* is small and it, like the other lemurs, is threatened by habitat destruction. It is probably a comparatively rare subspecies of the Brown Lemur and may be endangered (St Catherine's Workshop, 1986). It is hunted in Manombo Reserve (Nicoll and Langrand, 1989).

CONSERVATION MEASURES The only protected area in which *L. f. albocollaris* is reported to occur is Manombo Special Reserve (Nicoll and Langrand, 1989). Better protection and management of the Reserve is needed. Signs should be put up showing the limits of the protected area, reafforestation programmes are needed as are public awareness programmes to inform the local people about the importance of the forest (Nicoll and Langrand, 1989).

It would be useful to make some surveys in this area to determine the numbers and the distribution of all primates there, including the White-collared Lemur (St Catherines Workshop, 1986).

CAPTIVE BREEDING There is a pair of White-collared Lemurs at Strasbourg, which were imported in 1981, and they gave birth to an infant in 1988 (J.-M. Lernould, *in litt.*). These are the only individuals known to be in captivity.

REMARKS Though the females of this subspecies are indistinguishable from the females of *L. f. collaris*, the males have a white, rather than an orange, beard (Tattersall, 1982). The Malagasy name of this subspecies is varika (Tattersall, 1982).

Collared lemur   **Vulnerable**

Lemur fulvus collaris E. Geoffroy, 1796

DISTRIBUTION The Collared Lemur is found in south-eastern Madagascar, from Taolanaro (Fort Dauphin) northwards to the Mananara River (Tattersall, 1982; Petter *et al*, 1977; Petter and Petter-Rousseaux, 1979). Its exact northern and western limits are not well established (Tattersall, 1982).

POPULATION There are no estimates of population numbers or densities of this subspecies. Numbers are probably declining and it is possible that this subspecies is threatened (St Catherines Workshop).

HABITAT AND ECOLOGY This subspecies occurs in the eastern rain forest, but there have been no studies of its ecology or social organisation.

THREATS As with all the lemurs, habitat destruction is the main threat to the survival of the Collared Lemur. It is reported to be widely hunted and also occassionally trapped to sell as pets in Taolanaro (M. Pidgeon, *in litt.*).

CONSERVATION MEASURES *L. f. collaris* is common in Parcel 1 of Andohahela Special Reserve (O'Connor *et al*, 1986; M. Pidgeon, *in litt.*). There is a management and conservation development programme, proposed and funded by the Department of Water and Forests, the University of Madagascar, WWF and USAID currently underway in this Reserve (Nicoll and Langrand, 1989).

A few Collared Lemurs have been introduced to Berenty Private Reserve (Jolly *et al*, 1982) and it is suggested that these animals are removed (and taken to Duke Primate Center) to

The Collared Lemur, *Lemur fulvus collaris*, has a limited distribution in eastern Madagascar. Photo by Russell Mittermeier.

prevent hybridisation with the introduced *L. f. rufus* there (St Catherine's Workshop, 1986). A survey to determine the distribution and population number of the subspecies would be useful and could be combined with censuses of other lemurs (St Catherine's Workshop, 1986).

CAPTIVE BREEDING ISIS (June, 1989) records only 37 individuals in captivity and all of these are held at Duke Primate Center; 86% are captive born. A captive breeding programme is coordinated by Duke Primate Center and they are attempting to start colonies of this subspecies at other institutions (E. Simons, pers. comm.).

REMARKS Pelage differences between the sexes are comparatively slight. The males tend to have a black neck, face, ears and top of head while these parts are grey in the female. Both sexes have pale orange cheeks and these are bushy in the male. Upperparts are a darkish brown or grey-brown with a darker stripe down the spine, underparts are paler (Tattersall, 1982). Body weight has been recorded as between 2.1 and 2.8 kg. The Malagasy name of *L. f. collaris* is varika (Tattersall, 1982).

Brown Lemur   Rare

Lemur fulvus fulvus   E. Geoffroy, 1796

DISTRIBUTION Tattersall (1982) considers that this subspecies occurs in at least three distinct areas of Madagascar, though Petter *et al* (1977) and Petter and Petter-Rousseaux (1979) show it in only two areas. All these authors agree that *L. f. fulvus* occurs in the north-west, from north and east of the Betsiboka River to around Analava. Tattersall (1976) reports another small population, sympatric with *L. macaco*, further north just south of Beramanja to the east of the Galoka mountains. The other area where the Brown Lemur is found is in the east, southwards from approximately the latitude of Toamasina (according to Petter *et al*,1977 and Tattersall, 1982) or from Maningory River (according to Petter and Petter-Rousseaux, 1979) to at least Andasibé (Tattersall, 1982) or to as far as the Mangoro River (Petter *et el,* 1977; Petter and Petter-Rousseaux, 1979). *L. f. fulvus* has also recently been reported in Manongarivo Special Reserve (Raxworthy and Rakotondraparany, 1988; J. Andrews, pers. comm.) though the former authors only provisionally assigned subspecific status to the animals they saw. In addition, it has been reported in Bora Special Reserve (Nicoll and Langrand, 1989; O. Langrand, *in litt.*), which suggests it may be present, though perhaps scarce, along more of the north-west coast than has been thought previously. Nicoll and Langrand (1989) also report its presence in Ambohitantely Special Reserve, which is in central Madagascar between 18°04'S and 18°14'S latitude and 47°12'E and 47°20'E longitude.

POPULATION There are no estimates of numbers. Ganzhorn (1988) calculated densities of 170 individuals per sq. km in Ankarafantsika from Harrington's (1975) data. Pollock (1979) estimates densities of 40 to 60 individuals per sq. km in Analamazaotra, Vohidrazana and Fierenana forests near Andasibé (Perinet) in eastern Madagascar. The forests within the range of this subspecies are being destroyed so it is likely that numbers are declining (Sussman *et al*, 1985), but *L. f. fulvus* is not considered to be threatened at present (St Catherine's Workshop, 1986).

HABITAT AND ECOLOGY Harrington (1975) studied *L. f. fulvus* between February and July 1969 in Ankarafantsika in north-western Madagascar. The animals were active from sunrise to sunset, but were also frequently moving and feeding in the dark (Harrington, 1975). They were almost completely aboreal, spending less than 2% of their time on the ground. Most movement was quadrupedal on horizontal branches, though they also progressed by clinging and leaping between vertical branches (Harrington, 1975). Leaves, buds, flowers and fruits were eaten (Harrington, 1975).

Harrington's (1975) two study groups both had 12 members; one contained four adult males, three adult females, one subadult of each sex, two juvenile males and one juvenile female; while the other had four adults of each sex, one subadult female, two juvenile females and one juvenile male. It was estimated that the juveniles were born in October of the previous year (Harrington, 1975). There were few agonistic interactions within the groups, even during the mating season in May, and no dominance hierarchies could be discerned (Harrington, 1975). The home range of one group was at least 7 ha (Harrington, 1975). Though the ranges of the two groups overlapped, the members of each tended to avoid the other and their loud vocalisations may have served to maintain a distance between them (Harrington, 1975). In the same forest near Ampijoroa, Albignac (1981) reports groups of at least 12 individuals in a home range of more than 100 ha, possibly as much as 200-300 ha. He reports that they were more numerous and had smaller ranges in the wetter lowlands in the area than they were in his sandy study site.

In the east, there have been some brief observations of *L. f. fulvus*. Pollock (1979) reports group sizes of between three and ten individuals in the forests around Andasibé. In the same area, Ganzhorn (1988) observed Brown Lemurs in groups with a median size of two (range one to six) when they were feeding on leaves, and in larger groups with a median of six individuals (range 2 to 20) when they were feeding on fruits. *L. f. fulvus* frequently slept in eucalyptus and pine plantations near Andasibé, they also ate the flowers of both species. Ganzhorn (1985, 1987) suggests that this ability of the Brown Lemur to use new and unfamiliar food resources may contribute to its wide distribution in Madagascar.

THREATS As for the species as a whole, the main threat to *L. f. fulvus* is forest destruction. The eastern forests are being cleared principally by slash and burn agriculture, while the drier forests in the west are threatened mostly by fires. These are set each year to promote new grass growth for the numerous livestock in the area. Hunting of the Brown Lemur has been observed in Ambohitantely Special Reserve (M. Guis pers. comm. to O. Langrand.)

CONSERVATION MEASURES *L. f. fulvus* is found in Ankarafantsika Nature Reserve and Manongarivo and Bora Special Reserves in the north-west and in Analamazaotra and Ambohitantely Special Reserve in the east and centre of Madagascar (Nicoll and Langrand, 1989; J. Andrews, pers. comm.; Raxworthy and Rakotondraparany, 1988). The Department of Water and Forests with the World Bank have a management programme underway for Ankarafantsika Reserve. This includes more guards with better equipment to patrol the area, a reafforestation programme, the cutting of fire breaks and a conservation/education plan for the local people (Nicoll and Langrand, 1989). Ambohitantely Reserve, which contains one of the few remaining vestiges of the central plateau forest, is the focus for IUCN/WWF Project 1912. Studies of the flora and fauna, carried out by Antananarivo University, concentrate on plants of medicinal, ornamental and, possibly, economic, use and on the effects of fire on the vegetation. The other Reserves all need management programmes to ensure the survival of the lemurs within them.

A status survey would be useful to determine the distribution and numbers of this subspecies and a study should be conducted to determine if the east and west forms are distinct (St. Catherine's Workshop, 1986).

CAPTIVE BREEDING ISIS (June, 1989) lists 91 individuals in captivity of which 87% are captive born. There are a further 63 animals in European institutes that are not included in the ISIS lists (Wilde *et al*, 1988). Insitutes in Madagascar hold seven *L. f. fulvus* and they have bred in Parc Tsimbazaza (A. Katz, M. Pidgeon, G. Rakotoarisoa, *in litt*.).

REMARKS Unlike most subspecies of *L. fulvus,* there is relatively little difference in pelage colour between the sexes in *L. f. fulvus*. Upper parts and tail are greyish-brown, cheeks and beard are white, muzzle and forehead are black, underparts are creamy-tan. The females tend to be lighter in colour than the males. There is considerable variation in pelage colour within populations, but, generally, individuals from the east are darker (Tattersall, 1982). Body weight is between 2.1 and 4.2 kg (Tattersall, 1982). Malagasy names are gidro in the north-east, boromitoko in the Beramanja region and varika or varikosy in the east (Tattersall, 1982).

Mayotte Lemur   **Vulnerable**

Lemur fulvus mayottensis   Schlegel, 1866

DISTRIBUTION As its name suggests, this subspecies is found only on the island of Mayotte in the Comoro Islands (Tattersall, 1982; Petter *et al*, 1977; Petter and Petter-Rousseaux, 1979). It occurs wherever there is forest, but is rare at altitudes of more than 300 m (Tattersall, 1977a, 1977b, 1982).

POPULATION Tattersall (1977c), assuming, conservatively in 1974/75, that at least a quarter of the 375 sq. km of Mayotte Island was covered in forest, estimated a minimum population of 50,000 individuals of *L. f. mayottensis*. This figure is based on the densities of lemurs he found in his study area (10 per ha) and an assumption that densities in all other kinds of forest would not fall below 5 individuals per ha (Tattersall, 1977c). However, a survey in 1982 indicated that the rate of forest clearance was increasing and the lemur population declining (Tattersall, 1983). After a brief survey in 1987, Tattersall (*in litt*) estimated that the population of Mayotte Lemurs may have fallen by 50% or more from the numbers he estimated 12 years yearlier, i.e. there may be 25,000 or less remaining.

HABITAT AND ECOLOGY All the forest on Mayotte is secondary but the lemurs are able to thrive in it as long as there are enough of the large trees which provide for the bulk of their diet (Tattersall, 1977a, 1983). Rather than living in well-defined groups, the lemurs on Mayotte formed temporary associations the membership of which was constantly changing (Tattersall, 1977a). Average size of these associations was nine or 10, though they varied from two to 29 individuals (Tattersall, 1977a). There were no discernible dominance hierarchies in the associations and agonistic interactions were rare (Tattersall, 1977a). Home range size could not be measured because of the absence of stable identifiable groups (Tattersall, 1977a). The distance travelled in a day was measured once a month between February and May, the mean was 800 m (range 450-1150 m).

During the period of Tattersall's study in 1975 (the wet season), *L. f. mayottensis* ate 67.4% fruit, 27.3% leaves and 5% flowers. Although 32 different species of plants were eaten during this time, the fruit of three species alone accounted for over 60% of the feeding time (Tattersall, 1977a). In the dry season the proportion of leaves in the diet incresed to 53.8% while that of fruit decreased to 9.6% (Tattersall, 1979). Feeding occupied an average of 11.7% of each day in the wet season and 14.6 % in the dry season (Tattersall, 1979).

Resting accounted for 52% of the day in the wet season, but this dropped to 40% in the dry season (Tattersall, 1979). The lemurs were active at night as well during the day (Tattersall, 1977a, 1979). Activity was greatest in the early morning and late afternoon and there was a long rest period in the middle of the day, both the peaks and troughs of activity were accentuated in the dry season (Tattersall, 1977a, 1979).

THREATS After a survey in 1982, Tattersall considered that, though the Mayotte Lemur could not be considered threatened, it does face long term erosion of its habitat (Tattersall, 1983). There has been an accelerating decline in the number of lemurs on Mayotte and there is increasing exploitation of their habitat (Tattersall, 1983). Indeed, the forest of Mavingoni in which Tattersall studied this subspecies in 1974-5, and which he revisited in 1977 and 1980, had virtually disappeared when he returned to Mayotte in 1982 (Tattersall, 1983). By 1987, much of the secondary formation that supported lemurs in 1975 had been reduced to brush and eroding grassland (Tattersall, *in litt*). In 1975 there was only one tarred road on the island, by 1987 the island could be crossed in several places on all weather roads and they ring almost its entire periphery; there are no longer any inaccesible or remote areas remaining (Tattersall, *in litt*). The number of vehicles had increased from 30 to over 700 between 1975 and 1987 (Tattersall, in litt). Lemurs are hunted and eaten on Mayotte but, at least up to 1980, not to any great extent (Tattersall, 1983). The lemur population on Mayotte can no longer survive if left to manage for itself (Tattersall, *in litt*). There are no protected areas on the island.

CONSERVATION MEASURES It is reported that there is no political will on Mayotte to protect its forests and fauna, any initiative to do so will have to come from France and it will have to occur rapidly (Tattersall, *in litt*). Protected areas should be set up in the island and surveys are needed to determine which forested areas are most suitable for preservation (Tattersall, 1983, *in litt*).

A genetic study is needed to determine if this subspecies is actually distinct from *L. f. fulvus*. If it is not, then no special conservation measures are considered to be needed (St Catherine's Workshop). Neither E. Simons nor J.-J. Petter are of the opinion that this subspecies is distinct from *L. f. fulvus* (E. Simons, pers. comm.).

CAPTIVE BREEDING ISIS (June, 1989) lists 78 individuals in captivity of which 84% are captive born. Wilde *et al* (1988) report another 189 individuals in European institutes that are not listed by ISIS. The largest collection, of 40 animals, is held by Asson Zoo in France.

REMARKS This form is derived from *L. f. fulvus* and was probably introduced to the Comoros by man, maybe as long as several hundred years ago (Tattersall, 1977a, b and c). Its colouration is very variable but is similar to that of *L. f. fulvus* (Tattersall, 1982). There is some suggestion that the two forms are not distinct (St Catherine's Workshop, 1986; O. Langrand, *in litt.*). Its Comorian name is komba (Tattersall, 1982).

Red-fronted or Rufous Lemur   **Rare**

Lemur fulvus rufus Audebert, 1799

DISTRIBUTION *L. f. rufus* is widely distributed in western Madagascar and also occurs in the east (Tattersall, 1982; Petter *et al*, 1977; Petter and Petter-Rousseaux, 1979). In the west, it is found in the forests south-west of Betsiboka River and extends southwards to the

Fiherenana River, it has been recorded just south of the river in Lambomakandro Forest (Sussman, 1974, 1975, 1977a; Tattersall, 1982). Other authors (Petter *et al*, 1977; Petter and Petter-Rousseaux, 1979) show the Red-fronted Lemur extending only as far as the Mangoky River. In the east, its distribution is little known. It has been collected as far south and west as Ivohibé, and from just south of Manakara on the coast (Tattersall, 1982). Nicoll and Langrand (1989) report that it occurs in Kalambatritra Special Reserve, which is outside the range of this subspecies shown on any distribution maps. Although Petter *et al* (1977) and Petter and Petter-Rousseaux (1979) show the northern boundary of its range as the Mangoro River, Tattersall (1982) states that this limit is very uncertain.

POPULATION   There are no estimates of population numbers.   Population density, estimated from home range size of groups at Antserananomby and Tongobato Forests, has been calculated to be as high as 1061 individuals per sq. km (Sussman, 1974, 1975), a far higher density than has been reported for any of the other lemur species. After a brief study of this subspecies near Ranomafana in the eastern rain forest, Meyers (1988) estimated a population density of 70 individuals per sq. km.

HABITAT AND ECOLOGY   The Red-fronted Lemur has been studied at Antserananomby and Tongobato Forests just north of the Mangoky River (Sussman, 1974, 1975). These are primary deciduous forests, with a closed canopy of *Tamarindus indica* (kily) trees. Group size varied from four to 17 animals, and the groups were composed of between two and five adult males, between two and eight adult females and a small number of juveniles and infants (Sussman, 1974, 1975).   The groups were fairly cohesive, individuals remained in close proximity to each other and the entire group usually travelled together (Sussman, 1975). There was no noticeable dominance hierarchy within the groups (Sussman, 1975).

Both day ranges and home ranges of *L. f. rufus* were very small; the former were, on average, 125-150 m and the latter 0.75-1.0 ha (Sussman, 1974, 1975).   Home ranges of neighbouring groups overlapped extensively and were not rigidly defended (Sussman, 1974). Spatial separation between groups was probably maintained by frequent vocalisations (Sussman, 1975). The animals spent most of their time in the continuous canopy of the forest and were rarely seen on the ground (Sussman, 1974, 1975).

The Red-fronted Lemur eats leaves, fruit, flowers, bark and sap. During Sussman's study (1974, 1975) leaves from the kily tree were the main component of its diet, while pods, stems, flowers, bark and sap were also eaten from this tree species. Only 15 species of plant were eaten throughout Sussman's 13 month study (October 1969 - November 1970). Water was lapped from hollows in trees and licked off leaves (Sussman, 1975). Most feeding occurred early in the morning and late in the afternoon, while resting occupied over 60% of the time between 09.30 and 15.00h (Sussman, 1974, 1975). Some feeding took place after dark, but most activity was diurnal (Sussman, 1975).

As with the other lemurs, reproduction is seasonal. Gestation in the Brown Lemur is 120-135 days (Petter-Rousseaux, 1964). Infants were not born until mid September at Sussman's study sites (1977b). They are initially carried ventrally by their mother and do not begin to move about on her until they are two weeks old and it is a month or more before they transfer to ride regularly on her back (Sussman, 1977b). By the time the infants are 11-12 weeks old they are mostly moving around independently (Sussman, 1977b). By the age of two years the youngsters are adult size, but at Sussman's site they did not breed until they were 2.5 years old. However, M. Pidgeon and S O'Connor (*in litt.*) report breeding by 18 month old individuals at Berenty and that the females breed every year. At Berenty, mating took place in April/May (M. Pidgeon, *in litt.*).

In the eastern rain forest, near Ranomafana, *L. f. rufus* was watched for a total of 80h between June and August 1987 (Meyers, 1988). Here a group of 12 individuals had a home range of 22 ha; there was a 20% overlap in the home ranges of this and another group (Meyers, 1988). Fruit was the principal (94%) component of the Red-fronted Lemurs' diet at this site, some leaves and a few flowers were also eaten (Meyers, 1988). The animals were active at night here (pers. obs.), but no measures of the amount or kind of activity were taken.

At Berenty, the introduced Red-fronted Lemurs were seen in groups of between seven and 14 individuals (O'Connor,1987). Their home ranges were between six and 14 ha, and each overlapped with neighbouring ranges (M. Pidgeon, *in litt.*). The animals were very adaptabale, during periods of food shortage they spent a lot of their time on the ground and ate insects, other invertebrates and fungi as well as their usual diet of fruit, flowers and leaves (M. Pidgeon, *in litt.*).

THREATS The main threat to this subspecies is the destruction of its habitat. The western forests are being destroyed, largely by burning, while the eastern forest are being degraded and reduced in size principally by slash and burn agriculture but also by cutting for timber, fuel and building materials. In addition, Sussman (1975) reports that *L. f. rufus* is hunted by man.

CONSERVATION MEASURES This subspecies is found in the Isalo National Park, in the Nature Reserves of Tsingy Bemaraha and Namoroka and in the Special Reserves of Andranomena, Kalambatritra and Pic d'Ivohibé. It is also in Analabe Private Reserve and was introduced to Berenty Private Reserve in 1974, where the original eight or nine animals imported from Morondava had increased to 62 by 1985 (Jolly *et al,* 1982; M. Pidgeon, *in litt.*). *L. f. rufus* will also be protected near Ranomafana if the proposed National Park there is gazetted.

There are no particular conservation measures recommended except surveys to determine the range and numbers of the subspecies and to determine if the eastern and western populations are actually distinct (St Catherines Workshop, 1986).

CAPTIVE BREEDING ISIS (June, 1989) lists 64 individuals in captivity, of which 93% are captive born. European institutes not included in the ISIS list hold a further 10 animals (Wilde *et al,* 1988). In addition, there are 18 individuals in captivity in Madagascar in Ivoloina and Tsimbazaza and they breed well there (M. Pidgeon, A. Katz, G. Rakotoarisoa, *in litt.*).

REMARKS The sexes are dichromatic, but there is much individual variation. The males have grey upperparts and pale grey to grey-brown underparts. They have a bushy, rusty-orange head cap with a black muzzle, pale grey patches above the eyes and grey ears, bushy cheeks and throat. The upperparts of the females are a light to medium reddish-brown colour, underparts are pale golden brown or grey. The crown of their head is grey with light grey or white above the eye and on the cheeks, ears are reddish-brown (Tattersall, 1982). Pelage of the eastern *L. f. rufus* is much thicker than that of the western individuals (M. Pidgeon, *in litt.*). Body weight is 2.1 to 3.6 kg (Tattersall, 1982). Malagasy names are varika and gidro (Tattersall, 1982).

Sanford's lemur   **Vulnerable**

Lemur fulvus sanfordi **Archbold, 1932**

DISTRIBUTION This subspecies has a very restricted range in the north of Madagascar. Petter *et al* (1977) and Petter and Petter-Rousseaux (1979) both show the distribution of *L. f. sanfordi* extending southwards from Mt d'Ambre in the north to the latitude of Sambava. However, Tattersall (1977b, 1982) considers that its range is much smaller than this, he reports it as being restricted to the northern flanks of Mt d'Ambre extending only as far as the Ankarana Massif, between Anivorano Nord and Ambilobé. It may still be found as far south-east as Vohimarina (Tattersall, *in litt.*), which is where a specimen in the British Museum (Natural History) was collected in 1870 (Jenkins, 1987).

POPULATION Estimates of total population numbers have not been made. This subspecies has been recorded at densities as high as 221 $\pm$ 79 individuals per sq. km (mean and 95% confidence limits) in the canopy forest of the Canyon Grande in Ankarana Special Reserve (Hawkins *et al*, in press). In the humid forest of Montagne d'Ambre it was estimated that, excluding infants, there were 125 individuals per sq. km (Arbelot-Tracqui, 1983). Numbers are almost certainly declining as the forests within the range of this subspecies continue to diminish in area.

HABITAT AND ECOLOGY Sanford's Lemur has been studied briefly in Ankarana Special Reserve where it is reported to favour secondary forest and the forest bordering the savannah around the Massif, though it also frequented the canopy forest (Wilson *et al*, 1988, 1989; Fowler *et al*, 1989). In Mt d'Ambre Forest, activity was most common at above 10m (Arbelot-Tracqui, 1983). Peaks of activity occurred in the morning and evening, with a midday rest period between 10.30 and 13.00 hrs (Arbelot-Tracqui, 1983). The lemurs were active at night as well as during the day (Wilson *et al*, 1989). Fruit was the main component of the diet of this subspecies, but leaves and buds were also taken (Arbelot-Tracqui, 1983).

In Ankarana , *L. f. sanfordi* was seen in groups of up to 15 individuals, though an average group there contained nine animals, of these four were typically adult males and five were adult females (Wilson *et al*, 1989). In Mt d'Ambre, six groups were counted and these contained between six and nine individuals (Arbelot-Tracqui, 1983). Groups were cohesive and always led by a female during travel (Arbelot-Tracqui, 1983; Wilson *et al*, 1989). In Mt d'Ambre, the size of one home range, containing seven or eight individuals, was at least 14.4 ha; ranges of groups overlapped (Arbelot-Tracqui, 1983).

The first newborn Sanford's Lemur noted in Ankarana was seen on September 23rd (Wilson *et al*, 1989). In early November 1981 in the humid forests of Mt d'Ambre, Arbelot-Tracqui recorded that 15 of 16 females had infants riding on their backs that she estimated were approximately three weeks old, i.e. they were born around 24th October. She recorded births at around 12th October in the drier forests of Ankarana (Arbelot-Tracqui, 1983).

THREATS Though Sanford's Lemur appears able to survive in secondary and degraded forests, and may even prefer them, it is still threatened by the destruction of its habitat. It has a very restricted range. Poaching of lemurs in Montagne d'Ambre National Park is reported to be widespread and increasing, *L. f. sanfordi* is shot there (Nicoll and Langrand, 1989). Bush fires threaten the edges of the Park and there is illegal tree-felling within it (Nicoll and Langrand, 1989). Analamera Reserve is unguarded and unmanaged, it is being destroyed by logging, burning and grazing; lemurs are hunted in this area (Hawkins *et al*, in press). Until recently, Ankarana Reserve (where lemurs are not hunted) had remained relatively undisturbed, but the forest there is now being felled (P. Vaucoulon pers. comm. to Wilson, 1988)

CONSERVATION MEASURES Occurs in Analamera and Ankarana Special Reserves (Hawkins *et al,* in press; Wilson *et al,* 1989, Fowler *et al,* 1989) and the Montagne D'Ambre National Park (Nicoll and Langrand, 1989). These three protected areas are included in a management plan set up by the Department of Water and Forests, WWF, the Catholic Relief Service and US-AID (Nicoll and Langrand, 1989). The following are suggested: the area needs more, better-equipped guards to patrol it, an education programme for the local people would make them more aware of the importance of the forest, a development programme for the area is needed, cattle should not be allowed into the Reserves and fire breaks are necessary in some places (Nicoll and Langrand, 1989). The tourist potential of the area could be developed (Fowler *et al,* 1989).

Surveys are needed to determine remaining areas of suitable habitat for the Sanford's Lemurs and their population numbers.

CAPTIVE BREEDING ISIS (June, 1989) lists only 22 animals in captivity, all held at Duke Primate Center. Of these, 81% are captive born. A captive breeding programme is being coordinated by Duke Primate Center (E. Simons, pers. comm.).

REMARKS The sexes in this subspecies are easily distinguished. The upperparts of the males are brownish-grey, underparts are paler grey or cream. The crown of their head and their bushy cheeks are brown, the muzzle is black. The ears are tufted with white hairs and the forehead and areas around and below the eyes are white. Females have grey, sometimes grey-brown, upperparts and paler underparts. Their muzzle is black, but the rest of the head is darkish grey. They do not have tufted ears and the hair on their cheeks is not bushy (Tattersall, 1982). Body weight of one individual was 2.2 kg (Tattersall, 1982). Malagasy name is varika.

REFERENCES

Albignac, R. (1981). Lemurine social and territorial organisation in a north western Malagasy forest (restricted area of Ampijoroa). In: Chiarelli, A.B. and Corruccini, R.S. (Eds), *Primate Behavior and Sociobiology.* Springer-Verlag, Berlin. Pp. 25-29.
Arbelot-Tracqui, V. (1983). *Étude Éthoécologique de Deux Primates Prosimiens: Lemur coronatus Gray et Lemur fulvus sanfordi Archbold, Contribution a l'Étude des Mécanismes d'Isolement Reproductif Intervenant dans la Spéciation.* Unpublished PhD thesis, University of Rennes, France.
Conley, J.M. (1975). Notes on the activity pattern of *Lemur fulvus. Journal of Mammalogy,* 56: 712-715.
Constable, I.D., Mittermeier, R.A., Pollock, J.I., Ratsirarson, J. and Simons, H. (1985). Sightings of aye-ayes and red ruffed lemurs on Nosy Mangabe and the Masoala Peninsula. *Primate Conservation 5*: 59-62.
Fowler, S.V., Chapman, P., Checkley, D., Hurd, S., McHale, M., Ramangason, G.-S., Randriamasy, J.-E., Stewart, P., Walters, R. and Wilson, J.M. (1989). Survey and management proposals for a tropical deciduous forest reserve at Ankarana in northern Madagascar. *Biological Conservation* 47: 297-313.
Ganzhorn, J.U. (1985). Utilization of eucalyptus and pine plantations by brown lemurs in the eastern rainforest of Madagascar. *Primate Conservation* 6: 34-35.
Ganzhorn, J.U. (1987). A possible role of plantations for primate conservation in Madagascar. *American Journal of Primatology* 12: 205-215.
Ganzhorn, J.U. (1988). Food partitioning among Malagasy primates. *Oecologia* 75: 436-450.

Harrington, J.E. (1975). Field observations of social behaviour of *Lemur fulvus fulvus* E. Geoffroy 1812. In: Tattersall, I. and Sussman, R.W. (Eds), *Lemur Biology*. Plenum Press, New York. Pp. 259-279.

Hawkins, A.F.A., Ganzhorn, J.U., Bloxam, Q.M.C., Barlow, S.C., Tonge, S.J., and Chapman, P. (in press). A survey and assessment of the conservation status and needs of lemurs, birds, lizards and snakes in the Ankarana Special Reserve, Antseranana, Madagascar: with notes on the lemurs and birds of the nearby Analamera Special Reserve. *Biological Conservation*

ISIS (1989). *ISIS Species Distribution Report Abstract for Mammals,* 30 June 1989. International Species Information System, 12101 Johnny Cake Ridge Road, Apple Valley, MN, USA. Pp. 17-22.

Jenkins, P.D. (1987). *Catalogue of Primates in the British Museum (Natural History) and elsewhere in the British Isles Part IV: Suborder of the Strepsirrhini, including the Subfossil Madagascan Lemurs and the Family Tarsiidae.* British Museum (Natural History), London.

Jolly, A., Oliver, W.L.R., and O'Connor, S.M. (1982). Population and troop ranges of *Lemur catta* and *Lemur fulvus* at Berenty, Madagascar: 1980 census. *Folia Primatologica* 39: 115-123.

Meyers, D. (1988). Behavioral ecology of *L. f. rufus* in rain forest in Madagascar. *American Journal of Physical Anthropology* 75(2): 250.

Nicoll, M.E. and Langrand, O. (1989). *Revue Générale du Système d'Aires Protégées et de la Conservation à Madagascar.* Unpublished report to WWF.

O'Connor, S.M. (1987). *The Effect of Human Impact on Vegetation and the Consequences to Primates in two Riverine Forests, Southern Madagascar.* Unpublished PhD thesis, University of Cambridge.

O'Connor, S., Pidgeon, M. and Randria, Z. (1986). Conservation program for the Andohahela Reserve, Madagascar. *Primate Conservation* 7: 48-52.

Petter, J-J., Albignac, R. and Rumpler, Y. (1977). Mammifères lémuriens (Primates prosimiens). *Faune de Madagascar* No. 44. ORSTOM-CNRS, Paris.

Petter, J.-J. and Petter-Rousseaux, A. (1979). Classification of the Prosimians. In: Doyle, G.A. and Martin, R.D. (Eds), *The Study of Prosimian Behavior*. Academic Press, London. Pp. 1-44.

Petter-Rousseaux, A. (1964). Reproductive physiology and behaviour of the Lemuriodea. In: Buettner-Janusch, J. (Ed.), *Evolutionary and Genetic Biology of Primates*. Academic Press, London. Pp. 91-132.

Pollock, J.I. (1979). Spatial distribution and ranging behavior in lemurs. In: Doyle, G.A. and Martin, R.D. (Eds), *The Study of Prosimian Behavior*. Academic Press, New York. Pp. 359-409.

Pollock, J.I. (1984). *Preliminary report on a mission to Madagascar by Dr J. I. Pollock in August and September 1984.* Unpublished report.

Raxworthy, C. (1986). The lemurs of Zahamena Reserve. *Primate Conservation* 7: 46-48.

Raxworthy, C.J. and Rakotondraparany, F. (1988). Mammal report. In: Quansah, N. (Ed.), *Manongarivo Special Reserve (Madagascar): 1987/88 Expedition Report*. Madagascar Environmental Research Group, U.K.

Rumpler, Y. (1975). The significance of chromosomal studies in the systematics of the Malagasy lemurs. In: Tattersall, I. and Sussman, R.W. (Eds), *Lemur Biology*. Plenum Press, New York. Pp. 25-40.

St Catherine's Workshop (1986). Unpublished reports to participants of the conference on lemur conservation held on St Catherine's Island, Georgia on 26-27 April 1986.

Sussman, R.W. (1974). Ecological distinctions in sympatric species of lemur. In: Martin, R.D., Doyle, G.A. and Walker, A.C. (Eds), *Prosimian Biology*. Duckworth, London. Pp. 75-108.

Sussman, R.W. (1975). A preliminary study of the behavior and ecology of *Lemur fulvus rufus* Audebert 1800. In: Tattersall, I. and Sussman, R.W. (Eds), *Lemur Biology*. Plenum Press, New York. Pp. 237-258.

Sussman, R. W. (1977a). Distribution of the Malagasy lemurs. Part 2: *Lemur catta* and *Lemur fulvus* in southern and western Madagascar. *Annals New York Academy of Sciences 293*: 170-183.

Sussman, R.W. (1977b). Socialization, social structure and ecology of two sympatric species of lemur. In: Chevalier-Skolnikoff, S. and Poirer, F. (Eds), *Primate Bio-Social Development*. Garland, New York. Pp. 515-528.

Sussman, R.W., Richard, A.F. and Ravelojaona, G. (1985). Madagascar: current projects and problems in conservation. *Primate Conservation 5*: 53-59.

Tattersall, I. (1976). Notes on the status of *Lemur macaco* and *Lemur fulvus* (Primates, Lemuriformes). *Anthropological Papers of the Americam Museum of Natural History* 53(2): 255-261.

Tattersall, I. (1977a). Ecology and behavior of *Lemur fulvus mayottensis* (Primates, Lemuriformes). *Anthropological Papers of the American Museum of Natural History* 54: 423-482.

Tattersall, I. (1977b). Distribution of the Malagasy lemurs Part 1: the lemurs of northern Madagascar. *Annals New York Academy of Sciences* 293: 160-169.

Tattersall, I. (1977c). The lemurs of the Comoro Islands. *Oryx* 13: 445-448.

Tattersall, I. (1979). Patterns of activity in the Mayotte Lemur, *Lemur fulvus mayottensis*. *Journal of Mammalogy*, 60(2): 314-323.

Tattersall, I. (1982). *The Primates of Madagascar*. Columbia University Press, New York.

Tattersall, I. (1983). Studies of the Comoro lemurs: a reappraisal. *Primate Conservation* 3: 24-26.

Tattersall, I. (in litt). The Mayotte Lemur, *Lemur fulvus mayottensis:* cause for alarm. Submitted to *Primate Conservation*.

Wilde, J., Schwibbe, M. H. and Arsene, A. (1988). A census for captive primates in Europe. *Primate Report* 21: 1-120.

Wilson, J. M. (1988). Clear-felling of more lemur forest in Madagascar. *Primate Eye* 36: 21-22.

Wilson, J. M.; Stewart, P. D. and Fowler, S. V. (1988). Ankarana - a rediscovered nature reserve in northern Madagascar. *Oryx* 22: 163-171.

Wilson, J.M., Stewart, P.D., Ramangason, G-S., Denning, A.M., Hutchings, M.S. (1989). Ecology and Conservation of the Crowned Lemur, *Lemur coronatus*, at Ankarana, N. Madagascar: with notes on Sanford's Lemur, other sympatrics and subfossil lemurs. *Folia Primatologica* 52: 1-26.

The Ruffed Lemur, *Varecia variegata*, is common in captivity. Its numbers are declining in Madagascar as the eastern rain forest is destroyed. This is the more common subspecies *Varecia variegata variegata*.
Photo by Russell Mittermeier.

RUFFED LEMUR

Varecia variegata (Kerr, 1792)

Order PRIMATES   Family LEMURIDAE

SUMMARY The Ruffed Lemur is found in the eastern rain forest, but does not appear to be common anywhere. Two subspecies are commonly recognised, *Varecia variegata variegata* and *V. v. rubra,* both are considered Endangered, the latter is restricted to the Masoala Peninsula. Population numbers are unknown and there are no estimates of density. Numbers are certainly declining. A long term study of this species on Nosy Mangabe has recently been completed. It lives in small groups of up to five individuals. It is primarily frugivorous, though some leaves, nectar and seeds are also taken. The species is threatened by forest destruction and by hunting. *V. v. variegata* is found in at least five reserves; *V. v. rubra* does not occur in any protected area and this should be remedied. Surveys of the numbers and distribution of both subspecies are needed. There are over 700 individuals in captivity and they breed very well there. Listed in Appendix 1 of CITES, in Class A of the African Convention and protected by Malagasy law.

DISTRIBUTION *V. variegata* occurs in the eastern rain forest, but the details of its distribution are very poorly known. It is found on the Masoala Peninsula and extends southwards, possibly as far as just north of the Mananara River (Petter *et al*, 1977; Tattersall, 1982). The ranges of the two subspecies are given below.

POPULATION There are no estimates of population numbers or density for either subspecies, but numbers of the species are declining (Richard and Sussman, 1975; 1987; Richard, 1982).

HABITAT AND ECOLOGY See accounts below.

THREATS Both subspecies are threatened by habitat destruction. The forests within their range are being cleared for agriculture. In addition, they are hunted for food and are commonly kept as pets in Madagascar (O. Langrand, *in litt.*). See below for details.

CONSERVATION MEASURES See accounts for the separate subspecies below.

All species of Lemuridae are listed in Appendix 1 of the 1973 Convention on International Trade in Endangered Species of Wild Fauna and Flora. Trade in them, or their products, is subject to strict regulation and may not be carried out for primarily commercial purposes.

All Lemuroidea are listed in Class A of the African Convention, 1969. They may not, therefore, be hunted, killed, captured or collected without the authorization of the highest competent authority, and then only if required in the national interest or for scientific purposes.

All the lemurs in Madagascar are legally protected from hunting or unauthorised capture, but it is impossible to enforce this legislation.

CAPTIVE BREEDING Both subspecies breed well in captivity, a studbook is kept by San Diego Zoo. ISIS (1989) lists them as present (as *Lemur variegatus*) in at least 80 institutions, though most hold ten or less. The total numbers in captivity recorded on the ISIS lists are 593. Wilde *et al* list 40 European Institutes, most of which are not included on the ISIS lists, and these hold at least another 150 individuals. Both reports list many *Varecia* without specifying their subspecific names. Hybrids between *V. v. rubra* and *V. v. variegata* can be found in some zoos; it is strongly recommended that this

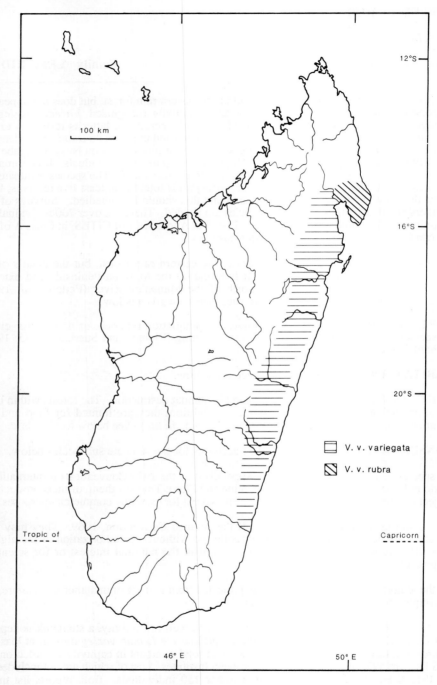

Figure 12: Distribution of both subspecies of *Varecia*. Shaded areas represent approximate limits of ranges.

interbreeding be stopped (SSP Master Plan, 1988; Lindsay, 1977). Details of numbers of each subspecies are shown below.

REMARKS The Ruffed Lemur is the biggest of the species within the family Lemuridae. Body weights of between 3293 and 4512 g have been recorded (Tattersall, 1982). In captivity at least, the females tend to be heavier than the males (Kress *et al*, 1978). This species is still frequently referred to as *Lemur variegatus*. See below for details of the two commonly recognised subspecies and the Remarks section of *V. v. variegata* for notes on the types found within this subspecies. It is possible that these different forms deserve subspecific status.

Black and White Ruffed Lemur   **Endangered**

Varecia variegata variegata (Kerr, 1792)

DISTRIBUTION The distribution of *V. v. variegata,* is poorly known (Tattersall, 1977,1982). It is found in the eastern rain forest, extending southwards from the Antainambalana River (which is the boundary between the two subspecies) as far as Manakara (Petter and Petter, 1971) or to just north of the Mananara River (Petter *et al*, 1977; Tattersall, 1982; Petter and Petter-Rousseaux, 1979). This subspecies is also found on the small island of Nosy Mangabe where it was introduced in the 1930s (J. Petter pers. comm. to Constable *et al*, 1985).

POPULATION Numbers are not known. The Black and White Ruffed Lemur does not appear to occur at high densities anywhere other than on Nosy Mangabe (Pollock, 1984). It is estimated (Simons Morland, in prep) that there may be as many as 100-150 individuals on the 520 ha island (i.e. approximately 20-30 individuals per sq. km). In 1984, Pollock estimated between 56 and 84 animals on the island. Density on the island in 1983 was estimated at 175 animals per sq km (Iwano, 1989), i.e. a total of 910 individuals, which is a much higher estimate than that of Simons Morland or Pollock.

HABITAT AND ECOLOGY A three month (June-August 1988) study of the Black and White Ruffed Lemur has been carried out near Ranomafana in the south-east of Madagascar (White, 1989). The results of a longer term study (1600 observation hours between July 1987 and January 1989) of the subspecies on Nosy Mangabe are currently being written up (Simons Morland, in prep). At Ranomafana, the study group consisted of an adult male and adult female which travelled through a large home range, of 197 ha, as a cohesive pair (White, 1989). A subadult was observed in the area but, though it exchanged calls with the adult pair, it did not associate with them. The pair frequently ranged more than 1 km each day, usually feeding, travelling and resting high (20-25 m) in the canopy. Locomotion was principally quadrupedal, with frequent leaping (White, 1989; Pereira *et al*, 1988). White *et al* (1989) suggest that the larger groups of *Varecia* with smaller home ranges that are found on islands and in isolated forest blocks may be a consequence of the limited space available there for dispersion. The diet of *V. variegata* in both Ranomafana and Nosy Mangabe was mostly fruit, supplemented with small amounts of nectar, seeds and leaves; on Nosy Mangabe, the diet varied seasonally (White, 1989; Simons Morland, in prep). Some earth was also eaten. Chorusing loud calls were used as territorial advertisment and for coordination of movement within the territory (White, 1989). Simons Morland (in prep) reports that it is female *V. v. variegata* which defend the territories. Other reports of group size are of between two and five individuals (Petter *et al*, 1977; Pollock, 1979; Jolly *et al*, 1984). On Nosy Mangabe, there was seasonal variation in activity levels and patterns;

levels were highest during the summer months and some nocturnal activity may have occurred (Simons Morland, in prep.). In general, the Ruffed Lemurs on the island were most active in the early morning and late afternoon/evening (Simons Morland, in prep). Pollock (1979) describes *Varecia* as crepuscular. In captivity, the animals were more active in the morning and evening and there was no sign of nocturnal activity (Klopfer and Dugard, 1976; Kress *et al*, 1978).

Most details of reproduction come from studies in captivity. Gestation period is 90-102 days (Hick, 1976; Bogart *et al*, 1977; Boskoff, 1977). Up to six offspring may be produced in a litter (Anon, 1984), although two or three is the most common number and primiparous females frequently have singletons (Boskoff, 1977; Foerg, 1982). On Nosy Mangabe, most females had twins, these were born in October and November (Simons Morland, in prep). When the infants are born, they do not cling to their mothers' fur, as happens in most other lemur species, but are left in nests (Petter *et al*, 1977; Klopfer and Dugard, 1976; Jolly *et al*, 1984). These may be constructed by the female, but are frequently just bundles of epiphytes (Jolly *et al*, 1984). On Nosy Mangabe, infants were kept in nests constructed by their mother, 15-20 m high in large trees; they were never seen in thick tangles of epiphytes but were parked in trees once they were one to two weeks old (Simons Morland, 1989, in prep). In a forest enclosure at Duke, nests were built by the female *Varecia* on the ground; infants remained in these until they were approximately three weeks old after which their mothers frequently left them parked high up in trees (Pereira *et al*, 1987). When they are carried, it is in their mothers' mouth (Klopfer and Dugard, 1976; Petter *et al*, 1977). The infants begin to follow their mother at three weeks of age and are as fully mobile and active as the adults at seven weeks old (Klopfer and Boskoff, 1979). In the wild, infants were close to adult size at six months of age (Simons Morland, in prep). Females can conceive at 20 months of age (Boskoff, 1977), but, in captivity, average age at first reproduction is 3.4 years (SSP Masterplan, 1988). Simons Morland (in prep.) suggests that the high rate of population increase seen in captive Ruffed Lemurs is not typical of wild populations.

THREATS There is considerable destruction of the eastern forests, these are being cleared principally for growing crops. The lemurs are heavily hunted for food, both trapping and shooting occurs (Nicoll and Langrand, 1989; Constable *et al*, 1985; Lindsay and Simons, 1986). Iwano (1989) implies that there was a considerable decline in the number of *Varecia* present on Nosy Mangabe between 1983 and 1984 because of the poaching of this species on the island.

CONSERVATION MEASURES The Black and White Ruffed Lemur is present in Betampona Nature Reserve, it is reported to be common in Zahamena Nature Reserve (Pollock, 1984; Nicoll and Langrand, 1989; Simons Morland, *in litt.*) and occurs in Andringitra Nature Reserve (Nicoll and Langrand, 1989). Nicoll and Langrand (1989) were informed that it was in Marojejy Nature Reserve but an expedition there in 1988 failed to see or hear them (Stafford *et al*, 1989; W. Duckworth, pers. comm.). The subspecies is also found in the Special Reserve of Nosy Mangabe and seems to be reappearing in Analamazaotra Special Reserve (Nicoll and Langrand, 1989).

A number of new protected areas, in which *Varecia* is present, have been proposed (Nicoll and Langrand, 1989). These are Ranomafana, Mantady (both proposed as National Parks) and Mananara (proposed as a Biosphere Reserve). Surveys to discover the distribution and numbers of existing populations of *V. v. variegata* are essential. Special attention should be paid to determining whether there are several subspecies within the Black and White Ruffed Lemur population, or whether the variation in colour is nothing more than individual variation (see Remarks below). If there are, in fact, distinct forms, the conservation problems for this species will be much greater than currently recognised (St Catherine's Workshop, 1986).

CAPTIVE BREEDING ISIS (1989) lists 243 Black and White Ruffed Lemurs (*Lemur variegatus variegatus* and *L. v. subcinctus*) in 49 institutes; about 95% of these are reported to be captive born. They also report a further 134 individuals of *Lemur variegatus* for which they give no subspecific name (ISIS, 1989). Wilde *et al* (1988) list a further 20 animals in four institutes that are not in the ISIS lists. The Species Survival Masterplan (1988) for the Ruffed Lemur records 265 individuals of this subspecies in North America. Duke Primate Center has the largest collection with 22 individuals held in February 1989 (Katz, *in litt.*). In Madagascar, there are six individuals held at Ivoloina, near Toamasina (Katz, *in litt.*). Two pairs of these were captive bred animals returned to Madagascar by Duke Primate Center in November 1988 (Katz, *in litt.*). The animals were supplied by San Diego and San Antonio Zoo as well as DPC. Brockman (1989) recommends equalization of founder representation and controlled reproduction for the captive population of this subspecies.

REMARKS There is considerable variation in coat colour and pattern within *V. v. variegata,* and it is possible that better knowledge of the distribution of the varieties may ultimately suggest their recognition as subspecies (Petter *et al*, 1977; Tattersall, 1982). Tattersall (1982) recognises four distinct and consistent coat patterns within the Black and White Ruffed Lemur: Type a) Face black except for short white hairs on muzzle below eyes; black forehead and crown; ears, cheeks and throat tufted white; otherwise white except for ventrum, tail, lateral aspect of thighs and shoulders, proximal part of forelimbs and extremities, all of which are black. Type b1) Resembles type a, except that the black shoulder patches extend posteriorly onto the flanks and medially to meet in the midline. Type b2) Pattern as in b1, except that a narrow white stripe runs forward in the dorsal midline, invading the back forequarters but not reaching the neck area. Type c) Entirely black except for white cheeks, ears and throat, a white transverse band extending across the back and sides just below the shoulders and another across the rump extending down the posterior aspect of the thighs onto the lateral surface of the lower leg. White patches also occur laterally on the lower arm. It is this dark type, often referred to as *V. v. subcintcus*, that is found on Nosy Mangabe and in the surrounding mainland forests (Simons Morland, *in litt.*). Adult sized animals weighed on Nosy Mangabe were between 2400 and 3700g; weights were seasonally variable (Simons Morland, in prep.). The Malagasy names of this subspecies are varikandana and varikandra (Tattersall, 1982).

Red-ruffed Lemur   **Endangered**

Varecia variegata rubra **(E. Geoffroy, 1812)**

DISTRIBUTION The Red-ruffed Lemur is restricted to the forests of the Masoala Peninusula (Petter *et al*, 1977; Petter and Petter-Rousseaux, 1979; Tattersall, 1977, 1982). During a survey in 1986, no Red-ruffed Lemurs were seen near the eastern bank of the Antainambalana River and it was suggested that the subspecies may occur at very low densities or that it is now locally extinct in the heavily disturbed parts of its range between the Andranofotsy and Antainambalana Rivers (Simons and Lindsay, 1987).

POPULATION Numbers are unknown but *V. v. rubra* is rare throughout its very small range, and possibly even extinct in the northern part (Tattersall, 1982). Numbers of the species as a whole are declining (Richard and Sussman, 1975; 1987; Richard, 1982) and this subspecies is rarer than *V. v. variegata*. There are no estimates of population density.

The Red-ruffed Lemur, *Varecia variegata rubra*, is restricted to the forests of Masoala Peninsula. It is threatened by hunting and habitat destruction.
Photo by Phillip Coffrey/Jersey Wildlife Preservation Trust.

HABITAT AND ECOLOGY This subspecies is found in rain forest but nothing is known of its ecology and social organisation as it has not been studied in the wild. However, it is probably similar to the Black and White Ruffed Lemur, i.e. living in small groups with a mainly frugivorous diet.

THREATS Parts of the Masoala Peninsula are heavily degraded: forest destruction for agriculture is particularly severe in the major river valleys in the north-east region, in coastal areas of the Peninsula and along the western side of the Bay of Antogil (Simons and Lindsay, 1987). The only Nature Reserve (No 2) on the Peninsula was degazetted in 1964 to permit timbering of the area (Andriamampianina, 1981; Simons and Lindsay, 1987). *V. v. rubra* is hunted on the Peninsula, many lemur traps can be found in the area and animals are shot there (Tattersall, 1977; Constable *et al*, 1985; Simons and Lindsay, 1987; Nicoll and Langrand, 1989).

CONSERVATION MEASURES The Department of Water and Forests in collaboration with MINESUP (Ministry of Higher Education), MRSTD (Ministry of Scientific Research and Technological Development) and the Missouri Botanical Garden are in the process of forming a plan for the conservation and sustainable development of the Masoala Peninsula (Nicoll and Langrand, 1989). They have proposed that a new National Park be set up in the area.

A study is needed of the Red-ruffed Lemur to identify the factors responsible for its limited distribution. Surveys are also needed to estimate present population numbers. It may be possible to reintroduce some of the many captive animals to the wild (Jolly, 1986).

CAPTIVE BREEDING ISIS (1989) lists 216 Red-ruffed Lemurs (as *Lemur variegata rubra*) in 38 different institutes; 96% of these are captive born. A further 20 are listed by Wilde *et al* (1988) in four European institutes not included in the ISIS lists. Within North America alone, the Species Survival Masterplan for Ruffed Lemurs (1988) records 149 individuals of this subspecies in 28 locations. Duke Primate Center has the largest collection, in February 1989 they held 36 individuals (Katz, in litt.). There was some concern over possible inbreeding problems in *V. v. rubra* as, until 1985, all Red-ruffed Lemurs in captivity traced their ancestory to seven wild caught individuals (Ryder *et al*, 1984). However, Mulhouse Zoo imported three animals in 1985 (J.-M. Lernould, *in litt.*) and Duke Primate Center received four more wild caught *V. v. rubra* in December 1987 (E.Simons, *in litt.*). In captivity, average age at first reproduction is 3.17 years (SSP Masterplan, 1988).

REMARKS The colour pattern of this subspecies is much more uniform than that of the Black and White Ruffed Lemur (Tattersall, 1982). Its body fur is mostly deep rusty red. Extremities, forehead, crown, ventrum and tail is black, a patch of white fur occurs on the neck. Malagasy names for this subspecies are varignena and varimena (Tattersall, 1982).

REFERENCES

Anon (1984). Red ruffed lemur *Lemur (Varecia) variegatus ruber*. *Dodo Dispatch* 11: 3-4.

Bogart, M.H., Cooper, R.W. and Benirschke, K. (1977). Reproductive studies of black and ruffed lemurs, *Lemur macaco macaco* and *L. variegatus* ssp. *International Zoo Yearbook* 17: 177-182.

Boskoff, K.J. (1977). Aspects of reproduction in ruffed lemurs (*Lemur variegatus*). *Folia Primatologica* 28: 241-250.

Brockman, D.K. (1989). Management imperatives for *Varecia* in Captivity. *Human Evolution* 4 (2-3): 217-222.

Constable, I.D., Mittermeier, R.A., Pollock, J.I., Ratsirarson, J. and Simons, H. (1985). Sightings of aye-ayes and red ruffed lemurs on Nosy Mangabe and the Masoala Peninsula. *Primate Conservation* 5: 59-62.

Foerg, R. (1982). Reproductive behaviour in *Varecia variegata*. *Folia Primatologica* 38 (1-2): 108-121.

Hick, U. (1976). The first year in the new lemur house at the Cologne Zoo. *International Zoo Yearbook* 16: 141-145.

ISIS (1989). *ISIS Species Distribution Report Abstract for Mammals,* 30 June 1989, pp. 17-22. International Species Information System, 12101 Johnny Cake Ridge Road, Apple Valley, MN, USA.

Iwano, T. (1989). Some observations of two kinds of Lemuridae (*Varecia variegata variegata* and *Lemur fulvus albifrons*) in the reserve of Nosy Mangabe. *Primates* 30(2): 241-248.

Jolly, A, Albignac, R. and Petter, J.-J. (1984). The lemurs. In: Jolly, A., Oberlé, P. and Albignac, R. (Eds), *Key Environments, Madagascar.* Pergamon Press, Oxford. Pp. 183-202.

Jolly, A. (1986). Lemur Survival. In: Benirshke, K. (Ed.), *The Road to Self-Sustaining Populations.* Springer-Verlag, New York. Pp. 71-98.

Klopfer, P.H. and Boskoff, K.J. (1979). Maternal behavior in prosimians. In: Doyle, G.A. and Martin, R.D. (Eds), *The Study of Prosimian Behavior.* Academic Press, London. Pp. 123-156.

Klopfer, P.H. and Dugard, J. (1976). Patterns of maternal care in lemurs: III: *Lemur variegatus. Zeitschrift fur Tierpsychologie* 40: 210-220.

Kress, J.H., Conley, J.M., Eaglen, R.H. and Ibanez, A.E. (1978). The behavior of *Lemur variegatus,* Kerr 1792. *Zietshcrift fur Tierpsychologie* 48: 87-99.

Lindsay, N.B.D. (1977). Notes on the taxonomic status and breeding of the ruffed lemur *Lemur (Varecia) variegatus. Dodo* 14: 65-69

Lindsay, N.B.D. and Simons, H.J. (1986). Notes on *Varecia* in the northern limits of its range. *Dodo* 23: 19-24.

Nicoll, M.E. and Langrand, O. (1989). *Revue Générale du Système d'Aires Protégées et de la Conservation à Madagascar.* Unpublished report to WWF.

Pereira, M.E., Klepper, A. and Simons, E.L. (1987). Tactics of care for young infants by forest-living ruffed lemurs (*Varecia variegata variegata*): Ground nests, parking and biparental care. *American Journal of Primatology* 13: 129-144.

Pereira, M.E., Seeligson, M.L. and Macedonia, J.M. (1988). The behavioral repertoire of the black-and-white ruffed lemur, *Varecia variegata variegata* (Primates: Lemuridae). *Folia Primatologica* 51: 1-32.

Petter, A. and Petter, J.J. (1971). Part 3.1 Infraorder Lemuriformes. In: Meester, J. and Setzer, H.W. (Eds), *The Mammals of Africa: An Identification Manual.* Smithsonian Institution Press, City of Washington. Pp. 1-10.

Petter, J.-J., Albignac, R. and Rumpler, Y. (1977). Mammifères lémuriens (Primates prosimiens) *Faune de Madagascar* No. 44. ORSTOM-CNRS, Paris.

Petter, J.-J. and Petter-Rousseaux, A. (1979). Classification of the Prosimians. In: Doyle, G.A. and Martin, R.D. (Eds), *The Study of Prosimian Behavior.* Academic Press, London. Pp. 1-44.

Pollock, J.I. (1979). Spatial distribution and ranging behavior in lemurs. In: Doyle, G.A. and Martin, R.D. (Eds), *The Study of Prosimian Behavior.* Academic Press, London. Pp. 359-409.

Pollock, J.I. (1984). *Preliminary report on a mission to Madagascar by Dr J. I. Pollock in August and September 1984.* Unpublished report to WWF.

Richard, A. (1982). The world's endangered primate species: a case study on the lemur fauna of Madagascar. In: Mittermeier, R.A. and Plotkin, M.J. (Eds), *Primates and the Tropical Forest.* World Wildlife Fund, U.S. and the L.S.B. Leakey Foundation.

Richard, A.F. and Sussman, R.W. (1975). Future of the Malagasy lemurs; conservation or extinction? In Tattersall, I. and Sussman, R.W. (Eds), *Lemur Biology.* Plenum Press, New York. Pp. 335-350.

Richard, A.F. and Sussman, R.W. (1987). Framework for Primate Conservation in Madagascar. In: Marsh, C.W. and Mittermeier, R.A. (Eds), *Primate Conservation in the Tropical Forest.* Alan R. Liss, Inc., New York. Pp. 329-341.

Ryder, O.A., Koprowski, M., Sexton, S., Gilpin, M.E., Brockman, D. and Benirschke, K. (1984). The status of the red ruffed lemur, *Varecia variegata ruber,* in captivity. Abstract, *American Society of Mammalogists.*

Safford, R.J., Durbin, J.C. and Duckworth, J.W. (1989). *Cambridge Madagascar Rainforest Expedition 1988 to R.N.I. No. 12 - Marojejy.* Unpublished preliminary report.

Simons Morland, H. (1989). Infant survival and parental care in ruffed lemurs (*Varecia variegata*) in the wild. *American Journal of Primatology* 18(2): 157.

Simons Morland, H.J. (in prep). *Social organisation and ecology of Varecia variegata on Nosy Mangabe.* PhD thesis, Yale University.

Simons, H.J. and Lindsay, N.B.D. (1987). Survey work on ruffed lemurs (*Varecia variegata*) and other primates in the northeastern rain forests of Madagascar. *Primate Conservation* 8: 88-91

St Catherine's Workshop (1986). Unpublished reports to paticipants of the conference on lemur conservation held on St Catherine's Island, Georgia on 26-27 April 1986.

Tattersall, I. (1977). Distribution of the Malagasy lemurs Part 1: the lemurs of northern Madagascar. *Annals of the New York Academy of Sciences* 293: 160-169.

Tattersall, I. (1982). *The Primates of Madagascar.* Columbia University Press, New York.

White, F.J. (1989). Diet, ranging behavior and social organisation of the black and white ruffed lemur, *Varecia variegata variegata,* in southeastern Madagascar. *American Journal of Physical Anthropology* 78(2): 323.

White, F., Burton, A., Buchholz, S. and Glander, K. (1989). Social organisation, social cohesion and group size of wild and captive black and white ruffed lemurs. *American Journal of Primatology* 18(2): 170.

Wilde, J., Schwibbe, M.H. and Arsene, A. (1988). A census for captive primates in Europe. *Primate Report* 21: 1-120.

The Grey Gentle Lemur, *Hapalemur griseus griseus*, lives in the eastern rain forests. Its principal diet is bamboo.
Photo by David Haring.

GREY GENTLE LEMUR

Hapalemur griseus (Link, 1795)

Order PRIMATES   Family LEMURIDAE

SUMMARY Three subspecies of the Grey Gentle Lemur are recognised. One of these (*H. g. griseus*) is widely distributed throughout the eastern rain forest, a second (*H. g. occidentalis*) occurs in two isolated populations in the west. Both of these subspecies are associated with bamboo, which is the principal component of their diet. The third subspecies (*H. g. alaotrensis*) occurs in the reed beds and marshes around Lake Alaotra, where the reeds and papyrus replace bamboo in its diet. The latter subspecies is especially threatened by habitat destruction and is classified as Endangered, but none is safe from destruction of the forests. However, it has been suggested that the eastern subspecies may be found at higher densities in areas where bamboo has colonised the cleared forests. There have been some brief studies of *H. g. griseus*. It lives in small groups and may be active during the night as well as during the day. *H. g. alaotrensis* is the only subspecies that is not found in any protected area. About 20 individuals are in captive colonies and most of these are wild caught, they do not appear to breed easily in captivity. Listed in Appendix 1 of CITES, Class A of the African Convention and is protected by Malagasy law.

DISTRIBUTION Three subspecies are now commonly recognised. These are found throughout the eastern rain forest and occur in restricted areas in the north-west and west of Madagascar. The species has a wide altitudinal range, from sea level to 2000m (Pollock, 1986). See below for details.

POPULATION Total numbers are unknown. Density estimates for *H. g. griseus* vary from 47 to 110 individuals per sq. km (see below). Numbers are almost certainly declining as the forests are destroyed (Richard and Sussman, 1975, 1987). *H. g. griseus* is the most numerous of the three subspecies, numbers of *H. g. alaotrensis* must be very low.

HABITAT AND ECOLOGY Bamboo or reeds appear to be vital to this species. Little is known of either *H. g. occidentalis* or *H. g. alaotrensis,* but there have been some short studies of the eastern subspecies. Details of each are given below.

THREATS All three subspecies, but particularly the Alaotran Gentle Lemur, are threatened by habitat destruction. *H. g. alaotrensis* is not found in any protected area. See below for details

CONSERVATION MEASURES *H. g. griseus* is found in many of the protected areas in the east; *H. g. occidentalis* is present in, perhaps, three reserves.

All species of Lemuridae are listed in Appendix 1 of the 1973 Convention on International Trade in Endangered Species of Wild Fauna and Flora. Trade in them, or their products, is subject to strict regulation and may not be carried out for primarily commercial purposes.

All Lemuroidea are listed in Class A of the African Convention, 1969. They may not, therefore, be hunted, killed, captured or collected without the authorization of the highest competent authority, and then only if required in the national interest or for scientific purposes.

In Madagascar, all lemurs are legally protected from unauthorised capture and from being killed. This is, however, very difficult to enforce.

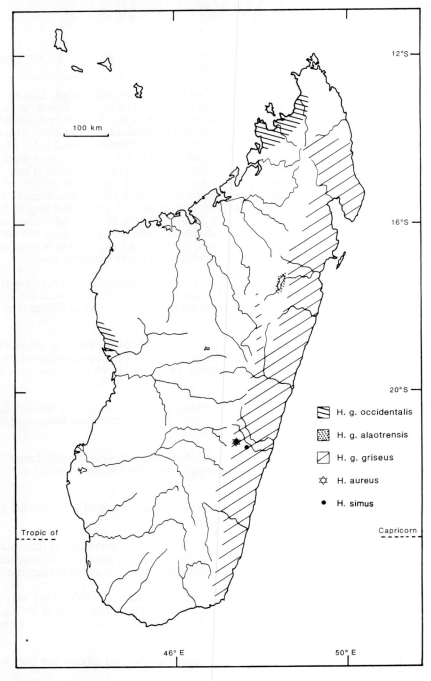

100 km

12°S

16°S

20°S

☒ H. g. occidentalis

▦ H. g. alaotrensis

▨ H. g. griseus

✪ H. aureus

● H. simus

Tropic of

Capricorn

46° E

50° E

Figure 13: Distribution of all species and subspecies of *Hapalemur*. Shaded areas represent approximate limits of ranges.

CAPTIVE BREEDING Only one of the subspecies, *H. g. griseus*, is recorded as being held in captivity by ISIS (June, 1989) and it has bred there, but it is not prolific. ISIS (June, 1989) list 22 individuals (no subspecies) held outside Madagascar and there are ten inside the country in 1989 (see below). There is one wild caught *H. g. alaotrensis* at Duke Primate Center (E. Simons, pers. comm.).

REMARKS Most recent authors consider that there are three subspecies within *H. griseus* (Petter *et al*, 1977; Petter and Petter Rousseaux, 1979; Tattersall, 1982; Jenkins, 1987). Two of these, *H. g. occidentalis* and *H. g. alaotrensis*, were first named by Rumpler in 1975. Pollock (1986) considers that there is no reason to regard the Lake Alaotra form as anything other than an isolated population of *H. g. griseus*. Warter *et al* (1987) describe a fourth subspecies (*H. g. meridionalis*), captured in a forest of bamboo, pandanus and travellers palm 10 km north of Taolanaro (Fort Dauphin). However, the authors themselves state that more information is needed on this form of Gentle Lemur before its subspecific status can be confirmed. It is reported to be slightly larger, to have a darker coat and a different karyotype from other *H. griseus* (Warter *et al*, 1987). Body weight of the species is probably from just under 700g to just over 1 kg. At one time Tattersall (1982) put *Hapalemur* in the family Lepilemuridae and this was followed by Jenkins (1987).

Grey Gentle Lemur   **Insufficiently known**

Hapalemur griseus griseus (Link, 1795)

DISTRIBUTION The nominate subspecies, *Hapalemur griseus griseus*, is the most widespread. It is found throughout the eastern forests from Tsaratanana Massif in the north to Taolanaro (Fort Dauphin) in the south (Tattersall, 1982). Tattersall (1982) reports that it is rare in the north-western part of its range, but Petter and Petter-Rousseaux (1979) show it occurring further north and west than does Tattersall.

POPULATION Population numbers are unknown. Pollock (1979) estimates a density of 47-62 individuals per sq. km in the eastern rain forest around Analamazaotra (Perinet). Richard (1982) gives densities of 1.1-1.2 per ha (i.e. 110-120 individuals per sq. km). Pollock (1986) suggests that the total population size must be substantial, though Tattersall (1982) considers that *H. g. griseus* is rarely found at great density and Richard and Sussman (1975, 1987) consider it to be declining. However, it has been suggested that *H. g. griseus* will not suffer from forest destruction as it apparently occurs at higher densities in areas where bamboo has replaced the original forest (Petter and Peyrieras, 1970, 1975; Jolly *et al*, 1984). Pollock (*in litt.*), however, considers it unlikely that the Grey Gentle Lemur will benefit from the destruction of the forests.

HABITAT AND ECOLOGY *H. g. griseus* is confined to forests characterised by bamboo or bamboo vines (Petter and Peyrieras, 1970; Tattersall, 1982). A two month study of this subspecies at Analamazaotra in "winter" found that 90% of feeding time was spent eating the new shoots, leaf bases and stem pith of the bamboo *Bambusa* (Wright, 1986). The Grey Gentle Lemur browsed continuously on the bamboo, at a rate of 10-12 leaf stems per minute and spent 48% of the day feeding. Other foods included fig leaves, leaf stems of terrestrial grasses, young leaves from trees and small berries (Wright, 1986). It was suggested that fruit eating might increase when more was available (Wright, 1986). The Gentle Lemurs ranged in all habitats that contained bamboo, including stream edges and ridge tops, feeding at all heights from the ground to tree canopies (Wright, 1986).

Group size ranged from between four and six individuals at Analamazaotra, eight groups were counted (Wright, 1986). Petter and Peyrieras (1970) found the most usual group size to be between three and five individuals and Pollock (1986) gives a mean group size of 2.6 individuals with sightings of between one and five individuals together. In Wright's study (1986), each group contained at least one adult pair, one juvenile and an infant (Wright, 1986). Petter and Peyrieras (1970) and Pollock (1986) found that it was not uncommon to have a second adult female in a group. Wright (1986) reported that home range sizes of between 6 and 10 ha; one group had a mean daily path length of 425 m (range 375-495m). At Ranomafana, a group of *H. g. griseus*, composed of an adult pair with two offspring, defended a 15 ha territory (Wright, 1989). Gentle Lemurs were active throughout the day except for an hour or so around midday when they rested, they were not active at night at Analamazaotra (Wright, 1986). Petter and Peyrieras (1970, 1975) found them to continue to be active for a couple of hours after sunset at Maroansetra. They are often considered to be crepuscular (Pollock, 1979; Jolly *et al*, 1984). In the wet season at Analamazaotra, Grey Gentle Lemurs can be active by 04.30 hr (Pollock, *in litt.*). During Wright's (1986) study, they left the emergent trees that they used as sleeping sites between 06.00 and 06.30 hours and returned between 15.45 and 17.25. The group members slept in contact in trees located throughout their home range (Wright, 1986).

In the area around Maroantsetra, the females give birth to single infants (Petter and Peyrieras, 1970), this is also the rule in captivity, (Pollock, 1979). Gestation period is reported to be 140 days and infants at Maroantsetra are born in December and January (Petter and Peyrieras, 1970). Pollock (1986) suggests a birth season from late October to January at Analamazaotra. The infants ride on their mothers back from when they are first born (Petter and Peyrieras, 1970), rather than initially in a ventral position as appears to be more common in most other lemurs. In captivity, both the male and the female carry the infant (Petter and Peyrieras, 1970, 1975).

THREATS The main threat to this subspecies is the destruction of the rain forest. FAO/UNEP (1981) estimated that in each year between 1976 and 1980, 40,000 ha of previously undisturbed forest was cleared and it is likely that most of this was in the eastern forests. It is, however, reported that in areas burned and abandoned long ago, where bamboo had entirely replaced the original forest, the density of *H. g. griseus* appeared to be higher than in undisturbed habitat (Petter and Peyrieras, 1975).

CONSERVATION MEASURES This subspecies is reported in Tsaratanana, Marojejy Zahamena, Betampona and Andohahela Nature Reserves and in Anjanaharibe-Sud, Analalmazaotra and Manombo Special Reserves (Pollock, 1984; Nicoll and Langrand, 1989; O'Connor *et al*, 1986; Safford *et al*, 1989). It is also found in Ranomafana, Masoala and Mananara, all of which have been proposed as protected areas (Nicoll and Langrand, 1989).

No conservation measures have been suggested for this subspecies other than a range wide survey (St Catherine's Workshop, 1986). It would be useful to ascertain if it does reach higher densities in disturbed areas where bamboo has replaced the original forest. Its conservation status cannot be assessed unless some estimates of its numbers are made.

CAPTIVE BREEDING There are around 35 *H. g. griseus* held in captivity. This subspecies has been bred in captivity at Duke Primate Center. However, apparently only certain females breed there, so only one or two infants are born in a year (E. Simons, *in litt.*). ISIS lists 17 individuals in Duke Primate Center in June 1989. Paris Zoo is recorded as having one pair in December 1988 (ISIS) and two pairs in June 1989 (ISIS). None has bred there (J.-J. Petter, *in litt.*). Cologne Zoo has one female (ISIS, June, 1989). Wilde *et al* (1988) report five individuals at Mulhouse Zoo, but these were not listed as being held there by J.-M. Lernould (*in litt.*) in March 1989. In Madagascar, there is a pair of this subspecies at Ivoloina and eight individuals at Parc Tsimbazaza, some of which were born there (A. Katz, M. Pidgeon, G. Rakotoarisoa, *in litt.*).

REMARKS *H. griseus griseus* is overall a brown-grey colour and it weighs around 700-1000g. (Tattersall, 1982). One individual trapped at Ranomafana weighed 770 g, whereas the average weight of five captive *H. griseus* at Duke Primate Center was 936 g (range 941-1226g) (Glander *et al*, in press). Its Malagasy names are bokombolo and kotrika.

Alaotran Gentle Lemur   **Endangered**

Hapalemur griseus alaotrensis **Rumpler, 1975**

DISTRIBUTION *H. g. alaotrensis* is restricted to the reed beds of Lake Alaotra and the surrounding marshes (Petter *et al*, 1977; Petter and Petter-Rousseaux, 1979; Tattersall, 1982).

POPULATION There are no estimates of population number or of density. This subspecies is certainly declining and its numbers are probably very low.

HABITAT AND ECOLOGY There have been only a few observations of this subspecies in the reed beds around Lake Alaotra. Local fishermen reported that *H. g. alaotrensis* are most commonly sighted in small groups of three to four individuals in July, while a few months later, groups of around a dozen animals are seen; during February at the height of the wet season, as many as 30-40 individuals gather together (Petter and Peyrieras, 1970, 1975). There is no bamboo in the region of Lake Alaotra, instead *H. g. alaotrensis* feeds on the leaves and the young shoots of the reed *Phragmites* and on the buds and pith of *Papyrus* (Petter and Peyrieras, 1970, 1975).

This subspecies is reported never to come to the ground, its usual mode of locomotion is vertical clinging and leaping (Petter and Peyrieras, 1975). It is said to be able to swim very well, even females carrying infants on their backs can cross canals over 15m wide (Petter and Peyrieras, 1975). The Alaotran Gentle Lemur is most active in the morning and evening (Petter and Peyrieras, 1975).

Alaotran Gentle Lemurs give birth in January and February (Petter and Peyrieras, 1970). Singletons are born and are carried on their mother's back from the moment of birth (Petter and Peyrieras, 1975).

THREATS The Alaotran Gentle Lemur is particularly threatened by the burning of the reed beds that occurs every year. As well as having their habitat destroyed, the Gentle Lemurs are caught for food as they flee the fires (Petter and Peyrieras, 1970; Jolly *et al*, 1984), though Pollock (1986) says they are not hunted directly. In addition, the lake is being drained for rice irrigation and both the papyrus and the reeds are cut for mats, fish traps, screens, barriers and fencing (Pollock, 1986). This subspecies is not found in any protected area.

CONSERVATION MEASURES A detailed ecological study and census of this subspecies is recommended to determine its status and ecological requirements (St Catherine's Workshop, 1986). It is suggested that translocation to a similar but better protected habitat is a possibility for the Alaotran Gentle Lemur (St Catherine's Workshop, 1986).

It is proposed that part of Lake Alaotra should be made into a reserve for the sake, particularly, of protecting *H. g. alaotrensis* and some of the aquatic birds which are also endemic to the area (Nicoll and Langrand, 1989; Collar *et al*, 1985).

CAPTIVE BREEDING There is one wild caught female of this subspecies in captivity in Duke Primate Center. She gave birth to twins in 1989 but they were sired by an *H. griseus griseus* (E. Simons, pers. comm.). Duke Primate Center is trying to obtain a male of *H. g. alaotrensis* for breeding purposes.

REMARKS Pelage of *H. g. alaotrensis* is grey-brown, similar to that of *H. g. griseus* but somewhat darker (Tattersall, 1982). No body weights are known, but it is said to be appreciably larger than *griseus* so probably weighs 1 kg or more. The Malagasy name of this subspecies is bandro.

Western Gentle Lemur   **Vulnerable**

Hapalemur griseus occidentalis **Rumpler, 1975.**

DISTRIBUTION *H. g. occidentalis* occurs in two isolated populations in the west of Madagascar (Petter *et al*, 1977; Petter and Petter-Rousseaux, 1979; Tattersall, 1982; Petter and Andriatsarafara, 1987). One of these is in the region of Lake Bemamba, between Maintirano and Belo-sur-Tsiribihina; and the other is in the Sambirano region, from Maromandia to Beramanja (Tattersall, 1982). There are also collecting records from the east of Lake Bemamba and in the Namoroka area but no *Hapalemur* have been reported there recently (Tattersall, 1982). There is a recent report of *H. griseus,* thought to be *H. g. occidentalis,* in Ankarana Special Reserve in the far north-west of Madagascar (Hawkins *et al*, in press).

POPULATION Total population number is not known but the restricted range of this subspecies suggests that it cannot be high. Numbers are probably declining as the forests in the west are being destroyed (Richard and Sussman, 1975; 1987).

HABITAT AND ECOLOGY This subspecies, like *H. g. griseus,* appears to be confined to forests that contain bamboo or bamboo vines (Petter and Peyrieras, 1970; Tattersall, 1982 In Manongarivo Special Reserve, *H. g. occidentalis* has been seen in groups of between one and four individuals. They were reported active during the day, foraging either on the ground or in understorey vegetation (Raxworthy and Rakotondraparany, 1988).

THREATS Destruction of the western forests, principally by fires set to promote new grass growth for the livestock in the area, is the major threat to this subspecies. Its apparent reduction in range within the last few decades suggests that it might be particularly susceptible to the disappearance of the forests.

CONSERVATION MEASURES The Western Gentle Lemur is found in Manongarivo Special Reserve (Raxworthy and Rakotondraparany, 1988) and it may be this subspecies that occurs in Ankarana Special Reserve (Hawkins *et al,* in press). It is also reported in Bemaraha Nature Reserve (Nicoll and Langrand, 1989).

No conservation measures have been suggested specifically for *H. g. occidentalis* except a range wide survey (St Catherine's Workshop, 1986). Knowledge of its numbers and distribution are needed before its conservation status can be ascertained.

CAPTIVE BREEDING No individuals of this subspecies are reported to be in captivity.

REMARKS Pelage is grey-brown, a bit lighter than that of *H. g. griseus*. It is also slightly smaller than the nominate subspecies, weighing maybe around 700 g. Malagasy names of *H. g. occidentalis* are bekola, kofi and ankomba valiha (Tattersall, 1982).

REFERENCES

Collar, N.J., Dee, T.J. and Goriup, P.D. (1985). La conservation de la nature à Madagascar la perspective du CIPO. In: *Priorités en Matière de Conservation des Espèces à Madagascar*. Occasional Papers of the IUCN Species Survival Commission, Number 2. Pp. 97-108.

FAO/UNEP (1981). *Tropical Forest Resources Assessment Project. Forest Resources of Tropical Africa. Part II Country Briefs*. FAO, Rome.

Glander, K.E., Wright, P.C., Seigler, D.S., Randrianasolo, V. and Randrianasolo, B. (in press). Consumption of cynogenic bamboo by a newly discovered species of bamboo lemur. *American Journal of Primatology*.

Hawkins, A.F.A., Ganzhorn, J.U., Bloxam, Q.M.C., Barlow, S.C., Tonge, S.J. and Chapman, P. (in press). A survey and assessment of the conservation status and needs of lemurs, birds, lizards and snakes in the Ankarana Special Reserve, Antseranana, Madagascar: with notes on the lemurs and birds of the nearby Analamera Special Reserve. *Biological Conservation*

ISIS (1989). *ISIS Species Distribution Report Abstract for Mammals*, 30 June 1989. International Species Information System, 12101 Johnny Cake Ridge Road, Apple Valley, MN, U.S.A. Pp. 17-22.

Jenkins, P.D. (1987). *Catalogue of Primates in the British Museum (Natural History) and elsewhere in the British Isles. Part IV: Suborder Strepsirrhini, including the Subfossil Madagascan Lemurs and Family Tarsiidae*. British Museum (Natural History), London.

Jolly, A., Albignac, R. and J.-J. Petter (1984). The lemurs. In: Jolly, A., Oberlé, P. and Albignac, R. (Eds), *Key Environments: Madagascar*. Pergamon Press, Oxford. Pp. 183-203.

Nicoll, M.E. and Langrand, O. (1989). *Revue Générale du Système d'Aires Protégées et de la Conservation à Madagascar*. Unpublished report to WWF.

O'Connor, S., Pidgeon, M. and Randria, Z. (1986). Conservation program for the Andohahela Reserve, Madagascar. *Primate Conservation* 7: 48-52.

Petter, J-J., Albignac, R. and Rumpler, Y. (1977). Mammifères lémuriens (Primates prosimiens). *Faune de Madagascar* No. 44. ORSTOM-CNRS, Paris.

Petter, J.-J. and Peyrieras, A. (1970). Observations éco-éthologiques sur les lémuriens malagache du genre *Hapalemur*. *La Terre et la Vie* 24: 356-382.

Petter, J.-J. and Peyrieras, A. (1975). Preliminary notes on the behavior and ecology of *Hapalemur griseus*. In: Tattersall, I. and Sussman, R.W. (Eds), *Lemur Biology*. Plenum Press, New York. Pp. 281-286.

Petter, J.-J. and Petter-Rousseaux, A. (1979). Classification of the Prosimians. In: Doyle, G.A. and Martin, R.D. (Eds), *The Study of Prosimian Behavior*. Academic Press, London. Pp. 1-44.

Petter, J.-J. and Andriatsarafara, F. (1987). Conservation status and distribution of lemurs in the west and northwest of Madagascar. *Primate Conservation* 8: 169-171.

Pollock, J. I. (1979). Spatial distribution and ranging behavior in lemurs. In: Doyle, G.A. and Martin, R.D. (Eds), *The Study of Prosimian Behavior*. Academic Press, New York. Pp. 359-409.

Pollock, J. I. (1984). *Preliminary Report on a mission to Madagascar by Dr J.I. Pollock in August and September 1984.* Unpublished report.

Pollock, J. (1986). A note on the ecology and behavior of *Hapalemur griseus*. *Primate Conservation* 7: 97-100.

Raxworthy, C. and Rakotondraparany, F. (1988). Mammals report. In: Quansah, N. (Ed.), *Manongarivo Special Reserve (Madagascar), 1987/88 Expedition Report.* Unpublished Report, Madagascar Environmental Research Group, U.K.

Richard, A. (1982). The world's endangered primate species: a case study on the lemur fauna of Madagascar. In: Mittermeier, R.A. and Plotkin, M.J. (Eds), *Primates and the Tropical Forest.* A seminar sponsored by the Leakey Foundation and WWF.

Richard, A.F. and Sussman, R.W. (1975). Future of the Malagasy lemurs; conservation or extinction? In: Tattersall, I. and Sussman, R.W. (Eds), *Lemur Biology.* Plenum Press, New York. Pp. 335-350.

Richard, A.F. and Sussman, R.W. (1987). Framework for Primate Conservation in Madagascar. In: Marsh, C.W. and Mittermeier, R. A. (Eds), *Primate Conservation in the Tropical Rain Forest.* Alan R. Liss Inc., New York. Pp. 329-341.

Rumpler, Y. (1975). The significance of chromosomal studies in the systematics of the Malagasy lemurs. In: Tattersall, I. and Sussman, R.W. (Eds), *Lemur Biology.* Plenum Press, New York. Pp. 25-40.

Safford, R.J., Durbin, J. C. and Duckworth, J.W. (1989). *Cambridge Madagascar Rainforest Expedition 1988 to RN12 - Marojejy.* Unpublished report.

St Catherine's Workshop (1986). Unpublished reports to participants of the conference on lemur conservation held on St Catherine's Island, Georgia on 26-27 April 1986.

Tattersall, I. (1982). *The Primates of Madagascar.* Columbia University Press, New York.

Warter, S., Randrianasolo, G., Dutrillaux, B. and Rumpler, Y. (1987). Cytogenetic study of a new subspecies of *Hapalemur griseus*. *Folia Primatologica* 48: 50-55.

Wilde, J., Schwibbe, M.H. and Arsene, A. (1988). A census for captive primates in Europe. *Primate Report* 21: 1-120.

Wright, P. C. (1986). Diet, ranging behavior and activity pattern of the gentle lemur (*Hapalemur griseus*) in Madagascar. *American Journal of Physical Anthropology* 69 (2): 283.

Wright, P.C.(1989). Comparative ecology of three sympatric bamboo lemurs in Madagascar. *American Journal of Physical Anthropology* 78(2): 327.

The Golden Bamboo Lemur, *Hapalemur aureus*, was discovered only in 1987. It has a very restricted distribution and its total population probably numbers in the low hundreds. Photo by Dick Byrne.

GOLDEN BAMBOO LEMUR

ENDANGERED

Hapalemur aureus Meier, Albignac, Peyrieras, Rumpler, Wright, 1987

Order **PRIMATES**

Family **LEMURIDAE**

SUMMARY The Golden Bamboo Lemur was discovered only in 1987 and is one of the most threatened primates in Madagascar. It is patchily distributed over a small area of rain forest in south-eastern Madagascar. All populations of this species are severely threatened by habitat destruction. Total population is estimated to be only 200-400 individuals. The species eats bamboo almost exclusively. It appears to live in small family groups. None is in a protected area but the forest near Ranomafana, where *Hapalemur aureus* has been briefly studied, is proposed as a National Park. One pair and their two offspring are in captivity in Madagascar. None is held outside Madagascar. Listed in Appendix 1 of CITES, in Class A of the African Convention and is protected by Malagasy law.

DISTRIBUTION The paratypes of this newly described species were caught 6.25 km and 250° from the village of Ranomafana (21°16'38"S, 47°23'50"E) in south-eastern Madagascar. It is also known from other bamboo areas south of the Namorona River and northwards to the village of Bevoahaza, eight kms north-east of Ranomafana (Meier *et al*, 1987). South of Ifanadiana was probably an important location for bamboo lemurs until 25 or so years ago (Meier and Rumpler, 1987). Now nearly all the bamboo and forest is destroyed and it is unlikely that any *Hapalemur* still surviving there will do so for much longer. "Red bamboo lemurs" were reported by local elders to have been present in the forest near Vondrozo (about 170 km north of Ranomafana) up until 10 years or so ago (Wright *et al*, 1987).

POPULATION Total population is estimated to be only 200-400 individuals (E. Simons, *in litt.*), it is, however, unclear how this figure was obtained. The Golden Bamboo Lemur is undoubtably declining in numbers and it is considered that the species may well be extinct by the year 2000 without immediate intervention to save some suitable habitat (Meier *et al*, 1987). Ranomafana forest may contain more than 10,000 ha of suitable habitat (Meier and Rumpler, 1987), but the density of *H. aureus* there, or elsewhere, is unknown. The status of this species is considered to be slightly better than that of the closely related *H. simus* (Meier, *in litt.*).

HABITAT AND ECOLOGY Found in rain forest, associated with patches of bamboo. At Ranomafana, it is sympatric with both of the other members of the genus *Hapalemur*, the larger *H. simus* and the smaller *H. griseus* (Meier *et al*, 1987). *H. aureus* feeds almost exclusively on plants of the Gramineae family, particularly the endemic giant bamboo or "volohosy" (*Cephalostachium viguieri*), but also on bamboo creeper and bamboo grass (Meier *et al*, 1987; Meier and Rumpler, 1987). It eats the base of bamboo leaves and all new growth (Wright *et al*, 1987). Chemical analysis has shown that the young shoots it eats, which are ignored by the other lemurs, are very high in protein and in toxins that are lethal to most mammals (Wright, 1989, Glander *et al*, in press). The Golden Bamboo Lemur has been seen in groups of between two and six individuals (Meier *et al*, 1987, Wright *et al*, 1987). The group studied at Ranomafana was composed of an adult male, adult female, a slightly smaller subadult and a large juvenile (Wright *et al*, 1987). Interbirth interval is estimated to be one year (Wright, 1989). Preliminary observations suggested that the group had a small home range of 16-18 ha and a mean daily path length of only 350m (Wright *et al*, 1987), but continued study showed that the exclusive territory of the Ranomafana group was approximately 80 ha (Wright, 1989). *H. aureus* appears to be most active in the early morning and evening and is probably also active for part of the night.

THREATS Destruction of the forest by slash and burn agriculture (tavy) is the main threat to this species. Indeed, all known populations of *H. aureus* are highly endangered because of this destruction (Meier *et al*, 1987). The forest at Ranomafana is threatened by tavy around its borders and by timber exploitation within the forest. In a 1973 map the forest is shown as 60 km in width; in 1987 it was only 7-15 km wide (Meier and Rumpler, 1987).

CONSERVATION MEASURES An area of 50,000 ha around Ranomafana has been proposed as a National Park. The Park will be made up of four separate areas of land, so that present villages are not included in the park and each will be surrounded by a buffer zone (Wright, 1988). Duke University has set up a research station in this area and further studies will be made on *H. aureus*. Detailed surveys of other forests are needed to ascertain if the Golden Bamboo Lemur does survive anywhere else. Preserving all areas of forest in which it is found will be of great benefit to the species.

All species of Lemuridae are listed in Appendix 1 of the 1973 Convention on International Trade in Endangered Species of Wild Fauna and Flora. Trade in them, or their products, is subject to strict regulation and may not be carried out for primarily commercial purposes.

All Lemuroidea are listed in Class A of the African Convention, 1969. They may not, therefore, be hunted, killed, captured or collected without the authorization of the highest competent authority, and then only if required in the national interest or for scientific purposes.

Malagasy law protects all lemurs from killing and unauthorised capture, but it is difficult to enforce this protection.

CAPTIVE BREEDING Two animals, a male and female, were captured in early 1987 and are now in Parc Tsimbazaza, Antananarivo. An infant was born to this pair in December 1988 (M. Pidgeon, *in litt.*) and a second infant was born in November 1989 (Meier, *in litt.*). All four animals were reported to be doing well in January 1990 (Meier, *in litt.*).

REMARKS *H. aureus* is a medium size lemur weighing around 1.5 kg. The average weight for three *H. aureus* captured in May 1987 in Ranomafana was 1569 g (range 1 500-1640 g) (Glander *et al*, in press). It has a black face with golden-yellow eyebrows, cheek and throat; underparts are yellow while dorsally there are greybrown guardhairs over pale orange fur. The sexes are difficult to distinguish. A more detailed description of this newly discovered species can be found in Meier *et al* (1987). There are no museum specimens, the paratypes are alive, in captivity in Parc Tsimbazaza, Antananarivo.

REFERENCES

Glander, K.E., Wright, P.C., Seigler, D.S., Randrianasolo, V. and Randrianasolo, B. (in press). Consuption of cyanogenic bamboo by a newly discovered species of bamboo lemur. *American Journal of Primatology* .

Meier, B., Albignac, R., Peyrieras, A., Rumpler, Y. and Wright, P. (1987). A new species of *Hapalemur* (Primates) from South East Madagascar. *Folia Primatologica* 48: 211-215.

Meier, B. and Rumpler, Y. (1987). Preliminary survey of *Hapalemur simus* and of a new species of *Hapalemur* in Eastern Betsileo, Madagascar. *Primate Conservation* 8: 40-43.

Wright, P.C., Daniels, P.S., Meyers, D.M., Overdorff, D.J. and Rabesoa, J. (1987). A census and study of *Hapalemur* and *Propithecus* in Southeastern Madagascar. *Primate Conservation* 8: 84-87.

Wright, P.C (1989). Comparative ecology of three sympatric bamboo lemurs in Madagascar. *American Journal of Physical Anthropology* 78 (2): 327.

Wright, P.C. (1988). IUCN Tropical Forest Programme, Critical Sites Inventory. Report held at the World Conservation Monitoring Centre, Cambridge, U.K.

The Greater Bamboo Lemur, *Hapalemur simus*, is one of the most endangered of Madagascar's primates. It used to be widespread but is now apparently confined to an area around Ranomafana in south-east Madagascar.
Photo by David Haring.

GREATER BAMBOO or
BROAD-NOSED GENTLE LEMUR

ENDANGERED

Hapalemur simus Gray, 1870

Order PRIMATES

Family LEMURIDAE

SUMMARY   The Greater Bamboo Lemur is extremely rare, now found patchily distributed in only a small area of south-eastern Madagascar around Ranomafana and Kianjavato. It was previously much more widespread, occurring in northern, north-western, central and eastern parts of the island.   It is severely threatened by habitat destruction and may not survive into the 21st century. Total population is estimated as no more than 200-400 individuals. Its main food source is bamboo, particularly the giant bamboo, but leaves, flowers and fruit of other species are eaten. Little is known about its social organisation, ranging or reproductive patterns. *H. simus* is not found in any protected area, but the area around Ranomafana, where it is has been briefly studied, has been proposed as a National Park. One pair is in captivity, in Paris Zoo. Listed in Appendix 1 of CITES and Class A of the African Convention and protected by Malagasy law.

DISTRIBUTION   Now known from only the humid forest east of Fianarantsoa (Tattersall, 1982; Meier & Rumpler 1987; Wright *et al*, 1987), but the species used to be distributed throughout northern, north-western, central and eastern Madagascar (Godfrey and Vuillaume-Randriamanantena, 1986).   Subfossil specimens have been found at Ampasambazimba in the Itasy Basin, in the Grotte D'Andrafiabe (Ankarana Massif) and near Mahajanga in the Grottes d'Anjohibe (Godfrey and Vuillaume-Randriamanantena, 1986; Wilson *et al*, 1988). The location of specimens collected at the end of the nineteenth century are mostly unclear but one, collected by J. Audebert in 1876, was within a day's walk of Mananara, far north of the present distribution of the species (Godfrey and Vuillaume-Randriamanantena, 1986). Certainly, even within the last 100 years, its range has been severely reduced.

In the mid sixties, Peyrieras bought an individual in Vondrozo market (Godfrey and Vuillaume-Randriamanantena, 1986; Wright *et al*, 1987). Then, in 1972, he and Petter captured two Greater Bamboo Lemurs near Kianjavato, about 80 kms east of Fianarantsoa (Godfrey and Vuillaume-Randriamanantena, 1986). The species is still present at this site, in an area of less than 100 ha around an agricultural research station, on the slope of Sangasanga Mountain (Meier and Rumpler, 1987).   It also occurs at Ranomafana (21°16'38"S, 47°23'50"E) about 50 kms west of Kianjavato (Wright *et al*, 1987), and has been seen in the region of Ambatovory, near the Farony River, 30kms or so south-west of Kianjavato (Meier & Rumpler, 1987).   In 1986, signs of the presence of *H. simus* (characteristic feeding marks on bamboo shoots) were noted by Meier and Rumpler in several other forests, all within a radius of approximately 50 kms of Kianjavato. One forest containing signs of the bamboo lemurs was near the village of Antafotenia just south of Ifanadiana, feeding traces were also found between Ifanadiana and Kianjavato near the village of Ambongo and in an area 10 kms south-east of the town of Manampatrana on the southern slope of Mt Ankelana (Meier and Rumpler, 1987).   This species may also occur in the forest of Ampasinambo, 80 km east of Ambositra (Meier, 1987). Local people in that area knew a "very big bamboo lemur" which B. Meier considers to be most probably *H. simus*.   There is a possibility that *H. simus* might be rediscovered at Ankarana as bamboo is plentiful in the area and recent feeding damage similar to that produced by Greater Bamboo Lemur was seen there in 1986 (Fowler *et al*, 1989; Wilson *et al*, 1989).

POPULATION Total population of this species is estimated at 200-400 individuals (E. Simons, *in litt.*), but it is unclear how this figure was reached. It is probably even less numerous than the recently discovered Golden Bamboo Lemur (E. Simons, *in litt.*). Numbers are certainly declining; it is estimated that, with the present rate of habitat destruction, the species may not survive the next 20 years (Meier *et al*, 1987; Meier and Rumpler, 1987; Richard and Sussman, 1987).

HABITAT AND ECOLOGY This species is found in rain forest areas where there is also considerable quantities of the giant bamboo *Cephalostachium viguieri*. Though *H. simus* eats mostly bamboo, particularly the woody pith inside the main stem (Petter *et al*, 1977; Wright *et al*, 1987), it has also been seen to feed on the flowers of *Ravenala madagascariensis*, on the fruits of *Arctocarpus integrifolius, Ficus* sp, *Dypsis* sp. and on the leaves of *Pennisetum clandestinum* (Meier *et al*, 1987). It has been seen in groups of up to seven individuals (Meier *et al*, 1987) though the age/sex composition of the groups is not known. A group of seven at Ranomafana ranged over an area greater than 100 ha (Wright, 1989).

THREATS Habitat destruction by slash and burn agriculture and the cutting of bamboo are the major threats to *H. simus*. The population at Kianjavato is threatened by habitat destruction, including cutting of the bamboo and by hunting with slingshots (Meier and Rumpler, 1987). In the past five years more than 50% of the bamboo in the research station area has been converted to rice plantations (Meier and Rumpler, 1987). In January 1990, it was reported that researchers from Duke Primate Center could not locate any Greater Bamboo Lemurs at Kianjavato (Meier, *in litt.*). The borders of Ranomafana forest are being invaded by local people clearing land for farming and timber is being extracted from within the forest. The extent of the forest has been considerably reduced in the last 15 years (Meier and Rumpler, 1987). In a 1973 map the forest is shown as 60 km in width, in 1987 it was only 7-15 km wide (Meier and Rumpler, 1987). Almost all the bamboo and forest south of Ifanadiana has now been destroyed; this area was probably an important locality for *H. simus* until quite recently (Meier and Rumpler, 1987). The animals in the region of Ambatovory, around Farony River, are endangered by hunting as well as by habitat destruction. There is a dense human population in this area (Meier and Rumpler, 1987).

CONSERVATION MEASURES Legally protected but enforcement is difficult and mostly nonexistent. An area of 50,000 ha around Ranomafana has been proposed as a National Park and it is hoped that this will become a sanctuary for the Bamboo Lemurs. The Park will be made up of four separate areas of land in order to exclude human settlement and each will be surrounded by a buffer zone (Wright, 1988). Integrated conservation and development strategies, as well as training of staff, are urgently needed to protect this area and the other reserves in Madagascar. Duke University has set up a research station in Ranomafana forest and attempts are being made to study the Greater Bamboo Lemur there. Surveys are needed in other areas, including Ankarana and Ampasinambo, to find out if *H. simus* still exists elsewhere.

All species of Lemuridae are listed in Appendix 1 of the 1973 Convention on International Trade in Endangered Species of Wild Fauna and Flora. Trade in them, or their products, is subject to strict regulation and may not be carried out for primarily commercial purposes.

All Lemuroidea are listed in Class A of the African Convention, 1969. They may not, therefore, be hunted, killed, captured or collected without the authorization of the highest competent authority, and then only if required in the national interest or for scientific purposes.

All lemurs are protected from killing or unauthorised capture by Malagasy law, but this is very difficult to enforce.

CAPTIVE BREEDING   One pair of Greater-Bamboo Lemurs is in Paris Zoo (J.-J. Petter, in litt.), although ISIS (June 1989) list two pairs. The two caught in 1972 were held in Parc Tsimbazaza, Antanarivo, but none is there now. That pair bred twice while in captivity, one of these offspring survived until 1984 (E. Simons, *in litt.*).

REMARKS   Largest species in the genus *Hapalemur*, an adult male weighed 2,365 g (Meier *et al*, 1987). Individuals have charcoal grey upperparts with paler, grey brown, underparts; their ears have white tufts (Tattersall, 1982). For a more detailed description of *H. simus* see Petter *et al*, 1977 and Tattersall, 1982. The Malagasy name for this species is varibolo in the east and tan-tang in the area around Maroantsetra (Tattersall, 1982).

REFERENCES

Fowler, S.V., Chapman, P., Hurd, S., McHale, M., Ramangason, G.-S., Randriamsy, J.-E., Stewart, P., Walters, R. and Wilson, J.M. (1989). Survey and management proposals for a tropical deciduous forest reserve at Ankarana in northern Madagascar. *Biological Conservation* 47: 297-313.

Godfrey, L. and Vuillaume-Randriamanantena, M. (1986). *Hapalemur simus*: Endangered lemur once widespread. *Primate Conservation* 7: 92-96.

ISIS (1989). *ISIS Species Distribution Report Abstract for Mammals,* 30 June 1989. International Species Information System, 12101 Johnny Cake Ridge Road, Apple Valley, MN, U.S.A. Pp. 17-22.

Meier, B. (1987). Unpublished letter sent to R. Mittermeier 27/8/87.

Meier, B. and Rumpler, Y. (1987). Preliminary survey of *Hapalemur simus* and of a new species of *Hapalemur* in Eastern Betsileo, Madagascar. *Primate Conservation* 8: 40-43.

Petter, J.-J., Albignac, R. and Rumpler, Y. (1977). Mammifères lémuriens (Primate prosimiens). *Faune de Madagascar* No. 44. ORSTOM-CNRS, Paris.

Richard, A.F. and Sussman, R.W. (1987). Framework for primate conservation in Madagascar. In: Marsh, C.W. and Mittermeier, R.A. (Eds), *Primate Conservation in the Tropical Rain Forest*. Alan R. Liss, Inc., New York. Pp. 329-341.

Tattersall, I. (1982). *The Primates of Madagascar*. Columbia University Press, New York.

Wilson, J.M., Stewart, P.D. and Fowler, S.V. (1988). Ankarana - a rediscovered nature reserve in northern Madagascar. *Oryx* 22:163-171.

Wilson, J.M., Stewart, P.D., Ramangason, G.-S., Denning, A.M. and Hutchings, M.S. (1989). Ecology of the crowned lemur, *Lemur coronatus*, at Ankarana, N. Madagascar. *Folia Primatologica* 52: 1-26.

Wright, P.C. (1989). Comparative ecology of three sympatric bamboo lemurs in Madagascar. *American Journal of Physical Anthropology* 78(2): 327.

Wright, P.C., Daniels, P.S., Meyers, D.M., Overdorff, D.J. and Rabesoa, J. (1987). A census and study of *Hapalemur* and *Propithecus* in Southeastern Madagascar. *Primate Conservation* 8: 84-87.

Wright, P.C. (1988). IUCN Tropical Forest Programme, Critical Sites Inventory. Report held at World Conservation Monitoring Centre, Cambridge, U.K.

The Woolly Lemur, *Avahi laniger*, is a monogamous species that eats leaves, an unusual diet for so small a primate. This subspecies, *Avahi laniger laniger*, lives in the eastern rain forest.
Photo by Caroline Harcourt.

WOOLLY LEMUR

Avahi laniger (Gmelin, 1788)

Order PRIMATES

Family INDRIIDAE

SUMMARY The Woolly Lemur is nocturnal and folivorous. There are two subspecies, one (*Avahi laniger laniger*) found throughout the eastern rain forest and the other (*A. v. occidentalis*) with a more restricted distribution in the north-west of Madagascar. Both subspecies used to be more widely distributed than they are today and both are classified as Vulnerable. Population numbers are unknown, but the species is declining because of habitat destruction. It is, however, unlikely that it is severely threatened. There have been a few brief studies of the species. *Avahi* is probably monogamous, it lives in family groups of two to five individuals in a small territory. The eastern form is found in at least six protected areas; the western form is reported in only two protected areas None is in captivity, they do not survive well there. Listed in Appendix 1 of Cites, Class A of the African Convention and is protected by Malagasy law.

DISTRIBUTION Two subspecies are generally recognised; the distribution of each is given below. Both subspecies used to be more widely distributed than they are today (Tattersall, 1982).

POPULATION There are no estimates of total population number for either subspecies. Estimates of density in different areas are given below. Numbers are probably declining due to habitat destruction (Richard and Sussman, 1975, 1987).

HABITAT AND ECOLOGY The Woolly Lemur is found in both rain forest and dry deciduous forest. It is seen in small groups and is probably monogamous. Its main food source is leaves. See below for further details

THREATS Habitat destruction is the major threat to both subspecies. However, it has been reported that *Avahi* may be more numerous in selectively logged or secondary forest, though it is possible that this is an artefact of better visibility (M. Pidgeon, *in litt.*). See separate accounts for details.

CONSERVATION MEASURES See separate accounts for the subspecies.

All species of Indriidae are listed in Appendix 1 of the 1973 Convention on International Trade in Endangered Species of Wild Fauna and Flora. Trade in them, or their products, is subject to strict regulation and may not be carried out for primarily commercial purposes.

All Lemuroidea are listed in Class A of the African Convention, 1969. They may not, therefore, be hunted, killed, captured or collected without the authorization of the highest competent authority, and then only if required in the national interest or for scientific purposes.

Malagasy law protects all lemurs from unauthorised capture and from hunting, but it is impossible to enforce this legislation.

CAPTIVE BREEDING There are no Woolly Lemurs in captivity. All specimens held in captivity have survived only briefly, perhaps due to some special dietary requirement. Some individuals were held at Parc Tsimbazaza in Antananarivo, but they lived only a few months (IUCN, 1972).

187

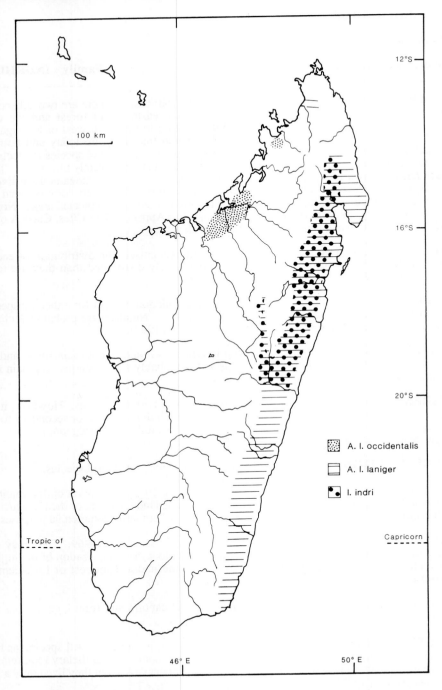

Figure 14: Distribution of both subspecies of *Avahi* and of *Indri*. Shaded areas represent approximate limits of ranges.

REMARKS The Woolly Lemur is the smallest and the only nocturnal member of the family Indridae. It is reported to weigh between 600-700 g by Petter *et al* (1977) and up to about 1300 g by other authors. See separate accounts for a description of the two subspecies. Tattersall (1982) is not convinced that two subspecies should be recognised.

Eastern Woolly Lemur **Vulnerable**

Avahi laniger laniger (Gmelin, 1788)

DISTRIBUTION Distribution maps in Petter *et al* (1977), Petter and Petter-Rousseaux (1979) and Tattersall (1982) show *A. l. laniger* in the rain forest from around the latitude of Sambava to near Taolanaro (Fort Dauphin) in the south. However, this subspecies has recently been found in Ankarana Special Reserve, considerably further north than indicated in the maps (Hawkins *et al*, in press; Fowler *et al*, 1989). Subfossil evidence indicates that *A. l. laniger* formerly occupied the centre of Madagascar, at least as far west as Analavory (Tattersall, 1982).

POPULATION Population numbers are unknown. This subspecies can be found at quite high densities in some forests (Ganzhorn *et al*, 1985), but it is suggested that it is not abundant throughout its range (Tattersall, 1982). In Analamazaotra Forest, Ganzhorn (1988) estimated densities of 72 ± 32 individuals per sq. km (mean and 95% confidence limits), while Charles Dominique and Hladik (1971) estimated a very similar figure of around 100 individuals per sq. km in the same forest. They counted both *Lepilemur* and *Avahi* in their census (as they found it difficult to distinguish between the two at night) and reported a combined density of 200 individuals per sq. km. They considered that there were approximately equal numbers of the two species.

HABITAT AND ECOLOGY The Eastern Woolly Lemur is found in rain forest. There have been no long term studies of *Avahi*, but all observations suggest that this species is monogamous. Pairs or trios of animals are seen most commonly though groups of up to five have been reported (Pollock, 1975; Petter and Charles-Dominique, 1979; Albignac, 1981; Ganzhorn *et al*, 1985; Harcourt, 1988). They are composed of an adult male and female pair and their offspring (Petter and Charles-Dominique, 1979; Albignac, 1981; Razanahoera-Rakotomalala, 1981; Harcourt, in press). Infants are born in August and September (Martin, 1972; Petter *et al*, 1977; Ganzhorn *et al*, 1985; Harcourt, 1988), apparently only one per female (Ganzhorn *et al*, 1985; Harcourt, pers obs.), but each adult female can probably give birth every year (Petter *et al*, 1977). The infant is initially carried on the front of the female but later transfers to ride on her back (Ganzhorn *et al*, 1985; Harcourt, pers. obs.).

Home range size of this subspecies is between 1 and 2 ha (Albignac, 1981; Ganzhorn *et al*, 1985; Harcourt, 1988). The ranges of groups do not overlap to any extent (Albignac, 1981; Ganzhorn *et al*, 1985; Harcourt, 1988); aggression between neighbours is frequent (Razanahoera-Rakotomalala, 1981) and increased calling and chasing has been seen at a home range boundary (Harcourt, pers. obs.). Harcourt (1988, in press) found mean distance travelled each night, measured for only seven nights, was about 450m (range 300-621m); while Razanahoera-Rakotomalala (1981) reports nightly ranges of more than 300m. Woolly Lemurs move around by leaping from trunk to trunk with the body held vertically (Petter and Peyriéras, 1974, Walker, 1979).

The predominate activity throughout the night was resting (Razanahoera-Rakotomalala, 1981 Ganzhorn *et al*, 1985; Harcourt, 1988). This inactivity is probably due to the comparatively low quality diet eaten *by Avahi*, its food is mostly leaves (Razanahoera-Rakotomalala, 1981; Albignac, 1981; Ganzhorn *et al*, 1985, 1988; Harcourt, 1988), an unusual diet for so small a primate. It has been reported eating flowers and fruits, but only in small amounts (Ganzhorn *et al*, 1985). Feeding and travelling are greatest at the beginning and end of the night and there is a prolonged rest period around midnight or a bit later (Harcourt, 1988; Razanahoera-Rakotomalala, 1981). Individuals generally move around alone, though members of a pair meet periodically to rest and groom each other (Harcourt, in press). A pair studied near Ranomafana were together for 40% of the night (Harcourt, in press). Though this species has been reported feeding during the day (Ganzhorn *et al*, 1985), it is more common for the individuals to retire to a sleeping site just before dawn (Razanahoera-Rakotomalala, 1981; Harcourt, in press). At Analamazaotra, sleeping sites were usually in trees with dense folige at a height of 2-9m (Ganzhorn, *et al*, 1985), though individuals at Ranomafana were also found low down, clinging to the base of a tree trunk but hidden in long grass (Harcourt, in press). Members of a group usually sleep huddled up together (Albignac, 1981; Harcourt, in press).

THREATS The major threat to the Woolly Lemur is destruction of its habitat. The forest is cut for timber and the local people need more agricultural land and they destroy the forest to obtain it. However, *Avahi's* nocturnal, secretive habits, comparatively small body size and use of a very small home range are all factors in favour of its survival.

CONSERVATION MEASURES Reported in the Nature Reserves of Betampona, Zahamena, Andohahela, Andringitra and Marojejy, (Safford *et al*, 1989; Nicoll and Langrand, 1989; O'Connor *et al*, 1986, Raxworthy, 1986; Pollock, 1984; Simons, 1984) and in the Special Reserves of Ankarana, Anjanaharibe-Sud, and Analamazaotra (Pollock, 1984; Hawkins *et al*, in press; Fowler *et al*, 1989; Nicoll and Langrand, 1989). However, most of the reserves are protected in name only and it is difficult to ensure that they are undisturbed. Better protection of all the reserves is needed. This has to be combined with conservation education programmes for the local people and alternative means of supplying the resources that they take from the forests at present. There are no measures suggested specifically for this species.

More protected areas have been proposed in the east: part of the Masoala Peninsula, an area near Ranomafana and an area (Mantady) just north of Analamazaotra are suggested as National Parks, while it is proposed that a Biosphere Reserve is created near Mananara (Nicoll and Langrand, 1989).

CAPTIVE BREEDING None is held in captivity. Individuals invariably die after a few days in captivity and it is not recommended that captive breeding is tried (E. Simons, *in litt.*).

REMARKS Dorsal fur is grey brown, sometimes with a rufous tinge. Ventrum is grey, tail is rusty red, insides of thighs are white. For a more detailed description see Tattersall (1982) and Jenkins (1987). Body weight has been recorded as 900-1200 g (Razanahoera-Rakotomalala, 1981), though Petter *et al* (1977) report weights of 600-700 g for the species. The Malagasy names for this subspecies are fotsifé, fotsiefaka, ampongy and avahy (Tattersall, 1982; Simons, 1984).

Western Woolly Lemur   **Vulnerable**

Avahi laniger occidentalis   (Lorenz, 1898).

DISTRIBUTION *A. l. occidentalis* is reported in a fairly restricted area to the north and east of the Betsiboka River, from the Ankarafantsika Reserve to the Bay of Narinda (Petter *et al*, 1977; Petter and Petter-Rousseaux, 1979; Tattersall, 1977, 1982). This subspecies has now been found further north, in the Manongarivo Special Reserve (Raxworthy and Rakotondraparany, 1988), which is where Tattersall (1982) reported that it had been collected in the late 19th and early 20th century. A specimen of *A. l. occidentalis* is said to have been collected from near Morondava (in 1868), which implies a vast earlier extension of its range to the south of that known today (Tattersall, 1982).

POPULATION There are no estimates of population number. Ganzhorn (1988) gives a density figure of 67 $\pm$ 66 individuals per sq. km (mean and 95% confidence limits) in Ankarafantsika Forest at Ampijoroa. Numbers are probably declining because of habitat destruction (Richard and Sussman, 1975, 1987).

HABITAT AND ECOLOGY In the dry deciduous forest in Ankarafantsika, this subspecies is reported to live in small family groups of between two and five individuals, three is the most common number seen (Razanahoera-Rakotomalala, 1981; Albignac, 1981). The groups are composed of an adult male and female and young of up to two years of age (Albignac, 1981). Territory size is 3 to 4 ha and there can be considerable overlap between the ranges of neighbouring groups (Albignac, 1981). Territorial cries are less common and there is less aggression between groups in this subspecies than in *A. l. laniger* (Razanahoera-Rakotomalala, 1981; Albignac, 1981).

The Western Woolly Lemur was seen to eat only young leaves and buds (Razanahoera-Rakotomalala, 1981; Albignac, 1981). It was recorded eating 20 different plant species in Ankarafantsika (Razanahoera-Rakotomalala, 1981), though it is not clear how long the animals there were studied. This subspecies, as well as *A. l. laniger,* is reported to feed more at the beginning and end of the night (Razanahoera-Rakotomalala, 1981). It rests between 21.30 and 00.30 h and is even less active than the eastern form, travelling only 180m in a night (Razanahoera-Rakotomalala, 1981).

THREATS The main threat to *A. l. occidentalis* is forest destruction. This destruction is due principally to fires set to encourage new grass growth.

CONSERVATION MEASURES This subspecies is found in Ankarafantsika Nature Reserve and Manongarivo Special Reserve (Raxworthy and Rakotondraparany, 1988; Nicoll and Langrand, 1989). A management plan for Ankarafantsika is being developed jointly by the Department of Water and Forests and the World Bank. This includes suggestions for better protection of the Reserve, recommendations for the cutting of fire breaks, public awareness campaigns for the local people and a reafforestation programme to provide fuel and building materials (Nicoll and Langrand, 1989). Manongarivo Reserve needs similar protection. As for *A. l. laniger,* no specific conservation measures are suggested for this subspecies.

CAPTIVE BREEDING There is none in captivity and they have never survived long there (Petter *et al*, 1977). The setting up of a captive colony is not recommended (E. Simons, *in litt.*).

REMARKS This subspecies is reported to weigh between 700 and 900 g (Razanahoera-Rakotomalala, 1981). Dorsal fur is a light to medium grey, with brown or olive elements. The face, throat, cheeks and ventrum are generally light coloured. For a more detailed description see Tattersall (1982) and Jenkins (1987). In Madagascar, it is known as fotsifé or tsarafangitra (Tattersall, 1982).

REFERENCES

Albignac, R. (1981). Variabilité dans l'organisation territoriale et l'écologie de *Avahi laniger* (Lémurien nocturne de Madagascar). *Compte Rendus Academie Science Paris* 292 Série III : 331-334.

Charles-Dominique, P. and Hladik, C.M. (1971). Le *Lepilemur* du sud de Madagascar : Ecologie, alimentation et vie sociale. *La Terre et la Vie* 25: 3-66

Fowler, S.V., Chapman, P., Checkley, D., Hurd, S., McHale, M., Ramangason, G-S., Randriamasy, J.-E., Stewart, P., Walters, R. and Wilson, J.M. (1989). Survey and management proposals for a tropical deciduous forest reserve at Ankarana in northern Madagascar. *Biological Conservation* 47: 297-313.

Ganzhorn, J.U. (1988). Food partitioning among Malagasy primates. *Oecologia* (Berlin) 75: 436-450.

Ganzhorn, J.U., Abraham, J.P. and Razanahoera-Rakotomalala, M. (1985). Some aspects of the natural history and food selection of *Avahi laniger*. *Primates* 26(4): 452-463.

Harcourt, C. (1988). *Avahi laniger*: A study in inactivity. *Primate Eye* 35: 9.

Harcourt, C. (in press). A study of the diet and behaviour of a nocturnal lemur, *Avahi laniger*, in the wild. *Journal of Zoology*.

Hawkins, A.F.A., Ganzhorn, J.U., Bloxham, Q.M.C., Barlow, S.C., Tonge, S.J. and Chapman, P. (in press). A survey and assessment of the conservation status and needs of lemurs, birds, lizards and snakes in the Ankarana Special Reserve, Antseranana, Madagascar: with notes on the lemurs and birds of the nearby Analamera Special Reserve. *Biological Conservation*.

IUCN (1972). Red Data Book - Mammalia. Sheet Code: 6.44.3.1.1. Western Woolly Lemur. Prepared by J.-J. Petter.

Jenkins, P. D. (1987). *Catalogue of Primates in the British Museum (Natural History) and elsewhere in the British Isles. Part IV: Suborder Strepsirrhini, including the Subfossil Madagascan Lemurs and Family Tarsiidae.* British Museum (Natural History), London.

Martin, R.D. (1972). Adaptive radiation and behaviour of the Malagasy lemurs. *Philosophical Transactions of the Royal Society of London* (Series B) 264: 295-352.

Nicoll, M.E. and Langrand, O. (1989). *Revue generale du système d'aires protégées et de la conservation à Madagascar.* Unpublished Report, WWF Project 3746.

O'Connor, S., Pidgeon, M. and Randria, Z. (1986). Conservation program for the Andohahela Reserve, Madagascar. *Primate Conservation* 7: 48-52.

Petter, J-J., Albignac, R. and Rumpler, Y. (1977). Mammifères lémuriens (Primates prosimiens). *Faune de Madagascar* No. 44. ORSTOM-CNRS, Paris.

Petter, J.-J. and Charles-Dominique, P. (1979). Vocal communication in prosimians. In: Doyle, G.A. and Martin, R.D. *The Study of Prosimian Behavior.* Academic Press, New York. Pp. 247-305.

Petter, J.-J. and Petter-Rousseaux, A. (1979). Classification of the Prosimians In: Doyle, G.A.and Martin, R.D. (Eds), *The Study of Prosimian Behavior.* Academic Press, London. Pp. 1-44.

Petter, J.-J. and Peyriéras, A. (1974). A study of population density and home ranges of *Indri indri* in Madagascar. In: Martin, R.D., Doyle, G.A. and Walker, A.C. (Eds), *Prosimian Biology.* Duckworth, London. Pp. 39-48.

Pollock, J.I. (1975). Field observations on *Indri indri*: A preliminary report. In: Tattersall, I. and Sussman, R.W. (Eds), *Lemur Biology.* Plenum Press, New York. Pp. 287-311.

Pollock, J.I. (1984). *Preliminary Report on a mission to Madagascar by Dr J. I. Pollock in August and September 1984.* Unpublished report to WWF.

Raxworthy, C. (1986). The lemurs of Zahamena Reserve. *Primate Conservation* 7: 46-48.

Raxworthy, C.J. and Rakotondraparany, F. (1988). Mammals report. In: Quansah, N. (Ed.),*Manongarivo Special Reserve (Madagascar) 1987/88 Expedition Report.* Unpublished report, Madagascar Environmental Research Group, U.K.

Razanahoera-Rakotomalala, M. (1981). Les adaptations alimentaires comparées de deux lémuriens folivores sympatriques: *Avahi* Jourdan, 1834 - *Lepilemur* I. Geoffroy, 1851. Unpublished PhD thesis, University of Madagascar, Antananarivo.

Richard, A.F. and Sussman, R.W. (1975). Future of the Malagasy lemurs; conservation or extinction? In: Tattersall, I. and Sussman, R.W. (Eds), *Lemur Biology.* Plenum Press, New York. Pp. 335-350.

Richard, A.F. and Sussman, R.W. (1987). Framework for primate conservation in Madagascar. In: Marsh, C.W. and Mittermeier, R.A. (Eds), *Primate Conservation in the Tropical Rain Forest.* Alan R. Liss, Inc., New York. Pp. 329-341.

Safford, R.J., Durbin, J.C. and Duckworth, J.W. (1989). *Cambridge Madagascar Rainforest Expedition 1988 to R.N.I. No. 12 - Marojejy.* Unpublished preliminary report.

Simons, H. (1984). Report on survey expedition to Natural Reserve No. 3 of Zahamena. Unpublished report.

Tattersall, I. (1977). Distribution of the Malagasy lemurs Part 1: The lemurs of northern Madagascar. *Annals New York Academy of Science* 293: 160-169.

Tattersall, I. (1982). *The Primates of Madagascar.* Columbia University Press, New York.

Walker, A. (1979). Prosimian locomotor behavior. In: Doyle, G.A. and Martin, R.D. (Eds), *The Study of Prosimian Behavior.* Academic Press, New York. Pp. 543-565.

The Indri, *Indri indri,* is the largest of the living lemurs and the only one without a long tail. It lives in small family groups in the eastern rain forests, where it is threatened principally by habitat destruction.
Photo by Russell Mittermeier.

INDRI   ENDANGERED

Indri indri   (Gmelin, 1788)

Order PRIMATES   Family INDRIIDAE

SUMMARY *Indri* is the largest of the living lemurs. It is now confined to a stretch of approximately 500 kms of the north and central eastern rain forest, a much smaller area than it was found in even a few decades ago. Population figures are not known, but it is not thought to occur at high densities anywhere. It is a diurnal, territorial, family-living species, which feeds principally on leaves and fruit. The species has been the subject of a 15 month study in the forest of Analamazaotra. Its numbers are declining as the eastern forest is destroyed for timber, fuel and agricultural land. *Indri indri* is found in at least four protected areas, one of which was created specifically for its protection. None is in captivity. Listed in Appendix 1 of CITES, Class A of the African Convention and protected by Malagasy law.

DISTRIBUTION Now confined to the eastern rain forest from the Mangoro River northwards to near the latitude of Sambava, but excluding the Masoala Peninsula (Petter *et al*, 1977; Tattersall, 1982). Other authors consider that *Indri* extends only to around Maroantsetra (Petter and Petter, 1971) or just north of there to the Antanambalana River (Petter and Petter-Rousseaux, 1979). However, it has recently (1989) been reported in the Special Reserve of Anjanharibe-Sud (Nicoll and Langrand, 1989). Tattersall, in 1982, considered that *Indri* was rare or even extirpated from the more northern extremities of its range. Whatever the present distribution, it has certainly been considerably reduced even within the past few decades (Petter *et al*, 1977). As recently as 1939, it was recorded by Lamberton as far south as Maranjary (noted in Tattersall, 1982). Subfossil evidence indicates that it used to occur in the interior of Madagascar, at least as far west as the Itasy Massif (Tattersall, 1982).

POPULATION Numbers are unknown and population density varies widely making it difficult to estimate even an approximate figure of the number of *Indri* in Madagascar (Pollock, 1975). In 1972 in the forest of Analamazaotra and those of Fierenana and Vohidrazana nearby, Pollock estimated densities of 9-16 individuals per sq. km (Pollock, 1975). He found no noticeable difference in the density of *Indri* between those in primary forest and those in selectively degraded forest, however his sample size was small (Pollock, 1975). Petter and Peyriéras (1974) found only one group (presumably three or four animals) per sq. km in undisturbed rain forest near Maroantsetra and they suggested that the higher densities in Analamazaotra (Perinet) were due to human interference.

HABITAT AND ECOLOGY Found in the eastern rain forest from sea level to 1500 m (Petter *et al*, 1977). *Indri* is one of the few lemurs that has been studied for more than a few months at a time. Pollock (1975, 1977, 1979) observed several groups in the forest of Analamazaotra for 15 months, from June 1972 to August 1973. He found, as Petter had reported earlier (Petter, 1962), that *Indri* lives in groups of between two and five individuals, these are usually an adult pair and their offspring. The two main groups studied by Pollock (1979) occupied defended territories of approximately 18 ha with little overlap between ranges. Petter and Peyriéras (1974) suggested a home range size for each group of 100 ha, but this was based on plotting the locations of calling groups rather than on direct observation. Loud morning calls advertise the presence of the groups within their ranges and these calls may be answered from as far as 3 km away (Petter and Peyriéras, 1974; Pollock, 1975, 1979, 1986). The Indris may also call at night (Oliver and O'Connor, 1980). Arboreal locomotion is principally by leaping from one vertical trunk to another. The daily distance travelled by the two groups in Analamazaotra was between 300 and 700 m (Pollock, 1979). *Indri indri* is strictly diurnal and has an activity period lasting 5-11 hours depending on season and weather (Pollock, 1975, 1979b). It sleeps in trees from 10-30 m above the ground, no more than two animals ever sleep in contact and distances between individuals can be 100 m or more (Pollock, 1975).

Indri feed on leaves (mostly young ones), flowers and fruits with feeding continuing throughout the day, reaching a peak at midday (Pollock, 1979). Females and very young individuals have priority of access to food (Pollock, 1977, 1979b). When certain plant species flushed into leaf, flowered or bore fruit, *Indri* groups made an early progression to these trees and then fed in them continuously for one to three hours. This was followed, in the early afternoon, by a series of short feeding bouts on a diverse array of plant species and usually ended in a central sleeping area (Pollock, 1979). Alternatively, when no concentrated source of food was present, the *Indri* ranged in a less predictable fashion with small feeding progressions scattered throughout the day (Pollock, 1979). All levels of the forest are used, including the ground to which the animals descend to eat earth exposed by upturned tree trunks (Pollock, 1979).

Infants are born in May after a gestation of 120-150 days and are carried on the front of the female until they are four or five months old, after which they transfer to ride on her back (Pollock, 1975). They move independently by the age of eight months but remain feeding closer to their mother than to any other group member into their second year (Pollock, 1975). The infants sleep with their mothers every night for the first year of life, but do so irregularly thereafter (Pollock, 1975). Females probably give birth no more than once every two or three years and reproductive maturity is not reached until between seven and nine years of age (Pollock, 1977, 1984).

THREATS *Indri indri* is severely threatened by destruction of its habitat for fuel, timber and, particularly, local agricultural development (Pollock, 1984). This destruction continues even in the protected areas as none of these eastern reserves is adequately guarded or financed. For instance, in 1984 over 3 000 people were reported to be living in a central valley enclave of Zahamena and more than 2000 ha of the forest there had been destroyed (Rabemazara pers. comm. to Pollock, 1984b). There is also a risk that the north/south paths from this legal central enclave to villages outside the reserve will bisect the protected area, hunting already occurs along these paths (Nicoll and Langrand, 1989). Hunting of lemurs does occur, even in the protected areas, but it is not clear if the Indri is killed. To some of the local groups it is taboo to hunt this species. The Indri is certainly declining in numbers (Richard and Sussman, 1975,1987). Its slow reproductive rate makes it more vulnerable to extinction.

CONSERVATION MEASURES *Indri* are found in several reserves in Madagascar including Zahamena and Betampona Natural Reserves and the Special Reserves of Anjanharibe-Sud and Analamazaotra (Nicoll and Langrand, 1989). The Reserve at Analamazaotra (Perinet) was created in 1970 specifically for the protection of *Indri* (Petter and Peyriéras, 1974; Pollock, 1984b) and it is here that tourists can most easily see this species. However, the Reserve is small and has become isolated from previously contiguous forest blocks so it is of greater educational than conservation value (Pollock, 1984b). Regular patrols of the Reserve are needed to protect it from encroachment and from hunters (Nicoll and Langrand, 1989). A local conservation group "Friends of the Reserve of Andasibé" has been created and it is suggested that this group could play a role in increasing local public awareness of the Special Reserve (Nicoll and Langrand, 1989). It has been proposed that a National Park be created in the region of Mantady just north of Analamazaotra and the management of the two areas could be combined (Nicoll and Langrand, 1989).

Indri is found in Zahamena Reserve, which is the largest protected area in the eastern rain forest, though it probably exists at a lower density there than in Analamazaotra (Raxworthy, 1986). Members of an expedition to Zahamena in 1985 suggested that fire breaks and boundary trails be cut round the Reserve and that more people were needed to guard it adequately (Thompson *et al*, 1986; Raxworthy, 1986). That expedition financed a two kilometre fire break in the south-west of the Reserve (Raxworthy, 1986). Several guard stations are probably essential to effect adequate control of Zahamena, one or more of these are needed within the central enclave (Pollock, 1984b). It may be that a new demarcation of the Reserve, excluding the central human settlement, is necessary in order to create a viable protected area (Pollock, 1984b).

Pollock (1984b) reports that a few *Indri* are present in Betampona Nature Reserve but he suggests that there may not be sufficient numbers left to create a self-sustaining population within the isolated forest island which is all that remains of the Reserve. It is surrounded by extensive agricultural development. As for the other reserves, funds are needed to support permanent guards within the area and frequent patrolling of the reserve is needed (Pollock, 1984b). Though there is already a good network of paths, some extra ones are needed for a comprehensive coverage of the region (Pollock, 1984b).

Petter *et al* (1977) suggests that it may be possible to introduce *Indri indri* onto the island of Nosy Mangabe. However, the small size of the island (520 ha) makes it unlikely that it would support many of these large, territorial lemurs. An area around Mananara has been proposed as a Biosphere Reserve and this would protect the Indris found there (Nicoll and Langrand, 1989).

Surveys are needed to make accurate estimates of population numbers and to determine the true distribution of this species so that these data can be used as the basis for conservation management of the species. Participants at the St Catherine's Lemur Workshop in 1986 suggested that range-wide surveys of this species are needed as soon as possible.

It may be possible to try breeding *Indri* in captivity, perhaps at an Eaux et Fôret station within the range of the species but this would need full time monitoring from a highly qualified lemur specialist (St Catherine's Workshop, 1986). If breeding in captivity is to be attempted at all, it is suggested that the individuals taken into captivity are from doomed habitats that have no long term hope for survival (St Catherine's Workshop, 1986).

All species of Indriidae are listed in Appendix 1 of the 1973 Convention on International Trade in Endangered Species of Wild Fauna and Flora. Trade in them, or their products, is subject to strict regulation and may not be carried out for primarily commercial purposes.

All Lemuroidea are listed in Class A of the African Convention, 1969. They may not, therefore, be hunted, killed, captured or collected without the authorization of the highest competent authority, and then only if required in the national interest or for scientific purposes.

Though legally protected from capture or killing within Madagascar, enforcement of this is difficult in practice.

CAPTIVE BREEDING *Indri* has never been successfully kept in captivity. One young individual was kept for more than a year at Ivoloina in Madagascar, but generally this species does not survive long when caged (Petter *et al*, 1977).

REMARKS *Indri indri* is the largest of the living lemurs, weighing 7-10 kg or more (Pollock, 1984). Pelage colouration and pattern are highly variable, mostly black with some white, grey or brown (Tattersall, 1982; Jenkins, 1987). It is the only lemur species with virtually no tail. For a more detailed description see Tattersall (1982) or Jenkins (1987). Babakota, one of the Malagasy names for this species, means "the father of man" or "the ancestor" (Petter et al, 1977). Other local names for the Indri are amboanala and endrina (Tattersall, 1982).

REFERENCES

Jenkins, P.D. (1987). *Catalogue of Primates in the British Museum (Natural History) and elsewhere in the British Isles. Part IV: Suborder Strepsirrhini, including the Subfossil Madagascan lemurs and Family Tarsiidae.* British Museum (Natural History), London.

Nicoll, M.E. and Langrand, O. (1989). *Revue Generale du Système d'Aires Protégées et de la Conservation à Madagascar.* Unpublished Report, WWF Project 3746.

Olivier, W.L.R. and O'Connor, S.M. (1980). Circadian distribution of *Indri indri* group vocalisations: a short sampling period at two study sites near Perinet, eastern Madagascar. *Dodo* (17): 19-27.

Petter, J. and Peyriéras, A. (1974). A study of population density and home ranges of *Indri indri* in Madagascar. In: Martin, R.D., Doyle, G.A. and Walker, A.C. (Eds), *Prosimian Biology.* Duckworth, London. Pp. 39-48.

Petter, J.-J. and Petter-Rousseaux, A. (1979). Classification of the Prosimians In: Doyle, G.A. and Martin, R.D. (Eds), *The Study of Prosimian Behavior.* Academic Press, London. Pp. 1-44.

Pollock, J. (1975). Field observations on *Indri indri*: A preliminary report. In: Tattersall, I. and Sussman, R.W. (Eds), *Lemur Biology.* Plenum Press, New York. Pp. 287-311.

Pollock, J. (1977). The ecology and sociology of feeding in *Indri indri*. In: Clutton-Brock, T. (Ed.), *Primate Ecology: Studies of feeding and ranging behaviour in lemurs, monkeys and apes.* Academic Press, London. Pp. 37-69.

Pollock, J. (1979). Spatial distribution and ranging behavior in lemurs. In: Doyle, G.A. and Martin, R.D. (Eds), *The Study of Prosimian Behavior.* Academic Press, London. Pp. 359-409.

Pollock, J. (1979b). Female dominance in *Indri indri*. *Folia Primatologica* 31: 143-164.

Pollock, J. (1986). The song of the Indris (*Indri indri*, Primates: Lemuroidea) natural history, form and function. *International Journal of Primatology* 7(3): 225-264.

Pollock, J.I. (1984). Indri and Sifakas - the leaping lemurs. In: Macdonald, D. (Ed.), *The Encyclopaedia of Mammals:1.* George Allen and Unwin, London. Pp. 327-329.

Pollock, J.I. (1984b). *Preliminary Report on a mission to Madagascar by Dr J. I. Pollock in August and September 1984.* Unpublished report to WWF.

Raxworthy, C.J. (1986). The lemurs of Zahamena Reserve. *Primate Conservation* 7: 46-47.

Richard, A.F. and Sussman, R.W. (1975). Future of the Malagasy Lemurs; Conservation or Extinction? In: Tattersall, I. and Sussman, R.W. (Eds), *Lemur Biology.* Plenum Press, New York. Pp. 335-350.

Richard, A.F. and Sussman, R.W. (1987). Framework for primate conservation in Madagascar. In: Marsh, C.W. and Mittermeier, R. A. (Eds), *Primate Conservation in the Tropical Rain Forest.* Alan R. Liss, Inc., New York. Pp. 329-341.

St Catherine's Workshop (1986). Unpublished reports to the participants of the conference on lemur conservation held on St Catherine's Island, Georgia on 26-27 April 1986.

Tattersall, I. (1982). *The Primates of Madagascar.* Columbia University Press, New York.

Thompson, P.M., Raxworthy, C.J., Murdoch, D.A., Quansah, N. and Stephenson, P.J. (1986). *Zahamena Forest (Madagascar) Expedition 1985.* International Council for Bird Preservation and University of London Union Natural History Society. Unpublished provisional final report.

This subspecies of the Diademed Sifaka, *Propithecus diadema edwardsi*, is found in the eastern rain forests. It is the most widely distributed of the subspecies.
Photo by David Haring.

DIADEMED SIFAKA

Propithecus diadema Bennett, 1832

Order PRIMATES   Family INDRIIDAE

SUMMARY The Diademed Sifaka is a comparatively large, diurnal lemur found in Madagascar's eastern rain forest. Opinions differ as to the number of subspecies. The distribution of each is not clear, but members of the species are found from Sambava in the north to, possibly, as far as Andohahela Reserve in the south. Population numbers are mostly unknown, but it was estimated in 1988 that there were a maximum of 2000 individuals remaining of the most endangered subspecies, *Propithecus diadema perrieri*. Density appears to be low in most subspecies and all are threatened by habitat destruction, all are classified as Endangered. There have been only a few brief studies of the species. It lives in small groups of up to eight animals, the composition of which is very variable. Its diet consists of fruit, leaves and flowers. There are no *P. diadema* in captivity. The species is found in most of the reserves in the east though one subspecies, *P. d. perrieri*, occurs in no protected area. Listed in Appendix 1 of CITES, Class A of the African Convention and protected by Malagasy law.

DISTRIBUTION *Propithecus diadema* occurs in the eastern rain forest southwards from near the Mananara River to near Anivorano in the north (Tattersall, 1982, 1986; also see Petter *et al,* 1997 and Petter and Petter-Rousseaux, 1979). It has been reported as far south as Andohahela Reserve (O'Connor *et al*, 1986, 1987), but this observation needs confirming (M. Pidgeon, *in litt.*). Distribution of the individual subspecies, and, indeed, the number of subspecies present, are a matter of debate. See below for details.

POPULATION Population numbers are unknown, but most estimates of densities of this species are low, a few individuals per square kilometre (e.g. Petter *et al*, 1977; Wright *et al* 1987). The species is considered to be declining (Richard and Sussman, 1975; 1987).

HABITAT AND ECOLOGY A large, diurnal lemur of the eastern rain forest. Generally little is known of its ecology or social organisation, but see accounts for the different subspecies.

THREATS The major threat to *P. diadema* is habitat destruction. The rain forest in Madagascar is being cut down for agricultural land and for timber. FAO/UNEP (1981) estimated that 40,000 ha of previously undisturbed forest was cleared each year between 1976 and 1980 and projected that 35,000 ha would be cleared yearly between 1981 and 1985; the great majority of this is expected to have been in the eastern forests. In addition, the species is hunted in some areas. Jolly *et al* (1984) report that the Diademed Sifaka is hunted for food more than is any other lemur.

CONSERVATION MEASURES Protected by Malagasy law but this, as for most of the lemurs, is difficult or impossible to enforce. The occurrence of the species in protected areas is considered for each subspecies, as are any specific recommendations.

All species of Indriidae are listed in Appendix 1 of the 1973 Convention on International Trade in Endangered Species of Wild Fauna and Flora. Trade in them, or their products, is subject to strict regulation and may not be carried out for primarily commercial purposes.

All Lemuroidea are listed in Class A of the African Convention, 1969. They may not, therefore, be hunted, killed, captured or collected without the authorization of the highest

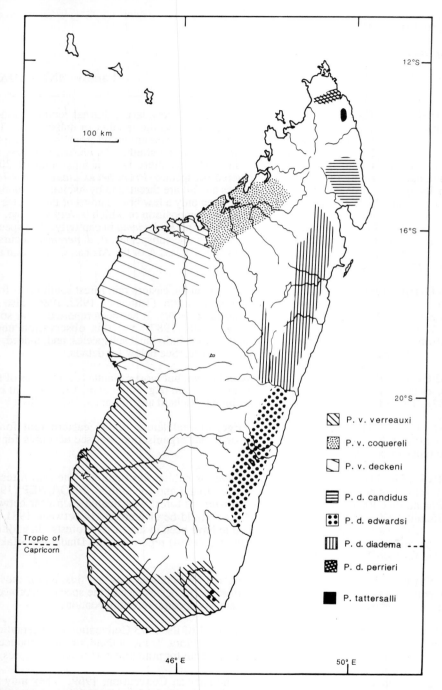

Figure 15: Distribution of all species and subspecies of *Propithecus*. Shaded areas represent approximate limits of ranges.

competent authority, and then only if required in the national interest or for scientific purposes.

CAPTIVE BREEDING None is known to be in captivity. However, members of Duke Primate Center believe that they now have sufficient experience with the other species in the genus to justify a captive conservation programme of *P. diadema* (Simons, 1988).

REMARKS *P. diadema* is the second largest of the living lemurs, weighing about 5 to 8 kg (Pollock, 1984a, Simons, 1988). Coat colour varies from all white to all black with extensive gold, grey or brown patches in some subspecies. For a brief description of each subspecies see below and see Tattersall (1982, 1986), Petter and Petter (1971), Petter *et al* (1977) and Jenkins (1987) for further details. Tattersall (1982), Petter and Petter (1971) and Petter *et al* (1977) suggest that there are five subspecies of *P. diadema* (*P. d. perrieri, P. d. candidus, P. d. diadema, P. d. edwardsi* and *P. d. holomelas*). However, Tattersall (1986) on the basis of recently discovered distribution data, now considers that the latter two subspecies are not distinct subspecies but are two forms of *P. d. edwardsi*.

Diademed Sifaka   **Endangered**

Propithecus diadema diadema Bennett, 1832

DISTRIBUTION This is the most widely distributed of the *P. diadema* subspecies, though the precise limits of its range are not known. It is found throughout the eastern primary rain forest from the Mangoro River in the south to near Maroantsetra in the north (Petter *et al*, 1977; Tattersall, 1982; Petter and Petter-Rousseaux, 1979).

POPULATION Numbers are unknown, but Pollock (1975) and Tattersall (1982) state that this subspecies is never found at high densities.

HABITAT AND ECOLOGY *P. d. diadema* has been observed in the forests around Analamazaotra in groups of two to five individuals (Pollock, 1979). One group had a home range size of at least 20 ha (Pollock, 1979). Petter *et al* (1977) estimate range sizes of between 25 ha to more than 50 ha.

THREATS The Diademed Sifaka is threatened by habitat destruction due to agricultural encroachment and extraction of timber and by hunting. They are reported to be commonly eaten in Zahamena (Simons, 1984).

CONSERVATION MEASURES Found in Analalmazaotra Special Reserve and in Zahamena Nature Reserve (Simons, 1984; Pollock, 1975, 1984b; Raxworthy, 1986, 1988; Nicoll and Langrand, 1989). It may still occur in Betampona Nature Reserve where it was reported by Andriamampianina and Peyrieras in 1972 but was not seen by Pollock in 1984. It is not common in either Analamazaotra or Zahamena. All the reserves need adequate protection. Studies of this subspecies are needed to determine population numbers, limits of its distribution and its ecological requirements. It has been suggested that it be introduced to the island of Nosy Mangabe (St Catherine's Workshop, 1986). Two new protected areas are proposed within the range of *P. d. diadema*: Mananara proposed as a Biosphere Reserve and Mantady as a National Park (Nicoll and Langrand, 1989).

CAPTIVE BREEDING There are no individuals in captivity.

REMARKS The face of *P. d. diadema* is black, as is its crown and this colour extends onto its neck and shoulders and for a variable distance along its back. In some individuals it shades immediately behind the shoulders into a light silver grey, in others it extends to the deep golden pygal (i.e. above the tail) region. Hindquarters and hindlimbs are usually a light gold; tail and forelimbs are usually white as are its forehead, throat and cheeks. Extremities are black. Ventral fur is light silver or gold. The Malagasy name of this subspecies is simpona (Tatersall, 1982)

Silky Sifaka   **Endangered**

Propithecus diadema candidus A. **Grandidier, 1871**

DISTRIBUTION *P. d. candidus* occurs throughout the humid forest belt north of Maroantsetra to the Andapa Basin and the Morojejy Massif (Tattersall, 1982). It is unclear whether it ever occurred in the Masoala Peninsula (Tattersall, 1982). Petter and Petter (1971) reports its distribution as "Sambava, Andapa", though Tattersall (1982) implies that it is no longer found as far north as Sambava. The population of *P. diadema* that Tattersall (1982) found near Daraina, which he provisionally included in *P. d. candidus, has* now been described as a separate species, *P. tattersalli* (Simons, 1988).

POPULATION Population numbers are unknown, but it is extremely rare throughout its range (Tattersall, 1982).

HABITAT AND ECOLOGY There has been no study of this subspecies, but from brief observations in Marojejy it has been suggested that groups may contain a dominant pair and their offspring (B.C. Sheldon, *in litt.*). Six groups were seen in Marojejy Reserve from 12th to 25th September 1988; one contained two adults with a single offspring carried ventrally, three groups contained four adult-sized individuals and two of these groups had a single infant (one of which was old enogh to be riding dorsally), the remaining two groups each contained five adult-sized animals and one of these groups included two infants, which were being carried on the front of their caretakers (B.C. Sheldon, *in litt.*). The presence of more than one offspring in a group implies that they may not be family groups as suggested by Sheldon, instead their social organisation is probably similar to that of *P. verreauxi*. This is described by Richard (1974) not as as a reproductive unit of predictable composition but rather a foraging party of mutually familar animals, the age and sex composition of which varies widely from group to group.

THREATS As for the other *P. diadema* subspecies, habitat destruction is the major threat. It is reported that lemurs are hunted in the Marojejy Reserve (Safford *et al*, 1989) and this probably occurs elsewhere as well.

CONSERVATION MEASURES Found in the Marojejy Nature Reserve and in Anjanaharibe-Sud Special Reserve (Safford *et al*, 1989; Nicoll and Langrand, 1989). Marojejy Reserve is listed by WWF and the Department of Water and Forests as one of the sites that is very important for conservation in Madagascar. In the preliminary management plan for the area it is recommended that Anjanaharibe is included in the conservation plans (Nicoll and Langrand, 1989).

CAPTIVE BREEDING None is in captivity.

REMARKS The dense silky pelage of this subspecies is mostly uniformaly white though some individuals may have pale to darkish silver grey tints on the crown, back and limbs (Tattersall, 1982). Its Malagasy name is simpona.

Milne-Edwards' Sifaka   Endangered

Propithecus diadema edwardsi   A. Grandidier, 1871

DISTRIBUTION Not known for certain, but this subspecies appears to occupy the eastern rain forest southwards from the Mangoro River to at least Manakara (Tattersall, 1982). Though O'Connor *et al* (1986, 1987) report the presence of *"P. d. holomelas"* in Andohahela, which is considerably further south than it has been noted before, this sighting needs confirmation (M. Pidgeon, S. O'Connor, *in litt.*)

POPULATION Total population numbers are unknown but *P. d. edwardsi* is reported to occur at very low population densities. In the Ranomafana area it has been estimated that there are four individuals per sq. km (Wright *et al*, 1987).

HABITAT AND ECOLOGY This subspecies has been studied in the eastern rain forest near Ranomafana. Group size, of nine groups counted, ranged from four to eight animals (Wright *et al*, 1987). In 1987, the study Group I contained an adult male and two adult females, while in Group II there were three adult females, one adult male, two subadult males and one juvenile male and an infant born June 30th (Wright 1988, pers. comm.). It is not clear what the mating system of *P. d. edwardsi* is, one male was seen to move between the two groups and spend time with each. It may well be similar to that of *P. verrauxi* as suggested above for *P. d. candidus*. Infants are born in late June and July and are initially carried on the belly of their mothers. An infant observed at Ranomafana was crawling on group members other than its mother by three weeks of age and was also occasionally being carried on its mother's back by that time (B. Greiser pers. comm.). At eight weeks old it was riding on her back more often than on her front (B. Greiser, pers. comm).

Group I had a home range of 100 ha, with a mean daily path length of 670m, whilst the range of the larger Group II was 254 ha and they had a mean daily path length of 1265m (Wright *et al*, 1987). For the four months that the species was studied in 1986, little overlap was reported between the ranges of these two neighbouring groups (Wright *et al*, 1987). The two groups ranged within 25m of each other two or three times each month but there was no aggression or calling when this occurred, the members of each group retreated without interacting (Wright, 1988). Peaceful intermingling of the two groups was also observed in 1987 (M. Willis, pers. comm.).

From June to September 1986, the Sifakas ate 58% leaves, 28% fruit (mostly *Gambeya madagascariensis*) and 14% flowers. Between 17 and 27 plant species were eaten each day (Wright *et al*, 1987). In 1987, a higher proportion of fruit was taken (P. Wright, pers. comm.). The Sifakas travelled and fed at all heights, including the ground, but they slept near ridge tops, generally 8-10m above the ground (Wright, 1987).

THREATS As with the other *P. diadema* subspecies, habitat destruction is the worst threat to *P. d. edwardsi*. During a survey by Wright *et al* (1987) it was reported that Sifakas used to live in the Vondrozo region but that they no longer do so. Agricultural encroachment and cutting for timber is occurring in the Ranomafana region.

CONSERVATION MEASURES A National Park is being set up near Ranomafana and it is hoped that the area can be adequately guarded to ensure the survival of the lemurs there (Wright, 1988). Duke Primate Center has a study site in the proposed park and work will be continued on *P. d. edwardsi* and other species in the region.

CAPTIVE BREEDING There is none in captivity.

REMARKS The pelage of Milne-Edwards' Sifaka is almost entirely black or chocolate brown with variably extensive white patches on the flanks and dorsum (Tattersall, 1982). Its Malagasy name is simpona.

Perrier's Sifaka   **Endangered**

Propithecus diadema perrieri Lavauden, 1931

DISTRIBUTION Initially thought to be restricted to the forests just south and east of Anivorano Nord (Petter *et al*, 1977; Tattersall, 1982). It has recently been recorded in the northern and north-eastern part of Ankarana Special Reserve, which extends its range further south and west than was thought (Hawkins *et al*, in press).

POPULATION Considered to be the rarest of the subspecies. It is reported to occur at very low population densities, only three to four individuals per sq. km (Petter *et al*, 1977). However, after a study of *P. d. perrieri* in Analamera Special Reserve, Meyers and Ratsirarson (1988) estimated a population density of 20 individuals per sq. km, but they considered this likely to be the highest density found anywhere. Estimates of population numbers differ considerably. In 1972, Petter estimated that about 500 animals remained (IUCN, 1972) while, in 1987, Richard and Sussman suggested that there may be as few as 100 individuals left. After their survey in 1988, Meyers and Ratsirarson estimated a maximum of 2000 individuals remaining.

HABITAT AND ECOLOGY This subspecies is associated with the drier forests of the north-east. Group size varies from one to six individuals with five adult-sized animals and an infant being the most commonly seen group (Meyers and Rasirarson, 1988). Home range size is estimated at 28 ha (Meyers and Rasirarson, 1988). The diet of *P. d. perrieri*, in the dry month of August, consisted of 33% mature leaves and 30% unripe fruit, with petioles, young leaves, stems and flowers making up the rest (Meyers and Ratsirarson, 1988).

THREATS The major threat to Perrier's Sifaka is destruction of its habitat for agricultural development. Fires, livestock grazing in the area and cutting of trees for charcoal are additional threats to the animals. The lemurs in Analamera region are hunted for food, though there is a local taboo on this in the Ankarana region (Fowler *et al*, 1989).

CONSERVATION MEASURES Most of the population of this subspecies is found within the Analamera Special Reserve (Meyers and Ratsirarson, 1988). Others have been found in Ankarana Special Reserve (Hawkins *et al*, in press). A management programme for Montagne d'Ambre National Park, Forêt d'Ambre and these two Special Reserves is being set up by the Department of Water and Forest, WWF, the Catholic Relief Service and US-AID (Nicoll and Langrand, 1989). Suggestions for the area include education and development programmes for the local people, better protection of the Reserves, prevention of cattle grazing within them and the cutting of fire breaks (Nicoll and Langrand, 1989). The narrow corridor of degraded forest between Analamera and Ankarana should be consolidated and protected. Encouraging tourism in the area would also help protect the lemurs (Fowler *et al*, 1989). Ecological surveys to determine the requirements of *P. d. perrieri* are needed.

CAPTIVE BREEDING No members of this subspecies are held in captivity.

REMARKS The fur of Perrier's Sifaka is long, dense and silky of a uniform black except for a brown tint on the ventrum (Tattersall, 1982). The Malagasy names for this subspecies are radjako and ankomba job (Petter *et al*, 1977; Tattersall, 1982).

REFERENCES

Andriamampianina, J. and Peyrieras, A. (1972). Les réserves naturelles intégrales de Madagascar. In: *Comptes rendus de la Conférence Internationale sur la Conservation de la Nature et de ses Ressources à Madagascar, Tananarive, Madagascar 7-11 Octobre 1970.* IUCN, Switzerland. Pp. 103-123.

FAO/UNEP (1981). *Tropical Forest Resources Assessment Project. Forest Resources of Tropical Africa. Part II Country Briefs.* FAO, Rome.

Fowler, S.V., Chapman, P., Checkley, D., Hurd. S., McHale, M., Ramangason, G.-S., Randriamasy, J.-E., Stewart, P., Walters, R. and Wilson, J.M. (1989). Survey and management proposals for a tropical deciduous forest reserve at Ankarana in Northern Madagascar. *Biological Conservation* 47: 297-313.

Hawkins, A.F.A., Ganzhorn, J.U., Bloxam, Q.M.C., Barlow, S.C., Tonge, S.J. and Chapman, P. (in press). A survey and assessment of the conservation status and needs of lemurs, birds, lizards and snakes in the Ankarana Special Reserve, Antseranana, Madagascar: with notes on the lemurs and birds of the nearby Analamera Special Reserve. *Biological Conservation.*

IUCN (1972). Red Data Book - Mammalia. Sheet Code: 6.44.2.2. Prepared by J.-J. Petter.

Jenkins, P.D. (1987). *Catalogue of Primates in the British Museum (Natural History) and elsewhere in the British Isles. Part IV: Suborder of the Strepsirrhini, including the Subfossil Madagascan Lemurs and the Family Tarsiidae.* British Museum (Natural History), London.

Jolly, A., Albignac, R. and Petter, J.-J. (1984). The lemurs. In: Jolly, A., Oberlé, P. and Albignac, R. (Eds), *Key Environments, Madagascar.* Pergamon Press, Oxford. Pp. 183-203.

Meyers, D.M. and Ratsirarson, J. (1988). Survey of the rare *Propithecus diadema* subspecies in Madagascar. Unpublished report to WWF. Project number 6384.

Nicoll, M.E. and Langrand, O. (1989). *Revue Générale du Système d'Aires Protégées et de la Conservation à Madagascar.* Unpublished report to WWF.

O'Connor, S, Pidgeon, M. and Randria, Z. (1987). Un programme de conservation pour la Réserve d'Andohahela. In: *Priorités en Matière de Conservation des Espèces à Madagascar.* Occasional Papers of the IUCN Species Survival Commission, Number 2. Pp. 31-36.

O'Connor, S., Pidgeon, M. and Randria, Z. (1986). Conservation program for the Andohahela Reserve, Madagascar. *Primate Conservation* 7: 48-52.

Petter, A. and Petter, J.-J. (1971). Part 3.1 Infraorder Lemuriformes. In: Meester, J. and Setzer, H.W. (Eds), *The Mammals of Africa: An Identification Manual.* Smithsonian Institution Press, City of Washington. Pp. 1-10.

Petter, J-J., Albignac, R. and Rumpler, Y. (1977). Mammifères lémuriens (Primates prosimiens). *Faune de Madagascar* No. 44. ORSTOM-CNRS, Paris.

Petter, J.-J. and Petter-Rousseaux, A. (1979). Classification of the Prosimians In: Doyle, G.A. and Martin, R.D. (Eds), *The Study of Prosimian Behavior.* Academic Press, London. Pp. 1-44.

Pollock, J. (1975). Field observations on *Indri indri*: a preliminary report. In: Tattersall, I. and Sussman, R.W. (Eds), *Lemur Biology*. Plenum Press, New York. Pp. 287-311.

Pollock, J.I. (1979). Spatial distribution and ranging behavior in lemurs. In: Doyle, G.A. and Martin, R.D. (Eds), *The Study of Prosimian Behavior*. Academic Press, London. Pp. 359-409.

Pollock, J.I. (1984a). Indri and Sifakas. In: Macdonald, D. (Ed.), *The Encyclopaedia of Mammals: 1*. George Allen and Unwin, London. Pp. 331.

Pollock, J.I. (1984b). *Preliminary Report on a Mission to Madagascar by Dr. J. I. Pollock in August and September 1984*. Unpublished report.

Raxworthy, C.J. (1986). The lemurs of Zahamena Reserve. *Primate Conservation* 7: 46-47.

Raxworthy, C. (1988). Expedition dans la Réserve de Zahamena. In: Rakotovao, L., Barre, V. and Sayer, J. (Eds), *L'Equilibre des Ecosystèmes forestiers à Madagascar: Actes d'un séminaire international*. IUCN Gland and Cambridge. Pp. 320-323.

Richard, A.F. (1974). Intra-specific variation in social organisation and ecology of *Propithecus verreauxi*. *Folia Primatologica* 22: 178-207.

Richard, A.F. and Sussman, R.W. (1975). Future of the Malagasy lemurs; conservation or extinction? In: Tattersall, I. and Sussman, R.W. (Eds), *Lemur Biology*. Plenum Press, New York. Pp. 335-350.

Richard, A.F. and Sussman, R.W. (1987). Framework for primate conservation in Madagascar. In: Marsh, C.W. and Mittermeier, R.A. (Eds), *Primate Conservation in the Tropical Forest*. Alan R. Liss, Inc., New York. Pp. 329-341.

Safford, R.J., Durbin, J.C. and Duckworth, J.W. (1989). *Cambridge Madagascar Rainforest Expedition 1988 to R.N.I. No. 12 - Marojejy*. Unpublished preliminary report.

Simons, E.L. (1988). A new species of *Propithecus* (Primates) from Northeast Madagascar. *Folia Primatologica* 50: 143-151.

Simons, H. (1984). Report on a survey expedition to Natural Reserve No. 3 of Zahamena. Unpublished report.

St Catherine's Workshop (1986). Unpublished reports to participants of the conference on lemur conservation held on St Catherine's Island, Georgia on 26-27 April 1986.

Tattersall, I. (1982). *The Primates of Madagascar*. Columbia University Press, New York.

Tattersall, I. (1986). Notes on the distribution and taxonomic status of some subspecies of *Propithecus* in Madagascar. *Folia Primatologica* 46: 51-63.

Wright, P.C. (1987). Diet and ranging patterns of *Propithecus diadema edwardsi* in Madagascar. *American Journal of Physical Anthropology* 72(2): 218.

Wright, P. (1988). *Social behavior of Propithecus diadema edwardsi* in Madagascar. *American Journal of Physical Anthropology* 75 (2): 289.

Wright, P.C., Daniels, P.S., Meyers, D.M., Overdorff, D.J. and Rabesoa, J (1987). A census and study of *Hapalemur* and *Propithecus* in Southeastern Madagascar. *Primate Conservation* 8: 84-87.

Wright, P.C. (1988). IUCN Tropical Forest Programme. Critical Sites Inventory. Report held by the World Conservation Monitoring Centre, Cambridge, U.K.

The Golden-crowned Sifaka, *Propithecus tattersalli*, was recognised as a distinct species in 1988. It is found in a very small area of northern Madagascar. Probably only a few hundred individuals survive.
Photo by David Haring.

GOLDEN-CROWNED or TATTERSALL'S SIFAKA   ENDANGERED

Propithecus tattersalli Simons 1988

Order PRIMATES   Family INDRIIDAE

SUMMARY The Golden-crowned or Tattersall's Sifaka is a newly described species with a very limited distribution around Daraina, in the north-east of Madagascar. Probably only a few hundred individuals exist and these are threatened by hunting, bush fires and clearance of the forest. Little is known about their ecology or social organisation. It is suggested that a National Park be set up to protect them. Duke Primate Center has the only three individuals known to be in captivity. Included in Appendix 1 of CITES, on Class A of the African Convention and is protected by Malagasy law.

DISTRIBUTION Confined to an approximately oval-shaped area with a diameter of about 25 km, around Daraina in the north-east of Madagascar (Simons, 1988). In 1974, Tattersall found a population of this species in dry forest near Daraina, 30 km north-east of Vohimarina (Vohémar), though it was not recognised as a separate species when he reported the sighting in 1982. In 1987, a group from Duke Primate Center found *P. tattersalli* individuals in the forest from about 6-7 km north-east of Daraina to approximately 5 km east of Daraina (Simons, 1988). In addition, the Duke team saw the Golden-crowned Sifaka 2 km east of the village of Ampandraha, a village 10 km north of Daraina (Meyers, *in litt.*, suggests this is a mispelling of Ampandrabe) and were told by local people that the species was also found near Madirabe, 15 km east of Daraina (Simons, 1988). Simons (1988) reports sightings by Andre Peyrieras in two forests, one 5 km east of Ampandraha and the second 7 km north-east of Daraina on the road to Ambilobé (presumably the forest in which the Duke team saw the Sifakas).

POPULATION It is estimated that a maximum of only several hundred individuals exist and these are in small and fragmented populations (Simons, 1988). Meyers and Ratsirarson (1988) report seeing 26 individuals along approximately 4 kms of trail in gallery forest near Daraina, a density that they consider high. Greatest numbers are found in the strip of forest north-east of Daraina, which is approximately 17 km in length and 7 km wide (Meyers, *in litt.*).

HABITAT AND ECOLOGY Tattersall's Sifaka is found in dry forests, but it makes extensive use of the gallery forest in the dry season at least (Meyers and Ratsirason, 1988). In a survey carried out in June and July of 1988, 26 individuals were seen along 4 km of trail in gallery forest, while only eight animals were seen in "large areas" of dry forest on the hills above the gallery forest (Meyers and Ratsirason, 1988). Little is known about the ecology of this species. In captivity it has been observed feeding at night as well as during the day, unlike captive *P. verreauxi* which feed only during the day (Simons, 1988). Simons (1988) suggested that this was an adaptation to escape high daytime temperatures in the dry forest or a response to human predation. Other species within the genus *Propithecus* eat mostly fruit and leaves and it is likely that the diet of *P. tattersalli* is similar. However, the individuals in captivity at Duke Primate Center did not initially accept ripe fruit (D. Meyers, *in litt.*), which suggests that this might not be taken naturally. As yet there are only a few observations of the Golden-crowned Sifaka feeding in the wild. *P. tattersalli* was seen feeding on *Poupartia caffra* (sakoa tree) in the forest near Daraina and was reported to feed in groves of mango trees (Simons, 1988). Tattersall's Sifaka has been seen in groups of three to six individuals, mean size of eight groups was 4.1 (Meyers and Ratsirason, 1988), but there is no information available on group composition.

THREATS No population of this species exists in any protected area. Its limited geographical distribution means that it is one of the most severely threatened of the lemurs (Meyers and Ratsirarson, 1988). The main threats to *P. tattersalli* include hunting, brush fires and competition for land with humans (Meyers and Ratsirarson, 1988). Though the customs of the local people from near Daraina forbid the consumption of lemurs, this is not so for those attracted in from outside the area. Daraina is on the only east/west road in the region and gold is found nearby. Though the miners, exploiting this gold, seem to have limited their hunting to the smaller lemurs so far, this may easily change (Meyers and Ratsirarson, 1988). The road between Ambilobé and Vohimarina (RN 5a) is due to be improved and easier access will almost certainly present an increased danger to *P. tattersalli* (Meyers and Ratsirarson, 1988). Hunting by people from Ambilobé has, apparently, eliminated the populations of the Golden-crowned Sifaka in the region of Maromakotra, 30 km or so north-west of Daraina (Meyers and Ratsirason, 1988).

Much of the area round the gallery forest in which the Golden-crowned Sifaka was seen in 1988 was already deforested (Meyers and Ratsirason, 1988) and fires, some probably set to increase grass growth, ensure that regeneration of trees is inhibited. The gallery forest itself is being cleared for agricultural land because of its proximity to water and this forest may well be critical to the Sifaka, particularly during the dry season (Meyers and Ratsirason, 1988).

CONSERVATION MEASURES It is suggested that a National Park of approximately 20,000 ha, divided into three different blocks, be set up in the area of Daraina to protect *P. tattersalli* (Meyers and Ratsirason, 1988). The Reserve would have to be well guarded and have clearly marked boundaries. In addition, education programmes are needed to increase the awareness of the local people to the economic and environmental importance of the forests (Meyers and Ratsirason, 1988).

Methods of sustainable use of the land around the proposed park need to be developed (Meyers and Ratsirason, 1988). Surveys to locate further populations are needed, as is an extensive ecological study of the species. Simons (1988) considers that the only hope against certain extinction of the species is a captive breeding programme combined with relocation of populations in Madagascar. However, the mortality rate of wild caught Sifakas taken into captivity remains high and there is little if any evidence that captive bred individuals could be successfully returned to a suitable area in Madagascar.

All species of Indriidae are listed in Appendix 1 of the 1973 Convention on International Trade in Endangered Species of Wild Fauna and Flora. Trade in them, or their products, is subject to strict regulation and may not be carried out for primarily commercial purposes.

All Lemuroidea are listed in Class A of the African Convention, 1969. They may not, therefore, be hunted, killed, captured or collected without the authorization of the highest competent authority, and then only if required in the national interest or for scientific purposes.

Malagasy law protects all lemurs from killing or unauthorised capture, but this is difficult to enforce.

CAPTIVE BREEDING There are three Golden-crowned Sifakas in captivity, one adult male and two females, all at Duke Primate Center (Simons, *in litt.*). Two are wild caught individuals and the third was born at the Center in July 1988 to the female caught earlier that month. The juvenile, in April 1989, is reported to be nearly adult size and doing well (Simons, *in litt.*).

REMARKS Initially attributed provisionally to the *candidus* subspecies of *Propithecus diadema* (Tattersall, 1982), but now considered to be a separate species (Simons, 1988). *P. tattersalli* is quite considerably smaller than *P. diadema*, mean weight of eight specimens of the former is recorded as 3.3 kg as opposed to 5.8 kg for the latter (Simons, 1988). Tattersall's Sifaka is mostly white with a gold or orange crown on its head and a wash of golden-orange across its upper chest and rump (Simons, 1988). It has completely furred ears with long hair tufts extending beyond their tips (Simons, 1988). For a more complete description of *P. tattersalli* and a comparison with other *Propithecus* species see Simons (1988). The holotype is at the American Museum of Natural History. The Malagasy name of this species is ankomba malandy (Simons, 1988).

REFERENCES

Meyers, D.M. and Ratsirarson, J. (1988). Survey of the rare *Propithecus diadema* subspecies in Madagascar. Unpublished report to WWF. Project number 6384.

Simons, E.L. (1988). A new species of *Propithecus* (Primates) from Northeast Madagascar. *Folia Primatologica* 50: 143-151.

Tattersall, I. (1982). *The Primates of Madagascar*. Columbia University Press, New York.

Verreaux's Sifaka, *Propithecus verreauxi*, is the most common species in the genus, but it is still not safe from destruction of its habitat. This photograph shows a female and her infant of the subspecies *Propithecus verreauxi verreauxi* in the spiny forest of southern Madagascar.
Photo by Russell Mittermeier.

VERREAUX'S SIFAKA

Propithecus verreauxi A. Grandidier, 1867

Order **PRIMATES**   Family **INDRIIDAE**

SUMMARY Verreaux's Sifaka is one of the larger, diurnal lemurs. It is found in the dry western and southern forests of Madagascar. The number of subspecies accepted varies from three to five. Population number is unknown, but it is almost certainly declining as the forests are destroyed. This species is also hunted in some places. *Propithecus verreauxi coquereli* is probably the most threatened of the three subspecies described here, although all are considered Vulnerable. *P. verreauxi* is one of the most studied of the lemur species. It lives in small groups and its diet is composed of varying amounts of leaves, fruit and flowers depending, principally, on season. There are 18 individuals in captivity, of which four are captive born; most are at Duke Primate Center. All subspecies are found in at least two protected areas. Listed in Appendix 1 of CITES, Class A of the African Convention and is protected by Malagasy law.

DISTRIBUTION *Propithecus verreauxi* is distributed in the dry western and southern forests from just west of Taolanaro (Fort Dauphin) to around Antsohihy in the north (Tattersall, 1982; also see Petter *et al*, 1977 and Petter and Petter-Rousseaux, 1979). For more detailed distributions of each subspecies, see the separate accounts below.

POPULATION There are no estimates of total population numbers. Estimates of density at Berenty have ranged from around 100 to 200 individuals per sq. km (O'Connor, 1987; Howarth *et al*, 1986; Richard, 1978a). The species is reported to be abundant but declining (Richard and Sussman, 1975, 1987).

HABITAT AND ECOLOGY *P. verreauxi* is found in the Didiereaceae and gallery forest of the south and in the dry deciduous forest of the west of Madagascar. It lives in small groups of between two and 12 individuals, the groups have a very varied age/sex composition (Richard, 1974, 1985; Albignac, 1981). Home range size varies from 2.5-11 ha and the ranges may or may not be defended (Jolly, 1966; Richard, 1974, 1985; O'Connor, 1987; Mertl-Millhollen, 1979). The diet of *P. verreauxi* is composed of varying amounts of leaves, fruit and flowers depending, principally, on season (Jolly, 1966; Richard, 1977; O'Connor, 1987). The Sifaka, like most lemurs, has a restricted breeding period; mating in this species occurs between January and March (Petter-Rousseaux, 1964; Jolly, 1966; Richard 1974; Petter *et al*, 1977). For more details see accounts of each subspecies.

THREATS Though this species has a wide geographic distribution, it is dependent on the two natural vegetation types of the south (Didiereaceae and riparian forest) and on the deciduous forests of the west. The southern forests are quite restricted in area and are becoming more so (Sussman and Richard, 1986). Destruction of these forests is, to a great extent, caused by the collection of wood for conversion to charcoal. Fires are used to encourage new grass growth for livestock, especially in the west, and these frequently destroy large areas of the dry forests. Overgrazing, which prevents forest regeneration is a problem in both the south and the west. The Sifaka is also an easy target for hunters and has probably been exterminated from some areas of its habitat as a result (Sussman and Richard, 1986). In 1971, Richard saw a hunter with 12 *P. verreauxi* corpses, the result of one afternoon's hunting (Richard and Sussman, 1975). In that incident, the hunter was a Chinese store owner from Fort Dauphin; it appears that the local Malagasy do not often kill the sifakas (A. Richard, *in litt.*).

CONSERVATION MEASURES The species is found in Isalo National Park as well as in Ankarafantsika, Bemaraha, and Andohahela Nature Reserves and in Ambohijanahary, Bora, Andranomena, Tsimanampetsotsa and Beza Mahafaly Special Reserves (Nicoll and Langrand, 1989). *P. verreauxi* is also found in the two Private Reserves, Berenty and Analabe, owned by M. de Heaulme. It has been studied in some detail, particularly by Alison Richard, but also by Jean-Jacques Petter, Alison Jolly, Sheila O'Connor and others.

All species of Indriidae are listed in Appendix 1 of the 1973 Convention on International Trade in Endangered Species of Wild Fauna and Flora. Trade in them, or their products, is subject to strict regulation and may not be carried out for primarily commercial purposes.

All Lemuroidea are listed in Class A of the African Convention, 1969. They may not, therefore, be hunted, killed, captured or collected without the authorization of the highest competent authority, and then only if required in the national interest or for scientific purposes.

Malagasy law protects all lemurs from unauthorised capture and from killing, but this is difficult to enforce. In addition, for some of the local people in Madagascar, there is a taboo against killing *P.verreauxi*.

CAPTIVE BREEDING There are 12 *P. verreauxi* in Duke Primate Center (ISIS, June 1989). Four of the individuals at Duke have been born in captivity. The only other institute listed by ISIS as holding *P. verreauxii* is Paris Zoo, which has four *P. v. coronatus*, all wild caught. This is confirmed by J.-J. Petter (*in litt.*), who adds that no infants have yet been born to this group.

REMARKS One of the larger lemurs, weighing between 2.0 and 5.1 kg (Simons, 1988). Coat colour varies from pure white to partly or largely brown, black or maroon (Pollock, 1984). The number of subspecies accepted within *P. verreauxi* varies from five (*verreauxi, coquereli, deckeni, coronatus* and *majori* (Petter *et al*, 1977; Petter and Petter-Rousseaux, 1979) to four (*verreauxi, coquereli, deckeni,* and *coronatus* (Tattersall,1982, 1986; Jenkins, 1987) to three (*verreauxi, coquereli* and *deckeni*) (Tattersall, in press). See below for more details.

Verreaux's Sifaka   **Vulnerable**

Propithecus verreauxi verreauxi **A. Grandidier, 1867**

DISTRIBUTION Occurs in the forested regions of south and south-west Madagascar from near Taolanaro (Fort Dauphin) to the Tsiribihina River (Petter *et al*, 1977; Petter and Petter-Rousseaux, 1979; Tattersall, 1982). It is found as far east as Andohahela Nature Reserve (O'Connor *et al*, 1986, 1987).

POPULATION The total number of *P. v. verreauxi* surviving in the wild is unknown. It is the most widely distributed and probably the most abundant of the subspecies. Counts of the animals at Berenty between 1963 and 1981 indicated that the population there had a stable density of around 150 individuals per sq. km (Jolly, 1972; Jolly *et al*, 1982; Howarth *et al*, 1986). The most recent count, in 1985, estimated a density of 211 individuals per sq. km (O'Connor, 1987). In the nearby disturbed forest of Bealoka, also on the Mandrare River, density was only 47 individuals per sq. km (O'Connor, 1987). In Antseranomby, 40-50 *P. v. verreauxi* lived at a density equivalent to 400-500 individuals per sq. km (Sussman, 1972 reported in Pollock, 1979).

216

HABITAT AND ECOLOGY Verreaux's Sifaka is found in all types of southern and south-western forests from the arid *Didierea* formations to riverine gallery forests (Tattersall, 1982). It has also been seen in a small, isolated patch of rain forest between Parcel 2 and 3 of Andohahela Nature Reserve (M. Pidgeon, *in litt.*). It is not, however, found in dense brush or scrub vegetation, nor is it successful in edge vegetation (Sussman and Richard, 1986).

Most of the studies of this subspecies have been in approximately 100 ha of the Private Reserve at Berenty in the south-east. Here, Jolly (1966) found groups of between two and 10 individuals, four of these groups, containing five individuals each, had home ranges of between 2.2 and 2.6 ha. A solitary male had a range of 1 ha. The ranges overlapped but each had a large nucleus that the others did not penetrate (Jolly, 1966). At Berenty, territorial battles occurred and marking was more frequent on the boundaries of the territory (Jolly, 1966; Mertl-Millhollen, 1979). Jolly (1966) reported that there was no dominance hierarchy within a group and that any individual could lead troop progressions. In the disturbed forest of Bealoka, home range sizes were between 9.5 and 11.3 ha (O'Connor, 1987).

Similar results were reported by Richard from her study of this subspecies at Hazafotsy, in Andohahela Nature Reserve. Group size there, and at other sites in the south, varied from three to 10 individuals, 34 groups were counted (Richard, 1974b). Richard (1974b, Richard and Heimbuch, 1975) suggests that the groups should be considered as foraging parties of mutually familar animals whose age/sex composition varies widely from group to group, rather than as reproductive units of predictable composition. Home ranges of *P. v. verreauxi* in her study varied in size from 6.75-8.5 ha and, as at Berenty, there was some overlap between ranges, but groups had exclusive use of about 90% of the range (Richard, 1974b,1985). Intergroup encounters occurred along the periphery of the area of exclusive use and apparently served to define and/or defend its borders (Richard, 1974b). In contrast to Jolly's observations (1966), Richard found that, outside the mating season, a linear dominance hierarchy incorporating all adults could be determined; females were dominant to males (Richard 1974a, 1987; Richard and Nicoll, 1987)

The diet of *P. v. verreauxi* consists principally of leaves, fruit and flowers, but there is considerable seasonal variation in the importance of the different components (Richard, 1977, 1978). It is suggested that Sifaka are opportunistic feeders in that they exploit the plant species that are most available (O'Connor, 1987). In the semi-arid forest near Hazafotsy, leaves constituted the most important part of the diet in the dry season, while fruit and flowers predominated in the wet season (Richard, 1977). The time spent feeding also changed seasonally, from 32.8% of the day in the wet season to 24.2% in the dry season (Richard, 1978). The Sifaka fed on fewer species in the wet season (Richard, 1974b). Jolly (1966) never saw *P. v. verreauxi* drink and she suggests that their survival in Didiereaceae forest, without access to gallery forest, indicates that they can tolerate extreme drought. However, Richard (1974b) observed the Sifakas eating bark and cambium of *Operculicarya decaryi* in the dry season. This contains a high percentage by weight of water and may have been critical to the animals' survival in the arid season. At the height of the dry season, heavy dew forms in the morning and the Sifakas do lick this moisture from their coats (M. Pidgeon, *in litt.*).

Activity patterns also changed between seasons. In the dry season, the Sifaka remained immobile for 1-2 hr after sunrise then moved to the tops of trees and sunned for an hour or so before moving off to feed (Richard 1974b). They fed more or less continuously until early afternoon, when they moved into forks of trees and took up their sleeping positions (Richard 1974b). In contrast, in the wet season, the animals were moving about and feeding before sunrise, most feeding stopped by mid-morning and the Sifakas then rested until the middle of the afternoon, before resuming feeding and foraging until after sunset

(Richard, 1974b). Related to this change in activity patterns, the mean distance moved in the dry season was only 550m, considerably less than the 1000m moved in the wet season (Richard, 1978). Jolly (1966) reported the Sifaka at Berenty moving only 2-300m each day, but O'Connor (1987) reported mean daily distances travelled of between 293 and 464 m there and distances of more than double these in the disturbed forest. In both seasons, the animals at Hazafotsy spent little time on the ground, but all the other levels of the forest were used extensively (Richard 1974b). Sifakas are typical vertical clingers and leapers (Petter *et al*, 1977) and they find it difficult to cross extensive open areas.

Breeding is seasonal in *P. v. verreauxi*. Petter-Rousseaux (1962) reports gestation time as 130 days. O'Connor (*in litt.*) has a single record of a gestation period of 165 days. At Berenty, infants were born in July (Jolly, 1966) or from July to October (S. O'Connor, *in litt.*), while at Hazafotsy, mating was seen in early March and infants were born in August (Richard, 1974 a). Richard (1974 a and b) noted an increase in intergroup aggression during the breeding season, at this time adult males left their own ranges and groups to make long excursions into neighbouring areas. Copulations took place between members of different groups (Richard 1974 a and b). The infants at Berenty were carried on their mother's belly until October and then on her back until December or January (Jolly, 1966). They are almost independent at six months of age (Jolly, 1966). Females generally give birth only once in two years (Jolly, 1966, 1972; Petter, 1962; Richard, 1978), but O'Connor (1987) reports two females giving birth in at least three successive years. The survivorship of infants to one year between 1983/84 was only 58%, whereas it approached 100% in 1984/85 (O'Connor, 1987).

THREATS Though this species has a wide geographic distribution, it is dependent on the two natural vegetation types of the south (Didiereaceae and riparian forest) and both of these are quite restricted in area and are becoming more so (Sussman and Richard, 1986; Sussman *et al*, 1987). The exploitation of wood for charcoal, timber and fuel is the major agent in the destruction of the spiny forest. Where good forest still exists, areas of vegetation are cleared and charcoal kilns are made within the forest. The trees not suitable for charcoal are used to build the kilns (M. Pidgeon, *in litt.*).

Some members of the Didiereaceae family, particularly *A. procera*, are heavily exploited for use in the timber trade. The removal of these trees has opened up the spiny forest to further encroachment and has drastically changed the stratification and forest type in some areas (M. Pidgeon, *in litt.*). In addition, there is overgrazing within the forest and fires are set to encourage new grass growth for the livestock and to clear land for cultivation.

CONSERVATION MEASURES *P. v. verreauxi* is found in the Private Reserve of Berenty where it has been studied at intervals over the years from 1963 (e.g. Jolly, 1966, 1972; O'Connor, 1987). The subspecies has also been studied near Hazafotsy in Andohahela Nature Reserve (Richard, 1974, 1977, 1978a and b) and in Beza Mahafaly Special Reserve (Richard *et al*, 1987; Rakotomanga *et al*, 1987). It is also found in Isalo National Park, Andranomena Special Reserve and in Analabe Private Reserve (Nicoll and Langrand, 1989). In 1988 it was heard, but not seen, in Tsimanampetsotsa Nature Reserve (L. Wilmé, pers. comm. to M. Pidgeon). There are management and conservation education plans underway or proposed for many of the reserves (e.g. Andohahela, Beza Mahafaly and Andranomena) in which Verreaux's Sifaka occurs (Nicoll and Langrand, 1989).

Participants at the St Catherine's Lemur workshop in 1986 suggested that a range-wide status survey of this subspecies be carried out but they did not consider this to be of high priority (St Catherine's Workshop, 1986).

CAPTIVE BREEDING There is only one pair of this subspecies in captivity (ISIS, June, 1989 listed as *P. v. majori*). These were acquired in mid-1984 by Duke Primate

Center, but they have not yet reared infants successfully. Two offspring have been born, but both were very small and did not survive. It is possible that the pair are members of the same family and there may be problems with inbreeding (E. Simons, pers. comm.).

REMARKS Some authors (e.g. Petter *et al*, 1977 and Petter and Petter-Rousseaux, 1979) recognise a second subspecies, *P. v. majori*, within the range of *P. v. verreauxi*. However, Jolly (1966) and Tattersall (1982) consider *majori* to be merely a melanistic variant within *verreauxi*. The two forms have been seen feeding, in separate groups, within 20 m of each other (F. Petter, quoted in Petter *et al*, 1977) and, in addition, they have been seen living together in the same group (Jolly, 1966; R.W. Sussman, quoted in Tattersall, 1982 and F. Petter, quoted in Petter *et al*, 1977). The subspecies is predominantly white, though it usually has a black or maroon cap on its head, this may be absent or extend on to the neck (Tattersall, 1982). The Malagasy name for this subspecies is sifaka (Tattersall, 1982) and the darker form may be called sifaka-avahi (M. Pidgeon, *in litt.*).

Coquerel's Sifaka   **Vulnerable**

Propithecus verreauxi coquereli   Milne-Edwards, 1867

DISTRIBUTION *P. v. coquereli* occurs in north-west Madagascar, north and east of the Betsiboka River. It extends from around Ambato-Boéni northwards to near Antsohihy, while its eastern limit is close to Antetemazy, a short distance to the west of Befandriana Nord (Tattersall, 1982).

POPULATION Total population is unknown. Ganzhorn (1988) has calculated density from mean group size and home range size (data in Richard, 1978) as 60 individuals per sq. km. Numbers are almost certainly declining (Richard and Sussman, 1987).

HABITAT AND ECOLOGY Coquerel's Sifaka lives in the mixed deciduous and evergreen forests of north-western Madagascar. Petter (1962) observed this subspecies in Ankarafantsika and reported that it lived in family groups. He found mean group size, of 27 groups, to be four and none of the groups contained more than one infant. However, in the same area, Richard (1974a) found groups ranging in size from four to 10, with a mean of 5.5 individuals in the 12 groups she counted. Age/sex composition of the groups was very variable and she suggests that the groups should be considered as foraging parties of mutually familar animals rather than as reproductive units of predictable composition (Richard, 1974a). Albignac (1981), also working in the same area, reported groups of three to five individuals.

Richard found home range sizes of between 6.75 and 8.5 ha, but her two study groups spent over 60% of their time in only 2.5 ha. The two study groups had exclusive use of 46% and 43% of their total home range, but these areas of exclusive use did not necessarily contain the heavily used areas (Richard, 1974b,1978b). Intergroup encounters occurred throughout the extensive areas of overlap with neighbouring groups, but there was no evidence that these encounters defined or defended the boundaries of the part of the home range used exclusively by the resident group (Richard, 1978b). In this subspecies, dispersion generally occurred through mutual avoidance between groups, rather than by defence of a territory (Richard, 1974b). Albignac (1981) found that each group of Coquerel's Sifaka occupied a home range of 4-6 ha and that there were areas of quite considerable overlap between ranges.

Coquerel's Sifaka, *Propithecus verreauxi coquereli*, occurs in north-west Madagascar. It is threatened by destruction of its habitat.
Photo by Mark Pidgeon.

P. v. coquereli fed chiefly on mature leaves and buds in the dry season and on a higher proportion of young leaves, flowers and fruit in the wet season (Richard, 1974b). The animals also ate bark during the dry season and dead wood in the wet season (Richard, 1974b). As many as 98 different plant species were eaten, though only 12 of these took up 65% of feeding time (Richard, 1978b). Between 30-37% of the Sifakas' time was occupied by feeding, but there were seasonal changes in the distribution of this time (Richard, 1974b, 1978b). During the wet season, feeding began early, often before sunrise even, reaching a peak between 07.00 h and 09.00 h. This was followed by a gradual decrease until midday by which time very little feeding was taking place. After a midday rest, feeding began to increase again, reaching a peak in late afternoon. However, during the dry season, intensive feeding began later in the day and ended earlier and there was only a slight midday depression (Richard, 1974b). Distances moved during the day were greater in the wet season than in the dry, means of 1100m and 750m respectively (Richard, 1974b, 1978b).

At Duke Primate Center, gestation period, presumably of this subspecies, has been reported as 162 days (Richard, 1987). Infants are born seasonally and Richard (1976) reports the birth of one in Ankarafantsika in mid June. An offspring initially rides on its mother's front until, at three to four weeks of age, it begins to be carried on her back, though it can still be periodically carried ventrally up to the age of seven weeks and may be occasionally riding on its mother up to six months of age (Richard, 1976).

THREATS The distribution of *P. v. coquereli* is the most restricted of the three subspecies described here and it is probably the most threatened as a result. Habitat destruction is the major cause of its decline. There are only two protected areas, Ankarafantsika and Bora, within the range of Coquerel's Sifaka. These reserves have been and continue to be badly damaged by fires, set each year to encourage new grass growth for domestic livestock to feed on (Nicoll and Langrand, 1989). Trees in both these protected areas are cut for charcoal and this is a major threat to the forests (Nicoll and Langrand, 1989). After exploitation by petrol companies and then by the local people, there is little if any intact forest left in the south of Bora Special Reserve. In Ankarafansika, poaching is limited at the moment as a local taboo forbids the killing of the animals (Nicoll and Langrand, 1989). However, as the region develops, people from other ethnic groups without this cultural restriction on hunting, may well hasten the demise of the lemurs in the area (Nicoll and Langrand, 1989).

CONSERVATION MEASURES *P. v. coquereli* is found in Ankarafantsika Nature Reserve and in Bora Special Reserve. The Department of Water and Forests, jointly with the World Bank, have set up a management programme for Ankarafantsika Nature Reserve and the Classified Forest of Ampijoroa (Nicoll and Langrand, 1989). A number of suggestions have been made for the area, these include the following: motorbikes are needed by the guards so that they can patrol the Reserve more effectively; fire breaks are necessary around the Reserve; conservation/education programmes should be set up; plantations are needed to supply the local people with wood for fuel and construction material (Nicoll and Langrand, 1989).

No conservation measures other than a range-wide survey have been suggested specifically for Coquerel's Sifaka (St Catherine's Workshop, 1986). The subspecies has been studied in some detail by Richard (1978) and by Petter (1962).

CAPTIVE BREEDING Duke Primate Center holds 12 of this subspecies, of which five are captive born (E. Simons. pers. comm.). The Center has a captive breeding programme for this subspecies and will be sending some of their animals to other institutions (E. Simons, pers comm,). There is also, in May 1989, one individual in Parc Tsimbazaza in Madagascar (M. Pidgeon, G. Rakotoarisoa, *in litt.*).

REMARKS Coquerel's Sifaka is white with extensive maroon patches on the anterior part of the ventrum and on the anterior and internal portions of the thighs and forelimbs (Tattersall, 1982). Malagasy names are tsibahaka, sifaka and, in the extreme north-eastern end of its range, ankomba malandy (Tattersall, 1982).

Decken's Sifaka   Vulnerable

Propithecus verreauxi deckeni Peters, 1870

DISTRIBUTION Found from west of the Betsiboka River southwards to near Antsalova at approximately 18°45'S (Tattersall, 1982, 1986, *in litt*). In addition, Petter *et al* (1977) show a population of *coronatus* (*deckeni* in the taxonomy used here) inland at Bongolava. It is reported that these animals occurred in Ambohitantely Reserve as little as twenty years ago (Petter and Andriatsarafara, 1987). This is considerable further east than is shown on any of the distribution maps.

POPULATION No estimates of population numbers or densities have been made. Decken's Sifaka is almost certainly declining in numbers (Richard and Sussman, 1987).

HABITAT AND ECOLOGY This subspecies lives in the dry deciduous forests in the west of Madagascar. There have been no studies of the ecology of *P. v. deckeni,* but it is unlikely to be very different from the other subspecies of *P. verreauxi.*

THREATS As for the other subspecies of *P. verreauxi,* the main threat to the survival of Decken's Sifaka is destruction of its habitat. The deciduous forests of the west are particularly susceptible to fires and these are set each year, usually in the dry season when the forest is most vulnerable, to provide fresh grass growth for livestock in the area. For instance, 500 ha of the forest in Namoroka Nature Reserve was burnt down in 1984 (Nicoll and Langrand, 1989).

CONSERVATION MEASURES Found in Bemaraha and Namoroka Nature Reserves and reported to be abundant in in Ambohijanahary Special Reserve (Nicoll and Langrand, 1989). Bemarivo, Maningozo and Kasijy Special Reserves are also located within the range of Decken's Sifaka, but no information on the vegetation or fauna of these sites has been located. Nicoll and Langrand (1989) have made a number of suggestions for the conservation of Bemaraha Nature Reserve. These include: increasing the awareness of the local people to the value of Bemaraha, many of them do not know that it is a protected area; the erection of notices at access points to mark entry into the reserve and to inform those entering that it is illegal to cut down any trees or hunt the animals and to warn them of the danger of fires; the construction of official access paths through the Reserve; better protection of the Reserve by more guards and the cutting of fire breaks. Similarly, conservation/education programmes for the villagers around Namoroka and Ambohijanahary Reserves would help to protect the areas. The latter is very isolated and rarely visited by government officials. As a result there has been a tendency to forget that the area is protected and much of it has been cleared for agricultural land (Nicoll and Langrand, 1989). It is not known which animal species survive in Ambohijanahary, a survey of the area is needed (Nicoll and Langrand, 1989).

It has been suggested that some individuals are captured and released into the well protected Ambohitantely Reserve (Petter and Andriatsarafara, 1987; St Catherine's Workshop, 1986). A range-wide status survey is also needed, particularly to ascertain if the two forms (*P. v.*

deckeni and *P. v. coronatus* of most authors) are merely variants of one subspecies as Tattersall (in press) considers them to be.

CAPTIVE BREEDING There are four wild born individuals of this subspecies (listed as *P. v. coronatus*) in Paris Zoo (ISIS, June, 1989).

REMARKS Though the ranges of *coronatus* and *deckeni* are shown as clearly distinct, separated by the Mahavavy River, on the distribution maps in both Petter *et al*, 1977 and Petter and Petter-Rousseaux, 1979, the situation is not this clear. In 1986, Tattersall reviewed reports on sightings, museum specimens and colour variations of these two forms and reports sightings of *deckeni* east of the Mahavay River. Though he did not have enough evidence then to synonymise *coronatus* and *deckeni*, a subsequent sighting of *coronatus* by Don Reid in 1987 near Katsepy (across the Bay of Bombetoka from Mahajanga) in the same forest as Sussman and Tattersall saw *deckeni* in 1973, is considered by Tattersall (in press) to be clear evidence that the two forms should be regarded as belonging to the chromatically variable subspecies *P. v. deckeni*. However, more work is needed to clarify the situation. It has been pointed out that *P. v. coronatus* has a much more bulbous muzzle than the other *verreauxi* subspecies (M. Pidgeon, S. O'Connor, *in litt.*) and M. Nicoll has never seen the two forms together or even in the same vicinity. He has found *coronatus* in the northern end of the Katsepy Peninsula and *deckeni* in the southern end (pers. comm. to S. O' Connor).

If the two forms are members of one subspecies then the colour variation within it is considerable. Some are completely white, in others the shoulders, limbs and/or backs are tinted, ranging from yellow gold to silver grey or brown (Tattersall, 1982). Those individuals previously classified as *P. v. coronatus* have a dark chocolate brown or black head and throat as well as a chestnut brown breast (Tattersall, 1982), while those classified as *P. v. deckeni* are mostly completely white. Malagasy names are sifaka and tsibahaka (Tattersall, 1982).

REFERENCES

Albignac, R. (1981). Lemurine social and territorial organisation in a north-western Malagasy forest (restricted area of Ampijoroa). In: Chiarelli, A.B. and Corruccini, R.S. (Eds), *Primate Behavior and Sociobiology*. Springer Verlag, Berlin. Pp. 25-29.

Ganzhorn, J.U. (1988). Food partitioning among Malagasy primates. *Oecologia* (Berlin) 75: 436-450.

Howarth, C.J., Wilson, J.M., Adamson, A.P., Wilson, M.E. and Boase, M. J. (1986). Population ecology of the ring-tailed lemur, *Lemur catta,* and the white sifaka, *Propithecus verreauxi verreauxi,* at Berenty, Madagascar, 1981. *Folia Primatologica* 47: 39-48.

ISIS (1989). *ISIS Species Distribution Report Abstract for Mammals,* 30 June 1989. International Species Information System, 12101 Johnny Cake Ridge Road, Apple Valley, MN, U.S.A. Pp. 17-22.

Jenkins, P. D. (1987). *Catalogue of Primates in the British Museum (Natural History) and elsewhere in the British Isles. Part IV: Suborder Strepsirrhini, including the Subfossil Madagascan Lemurs and Family Tarsiidae.* British Museum (Natural History), London.

Jolly, A. (1966). *Lemur Behavior*. Chicago University Press, Chicago.

Jolly, A. (1972). Troop continuity and troop spacing in *Propithecus verreauxi* and *Lemur catta* at Berenty (Madagascar). *Folia Primatologica* 17: 335-362.

Jolly, A., Gustafson, H., Oliver, W.L.R. and O'Connor, S.M. (1982). *Propithecus verreauxi* population and ranging at Berenty, Madagascar, 1975 and 1980. *Folia Primatologica* 39: 124-144.

Mertl-Millhollen, A.S. (1979). Olfactory demarcation of territorial boundaries by a primate - *Propithecus verreauxi*. *Folia Primatologica* 32: 35-42.

Nicoll, M. and Langrand, O. (1989). *Revue Generale du Système d'Aires Protégées et de la Conservation à Madagascar.* Unpublished Report, WWF Project 3746.

O'Connor, S.M. (1987). *The Effect of Human Impact on Vegetation and the Consequences to Primates in two Riverine Forests, Southern Madagascar.* Unpublished PhD thesis, Cambridge University.

O'Connor, S., Pidgeon, M. and Randria, Z. (1986). Conservation program for the Andohahela Reserve, Madagascar. *Primate Conservation* 7: 48-52.

O'Connor, S., Pidgeon, M. and Randria, Z. (1987). Un programme de conservation pour la Réserve d'Andohahela. In: *Priorités en Matière de Conservation des Espèces à Madagascar.* Occasional Papers of the IUCN Species Survival Commission, Number 2. Pp. 31-36.

Petter, J.-J. (1962). Recherches sur l'écologie et l'éthologie des lémuriens malagache. *Memoires de Museum National d'Histoire Natural* (Paris) 27: 1-146.

Petter, J-J., Albignac, R. and Rumpler, Y. (1977). Mammifères lémuriens (Primates prosimiens). *Faune de Madagascar* No. 44. ORSTOM-CNRS, Paris.

Petter, J.-J. and Petter-Rousseaux, A. (1979). Classification of the Prosimians In: Doyle, G.A. and Martin, R.D. (Eds), *The Study of Prosimian Behavior.* Academic Press, London. Pp. 1-44.

Petter-Rousseaux, A. (1962). Recherches sur la biologie de la réproduction des primates inférieurs. *Mammalia* 26 (Supplement 1): 1-88.

Petter-Rousseaux, A. (1964). Reproductive physiology and behavior of the Lemuroidea. In: Buettner-Janusch, J. (Ed.), *Evolution and Genetic Biology of the Primates.* Academic Press, New York. Pp. 91-132.

Pollock, J.I. (1979). Spatial distribution and ranging behavior in lemurs. In: Doyle, G.A. and Martin, R.D. (Eds), *The Study of Prosimian Behavior.* Academic Press, London. Pp. 359-409.

Pollock, J.I. (1984). Indri and sifakas. In: Macdonald, D. (Ed.), *The Encyclopaedia of Mammals: 1.* George Allen and Unwin, London. P. 330.

Rakotomanga, P., Richard, A.F. and Sussman, R. W. (1987). Beza-Mahafaly: formation et mesures de conservation. In: *Priorités en Matière de Conservation des Espèces à Madagascar.* Occasional Papers of the IUCN Species Survival Commission, Number 2. Pp. 41-43.

Richard, A. (1974a). Patterns of mating in *Propithecus verreauxi verreauxi.* In: Martin, R.D., Doyle, G.A. and Walker, A.C. (Eds), *Prosimian Biology.* Duckworth, London. Pp. 49-74.

Richard, A.F. (1974b). Intra-specific variation in the social organisation and ecology of *Propithecus verreauxi. Folia Primatologica* 22: 178-207.

Richard, A.F. (1976). Preliminary observations on the birth and development of *Propithecus verreauxi* to the age of six months. *Primates* 17: 357-366.

Richard, A. (1977). The feeding behaviour of *Propithecus verreauxi.* In: Clutton-Brock, T. (Ed.), *Primate Ecology: Studies of Feeding and Ranging Behaviour in Lemurs, Monkeys and Apes.* Academic Press, London. Pp. 71-96.

Richard, A.F. (1978a). *Behavioural Variation: Case Study of a Malagasy Lemur.* Bucknell University Press, Lewisburg.

Richard, A.F. (1978b). Variability in the feeding behaviour of a Malagasy prosimian, *Propithecus verreauxi:* Lemuriformes. In: Montgomery, G. G. (Ed.), *The Ecology of Aboreal Folivores.* Smithsonian Institution Press, Washington D. C. Pp. 519-533.

Richard, A.F. (1985). Social boundaries in a Malagasy prosimian, the sifaka (*Propithecus verreauxi). International Journal of Primatology* 6(6): 553-568.

Richard, A.F. (1987). Malagasy prosimians: Female dominance. In: Smuts, B.B., Cheney, D.L., Seyfarth, R.M., Wrangham, R.W. and Struhsaker, T.T. (Eds), *Primate Societies.* University of Chicago Press, Chicago. Pp. 25-33.

Richard, A.F. and Heimbuch, R. (1975). An analysis of the social behavior of three groups of *Propithecus verreauxi.* In: Tattersall, I. and Sussman, R.W. (Eds), *Lemur Biology.* Plenum Press, New York. Pp. 313-333.

Richard, A.F. and Nicoll, M.E. (1987). Female social dominance and basal metabolism in a Malagasy primate, *Propithecus verreauxi. American Journal of Primatology* 12: 309-314.

Richard, A.F. and Sussman, R.W. (1975). Future of the Malagasy lemurs; conservation or extinction? In: Tattersall, I. and Sussman, R.W. (Eds), *Lemur Biology.* Plenum Press, New York. Pp. 335-350.

Richard, A.F. and Sussman, R.W. (1987). Framework for primate conservation in Madagascar. In: Marsh, C.W. and Mittermeier, R. A. (Eds), *Primate Conservation in the Tropical Forest.* Alan R. Liss, Inc., New York. Pp. 329-341.

Richard, A.F., Rakotomanga, P. and Sussman, R.W. (1987). Beza-Mahafaly: recherches fondamentales et appliquées. In: *Priorités en Matière de Conservation des Espèces à Madagascar.* Occasional Papers of the IUCN Species Survival Commission, Number 2. Pp. 45-49.

St Catherine's Workshop (1986). Unpublished reports to the participants of the conference on lemur conservation held on St Catherine's Island, Georgia on 26-27 April 1986.

Sussman, R.W. (1972). An Ecological Study of two Madagascan Primates: *Lemur fulvus rufus* Audebert and *Lemur catta* Linnaeus. Unpublished PhD thesis , Duke University.

Sussman, R.W. and Richard, A.F. (1986). Lemur conservation in Madagascar: The status of lemurs in the south. *Primate Conservation* 7: 86-92.

Sussman, R.W., Richard, A.F. and Rakotomanga, P. (1987). La conservation des lémuriens à Madagascar: Leur statut dans le sud. In: *Priorités en Matière de Conservation des Espèces à Madagascar.* Occasional Papers of the IUCN Species Survival Commission, Number 2. Pp. 75-81.

Tattersall, I. (1982). *The Primates of Madagascar.* Columbia University Press, New York.

Tattersall, I. (1986). Notes on the distribution and taxonomic status of some subspecies of *Propithecus* in Madagascar. *Folia Primatologica* 46: 51-63.

Tattersall, I. (in press). Distribution survey of the Malagasy lemurs: Request for information and initial report. *Primate Conservation.*

The Aye-aye, *Daubentonia madagascariensis*, is the strangest looking of Madagascar's lemurs. It was initially classified as a rodent, not a primate.
Photo by A. Visage/Bios.

AYE-AYE   ENDANGERED

Daubentonia madagascariensis (Gmelin, 1788)

Order PRIMATES   Family DAUBENTONIIDAE

SUMMARY The Aye-aye is probably widely but sparsely distributed in the forests of the east, north and north-west of Madagascar. Population numbers are unknown. It may be that this species is not as rare as previously thought, it is possibly merely very elusive. It is, however, threatened by habitat destruction and is frequently killed by local people. Very little is known about its ecology and social organisation. It is nocturnal and mostly solitary. Its diet is reported to consist of fruit, especially coconuts, and insect larvae. Some short studies have been undertaken and an 18 month study began in July 1989. There are ten individuals in captivity, but none has been born there. *Daubentonia madagascariensis* is reported present in ten protected areas. Listed in Appendix 1 of CITES, in Class A of the African Convention and is protected by law in Madagascar.

DISTRIBUTION The Aye-aye is probably still widely, but apparently very sparsely, distributed throughout the eastern rain forests. It is also in the north, in the north-west in the Sambirano Region and occurs as far south as Bemaraha Nature Reserve. Within the past five years, its presence or signs of it have been reported in Andohahela Nature Reserve (O'Connor *et al*, 1986), in Manomba Special Reserve (Nicoll and Langrand, 1989), near Ranomafana (P. Wright, pers. comm.), in Analamazaotra (Ganzhorn, 1986), in Zahamena Nature Reserve (Pollock, 1984), near Mananara and Maroantsetra (Albignac, 1987), on the Masoala Peninsula (Nicoll and Langrand, 1989, reported present), in Marojejy Nature Reserve (Safford *et al*, 1989 signs seen), in Analamera and Ankarana Special Reserves (Hawkins *et al*, in press), in Montagne d'Ambre National Park (Nicoll and Langrand, 1989), just south of both Ambilobé and Ambanja (J. Andrews, pers. comm.), in Manongarivo Special Reserve (Raxworthy and Rakotondraparany, 1988, reported by local people; Nicoll and Langrand, 1989) and in Bemaraha Nature Reserve (Petter and Andriatsarafara, 1987). Iwano (*in litt*) reported that natives had killed and eaten individuals from two sites in northern Madagascar, one about latitude 16°S and the other just west and north of Befandriana Nord.

POPULATION Numbers are not known, but there are probably more Aye-aye than was thought (Ganzhorn and Rabesoa, 1986). It appears to be very elusive rather than very rare. It is, however, unlikely that it is found, or was ever found, in very high densities (Tattersall, 1982). In Analamazaotra, it took 60 to 70 hours of intensive night work to find one animal (Ganzhorn, 1986). Population numbers are almost certainly declining (Sussman *et al*, 1985).

HABITAT AND ECOLOGY The Aye-aye appears to be very adaptable in its choice of habitat. It is, or was, found in areas of primary rain forest, deciduous forest, secondary growth, cultivation (particularly coconut groves) and possibly even in mangrove swamps and dry scrub forest (Tattersall, 1982). It has been seen in an area of open brush and low trees several miles from any real forest (Rand, 1935).

Daubentonia is a nocturnal species. It spends the day in a nest, which it usually builds in a fork of a tree or in a dense tangle of lianes at a height of between 10 and 15 m (Petter and Peyrieras, 1970; Petter, 1977). At night, it is usually seen singly, though three were seen within about 50 m of each other in the forests of Mahambo (Petter *et al*, 1977), two adults were together in Analamazaotra (E. Stirling, pers. comm.) and three individuals were observed within 10 m of each other on Nosy Mangabe, one of these was an adult male (Iwano and Iwakawa, 1988).

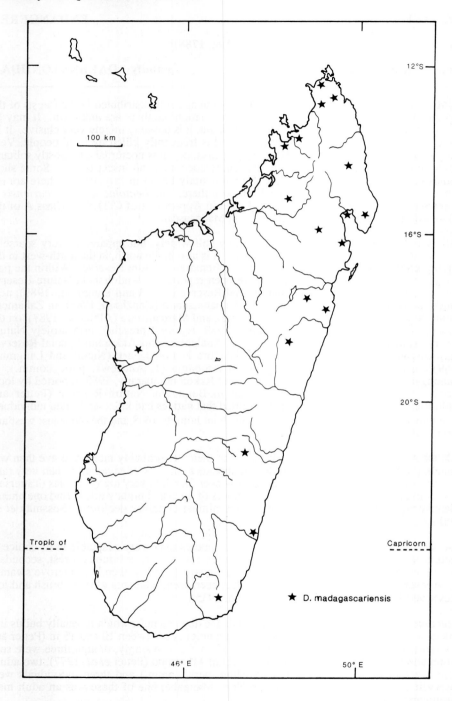

Figure 16: Recent sightings or reports of *Daubentonia*.

The Aye-aye's diet is reported to consist of fruit, especially coconuts, and insect larvae (Petter, 1977). They have been seen eating lychees and mangoes (Petter, 1977). The larvae are extracted from dead branches and from the nuts in *Terminalia* fruits (Petter and Petter-Rousseaux, 1967; Petter, 1977). Pollock *et al* (1985) record an adult male Aye-aye on Nosy Mangabe feeding on gall-like protuberances on an *Afzelia bijuga* tree. The Aye-aye appeared to consume the fibrous bark of the tree, the clay-like tissue beneath the galls, the insects and, perhaps, vertebrates located within the galls' crevices. There were elaterid larvae in the galls and a frog was found there. Though Petter (1977; Petter *et al*, 1977) notes that Aye-ayes do not feed on adult insects, Pollock *et al* (1985) suggest that they are eaten. The *D. madagascariensis* observed on Nosy Mangabe also fed briefly on the shoots of the large variegated bamboo species, *Bambusa striata* (Pollock *et al*, 1985). Iwano and Iwakawa (1988) observed an Aye-aye on Nosy Mangabe feeding on "ramy" fruits (*Canarium madagascariensis*). It scraped off the outer pulp, gnawed into the hard nut then extracted and ate its contents.

It has been reported that Aye-aye may give birth only once in two or three years (Petter and Peyrieras, 1970; Petter, 1977). However, it is unclear why this is suggested. Singletons are said to be born in October and November (Petter and Peyrieras, 1970; Petter, 1977), but Albignac (1987) reports finding a three week old infant at the end of March.

THREATS   The main threat to the Aye-aye is the destruction of its habitat. It is not known if it can survive in degraded areas; it is suggested that it, at least, needs large trees in which to build its nests (Petter, 1977; Iwano and Iwakawa, 1988). In some areas of Madagascar it is killed on sight as it is regarded as a harbinger of misfortune. It is also reported to be killed when raiding crops (Albignac, 1987). It appears to be unafraid of humans and it is easy to capture (Petter, 1977). Two of the tree species which *D. madagascariensis* appears to use as a food source (*Afzelia bijuga* and *Canarium madagascariensis*) occur throughout the eastern rain forest, but they are frequently cut down as their wood is used in the construction of boats, houses and coffins (Pollock *et al*, 1985; Iwano and Iwakawa, 1988).

CONSERVATION MEASURES   The Aye-aye has been reported in Montagne d'Ambre National Park, in Andohahela, Bemaraha, Marojejy and Zahamena Nature Reserves and in Analamazaotra, Manomba, Manongarivo, Analamera and Ankarana Special Reserves; it was introduced to Nosy Mangabe Special Reserve (Nicoll and Langrand, 1989; Ganzhorn, 1986; Pollock, 1984; Safford *et al*, 1989; Hawkins *et al*, in press; Raxworthy and Rakotondraparany, 1988; Petter and Andriatsarafara, 1987; O'Connor *et al*, 1986). It is also found, or is reported to occur, in three of the areas in the east that have been proposed as protected areas. These are Ranomafana, Mananara and Masoala (Nicoll and Langrand, 1989; Wright, 1988; Albignac, 1987). Most of these areas need better protection. In addition, conservation/education and development programmes are needed for the local people. The laws against killing Aye-ayes (or any other lemurs) require better enforcement, but local people should be compensated for any damage done to their crops by Aye-ayes (Albignac, 1987).

An Aye-aye conservation programme, funded by WWF, was set up by the Department of Water and Forests, the Museum of Natural History in Paris and IUCN (Constable *et al*, 1985). This programme included the release of nine Aye-aye in 1966/67 on to Nosy Mangabe, a 520 ha island off the east coast of Madagascar in the Bay of Antogil. This island was set up as a Special Reserve in December 1966 (Petter and Peyrieras, 1977; Constable *et al*, 1985). The number of animals on the island now are not known, but some are certainly still present (Constable *et al*, 1985; H. Simons, E. Sterling, pers. comm.).

E. Sterling (Anthropology Department, Yale University) began an eighteen month study of the Aye-aye on Nosy Mangabe in the summer of 1989 and T. Iwano intends to return for several months to continue his work. It is hoped that these studies will help ascertain the habitat requirements of the Aye-aye and its ability to adapt to environments modified by humans. Extensive surveys are needed to determine the extent of the present range of *D. madagascariensis,* its true population numbers and, thereby, its actual conservation status.

Participants at the St Catherine's Lemur Workshop held in Georgia in 1986 suggested that 10-20 individuals of this species be brought into captivity as they "should breed well". They regarded the Aye-aye as probably the single highest breeding priority for Malagasy lemurs.

Daubentoniidae is listed in Appendix 1 of the 1973 Convention on International Trade in Endangered Species of Wild Fauna and Flora. Trade in it, or its products, is subject to strict regulation and may not be carried out for primarily commercial purposes.

All Lemuroidea are listed in Class A of the African Convention, 1969. They may not, therefore, be hunted, killed, captured or collected without the authorization of the highest competent authority, and then only if required in the national interest or for scientific purposes.

Malagasy law prohibits the killing or unauthorised capture of any lemurs. This is, however, evidently impossible to enforce.

CAPTIVE BREEDING Outside Madagascar, there are only seven individuals in captivity, two of each sex in Duke Primate Center, which were acquired in December 1987 and August 1988, and three at Paris Zoo which were taken there in 1986 (ISIS, June 1989; Albignac, 1987; Winn, 1989; A. Katz, J.-J. Petter, *in litt.*). In Madagascar, two Aye-ayes were reported to have been taken to Ivoloina in February 1989 but these became ill and had died by early 1990 (E. Simons, pers. comm.); there is a single animal in Parc Tsimbazaza (A. Katz, M. Pidgeon, G. Rakotoarisoa, *in litt.*). No Aye-ayes, however, have yet bred successfully in captivity. A pair were held for four years at Analamazaotra and they had two infants but these were eaten by the mother (Petter *et al,* 1977). Duke Primate Center intends to coordinate a breeding programme for animals of this species being held both inside and outside Madagascar (E. Simons, pers. comm.).

REMARKS The Aye-aye is the only living representative of its family. It was originally classified as a squirrel and it was not until 1800 that it was recognised as a primate (see Jenkins, 1987). Long, coarse blackish-brown guard hairs overlay a dense layer of relatively short white hair, giving the overall impression of dark brown pelage suffused with white. The tail is bushy; ears are large, naked and mobile; incisors are long and continually growing; digits are elongated, particularly the middle finger, and most are clawed. *D. madagascariensis* weighs about 3 kg (Tattersall, 1982 Winn, 1989). See Petter (1977), Petter *et al* (1977), Jenkins (1987) and Tattersall (1982) for more details. Malagasy names for the species are hay-hay, ahay and aiay (Tattersall, 1982).

REFERENCES

Albignac, R. (1987). Status of the aye-aye in Madagascar. *Primate Conservation* 8: 44-45.

Constable, I.D., Mittermeier, R.A., Pollock, J.I., Ratsirarson, J. and Simons, H. (1985). Sightings of aye-ayes and red ruffed lemurs on Nosy Mangabe and the Masoala Peninsula. *Primate Conservation* 5: 59-62.

Ganzhorn, J.U. and Rabesoa, J. (1986). Sightings of aye-ayes in the eastern rainforest of Madagascar. *Primate Conservation* 7: 45.

Ganzhorn, J.U. (1986). The aye-aye (*Daubentonia madagascariensis*) found in the eastern rainforest of Madagascar. *Folia Primatologica* 46: 125-126.

Hawkins, A.F.A., Ganzhorn, J.U., Bloxham, Q.M.C., Barlow, S.C., Tonge, S.J. and Chapman, P. (in press). A survey and assessment of the conservation status and needs of lemurs, birds, lizards and snakes in the Ankarana Special Reserve, Antseranana, Madagascar: with notes on the lemurs and birds of the nearby Analamera Special Reserve. *Biological Conservation.*

ISIS (1989). *ISIS Species Distribution Report Abstract for Mammals,* 30 June 1989. International Species Information System, 12101 Johnny Cake Ridge Road, Apple Valley, MN, U.S.A. Pp. 17-22.

Iwano, T. and Iwakawa, C. (1988). Feeding behaviour of the aye-aye (*Daubentonia madagascariensis*) on nuts of Ramy (*Canarium madagascariensis*). *Folia Primatologica* 50: 136-142.

Jenkins, P.D. (1987). *Catalogue of Primates in the British Museum (Natural History) and elsewhere in the British Isles. Part IV: Suborder Strepsirrhini, including the Subfossil Madagascan Lemurs and Family Tarsiidae.* British Museum (Natural History), London.

Nicoll, M.E. and Langrand, O. (1989). *Revue Generale du Système d'Aires Protégées et de la Conservation à Madagascar.* Unpublished Report, WWF Project 3746.

O'Connor, S., Pidgeon, M. and Randria, Z. (1986). Conservation program for the Andohahela Reserve, Madagascar. *Primate Conservation* 7: 48-52.

Petter, J-J., Albignac, R. and Rumpler, Y. (1977). Mammifères lémuriens (Primates prosimiens). *Faune de Madagascar* No. 44. ORSTOM-CNRS, Paris.

Petter, J.-J. (1977). The aye-aye. In: Prince Rainer and Bourne, G.H. (Eds), *Primate Conservation.* Academic Press, New York. Pp. 37-57.

Petter, J.-J. and Andriatsarafara, F. (1987). Conservation status and distribution of lemurs in the west and northwest of Madagascar. *Primate Conservation* 7: 169-171.

Petter, J.-J. and Petter-Rousseaux, A. (1967). The aye-aye of Madagascar. In: Altman, S.A. (Ed.), *Social Comminication Among Primates.* University of Chicago Press, Chicago. Pp. 195-205.

Petter, J.-J. and Peyrieras, A. (1970). Nouvelle contribution a l'étude d'un lémurien malagache, le aye-aye (*Daubentonia madagascariensis* E. Geoffroy). *Mammalia* 34 (2): 167-193.

Pollock, J.I. (1984). *Preliminary Report on a Mission to Madagascar by Dr J. I. Pollock in August and September 1984.* Unpublished report to WWF.

Pollock, J.I., Constable, I.D., Mittermeier, R.A., Ratsirason, J. and Simons, H. (1985). A note on the diet and feeding behaviour of the aye-aye *Daubentonia madagascariensis. International Journal of Primatology* 6(4): 435-447.

Rand, A.L. (1935). On the habits of some Madagascar mammals. *Journal of Mammalogy* 16(2): 89-104.

Raxworthy, C.J. and Rakotondraparany, F. (1988). Mammals report. In: Quansah, N. (Ed.),*Manongarivo Special Reserve (Madagascar) 1987/88 Expedition Report.* Unpublished report, Madagascar Environmental Research Group, U.K.

Safford, R.J., Durbin, J.C. and Duckworth, J.W. (1989). *Cambridge Madagascar Rainforest Expedition 1988 to R.N.I. No. 12 - Marojejy.* Unpublished preliminary report.

St Catherine's Lemur Workshop (1986). Unpublished reports to participants of the conference held on St Catherine's Island, Georgia on 26-27 April 1986.

Sussman, R.W., Richard, A.F. and Ravelojaona, G. (1985). Madagascar: current projects and problems in conservation. *Primate Conservation* 5: 53-58.

Tattersall, I. (1982). *The Primates of Madagascar.* Columbia University Press, New York.

Winn, R.M. (1989) The Aye-Ayes, *Daubentonia madagascariensis,* at the Paris Zoological Gardens: maintenance and preliminary behavioural observations. *Folia Primatologica* 52: 109-23

Wright, P. (1988). IUCN Tropical Forest Programme. Critical Sites Inventory Report held by the World Conservation Monitoring Centre, Cambridge, U.K.

APPENDIX A

Population Viability Analysis Data Form

Report to be mailed to:
World Conservation Monitoring Centre
219(c) Huntingdon Road
Cambridge CB3 0DL, U.K.

Species:

Species distribution:

Study taxon (subspecies):

Study population location:

Metapopulation - are there other separate populations? Are maps available (Separation by distance, geographic barriers?):

Specialised requirements (Trophic, ecological):

Age of first reproduction for each sex (population breeding):
    a) Earliest:
    b) Mean:

Gestation period (days or weeks):

Litter size (N, mean, SD, range) (at birth?, weaning?):

Birth season:

Birth frequency (interbirth interval):

Reproductive life-span (male and female, range):

Life time reproduction (mean, male and female):

Adult sex ratio:

Adult body weight of males and females:

Past population estimates (5, 10, 20 years- dates, reliability estimates):

Population sex and age structure (young, juvenile and adults) - time of year:

Fecundity rates (by sex and age class):

Mortality rates and distribution (by sex and age) (neonatal, juvenile adult):

Population density estimate. Area of population. Attach marked map:

Sources of mortality - % (natural, poaching, harvest, accidental, seasonal?):

Present habitat protection status:

Projected habitat protection status (5, 10, 50 years):

Environmental variance affecting reproduction and mortality (rainfall, prey, predators, disease, snow cover?):

Is pedigree information available?:

Attach life table if available

Social structure in terms of breeding (random, pair-bonded, polygyny, polyandry, etc.; breeding male and female turnover each year?):

Proportion of adult males and females breeding each year:

Dispersal distance (mean, sexes):

Migration (months):

Territoriality (home range, season):

Birth sex ratio:

Birth weights (male and female):

Ovulation - induced or spontaneous:

Implantation - immediate or delayed (duration):

Oestrous cycles (seasonal, multiple or single, post partum):

Duration of lactation:

Post-lactational oestrus:

Age of dispersal:

Maximum longevity:

Population census - most recent. Date of last census. Reliability estimate:

Projected population (5, 10, 50 years):

Date form completed:

Correspondent/Investigator:
    Name:
    Address:

    Telephone:
    Fax:

References:

Comments:

APPENDIX B

Distribution Survey of the Malagasy Lemurs: Request for information.

Despite over a century of exploration and zoological collection in Madagascar, we still know remarkably little about the geographical distribution of the Malagasy primates. True, in most cases we know where to go to see representatives of this species/subspecies or that; but in no case do we have a precise idea of the boundaries, geographical or ecological, that limit such populations. Nevertheless, even as primate habitat in the island inexorably disappears, a steady stream of discoveries is being made of range extensions or of previously unknown isolates (or even species). Clearly, Madagascar is so vast, our knowledge so rudimentary, that almost any journey into the field there may reveal new and unexpected information about what species or subspecies occur where. Such discoveries are often made by field workers who are not primatologists, or to whom zoogeographical survey is not a priority. In instances of this kind observations of the greatest potential interest may well go unreported in the literature; when this occurs, the information will at best be reduced to anecdotal hearsay, and at worst will be lost altogether, as over the years much undoubtedly has been.

In an attempt to provide a mechanism for placing observations of this sort on record, I am offering to act as a clearinghouse for them. Questionnaires have been prepared, and are available from me at the address below, which those working in the field in Madagascar are invited to fill out when casual sightings of interest are made. The basic questions relate to identity and locality, with the option of furnishing additional information on habitat, group size, and so forth. Information would ideally also include description of external and pelage characters observed, and of any variations noted in them. It is important to emphasise here that I am requesting only information for which publication plans do not otherwise exist; my concern is simply that valuable information not be lost. If response justifies it, I will prepare periodic summaries. Ultimately, I hope, a permanent home for this clearinghouse will be found in Madagascar itself.

Ian Tattersall
Department of Anthropology
American Museum of Natural History
New York
NEW YORK 10024
U.S.A.

APPENDIX C

National and International Legislation Protecting Lemurs

National Legislation

In Madagascar

Legislation for particular species in Madagascar is based primarily on the 1933 London Convention and on Ordonnance No. 60-126 of 03.10.60. The fauna has been divided into three categories (protected, game or vermin) and is now considered under a series of dispositions controlling hunting and fishing. Some species can be captured for commercial purposes, others under only "exceptional" circumstances. Such exploitation is controlled by Decrees (mainly No. 61-093) which lay down the means, time and area of capture. Capture for scientific purposes is controlled by Decree No. 71-006.

All lemurs are listed as protected species and there are also restrictions on their being kept in captivity (Decree No. 62-020).

In the Comoros

In the Comoros, it has been illegal to kill lemurs or to keep them without a licence since 1974. Exports are restricted to a maximum of 10 females and 20 males each year.

International Legislation

In 1969 Madagascar signed and ratified the 1933 African Convention. All the lemurs are listed in Class A and they, therefore, may not be hunted, killed, captured or collected except with the authorisation of the highest competent authority and then only if required in the national interest or for scientific purposes.

Madagascar has been a member of the Convention on International Trade in Endangered Species of Wild Fauna and Flora (CITES) since November 1975. All the lemurs are listed in Appendix 1 of CITES. Trade in the species or their products listed in this Appendix is subject to strict regulation by ratifying nations and trade for primarily commercial purposes is banned.

REFERENCES

Randrianarijaona, P. and Razafimbelo, E. (1983). *Rapport national pour Madagascar.* Report prepared for UNEP Regional Seas East Africa Programme.
Tattersall, I. (1977). The lemurs of the Comoro Islands. *Oryx* 13(5): 445-448.

SPECIES INDEX